Careers and Training in Hotels, Catering and Tourism

Published in association with

HOTEL&
CATERING
TRAINING
COMPANY

Careers and Training in Hotels, Catering and Tourism

Roy Hayter

Research and profiles: Pam Frediani

BUTTERWORTH
HEINEMANN

Butterworth-Heinemann Ltd
Linacre House, Jordan Hill, Oxford OX2 8DP

ℛ A member of the Reed Elsevier plc Group

OXFORD   LONDON   BOSTON
MUNICH   NEW DELHI   SINGAPORE   SYDNEY
TOKYO   TORONTO   WELLINGTON

First published 1993
Reprinted 1994

© Hotel & Catering Training Company Ltd 1993

British Library Cataloguing in Publication Data
Hayter, Roy
   Careers and Training in Hotels, Catering
   and Tourism
   I. Title
   647.9

ISBN 0 7506 0166 3

Printed and bound in Great Britain by
Redwood Books, Trowbridge, Wiltshire

Contents

Preface

There is increasingly widespread recognition of the importance of the hotel, catering and tourism industry – in terms of its contribution to the UK economy, the number of people it employs, and the growth prospects for the 1990s and beyond. There have never been such good education and training opportunities to encourage people of all ages to join the industry, and to develop them as their careers progress.

In spite of this there are some who still regard the industry as a second-best career choice, to be explored, with considerable reservation, if all other avenues seem closed. It is clear that a communication and information gap remains and this book is intended to make a contribution to filling that gap.

It can only be a snapshot, for events are moving rapidly in all areas of education and training. However, if it was necessary to wait until things were settled, there would never be a right time for such a book. That there are still enquiries about my two previous career books, written ten and five years ago, confirms that a comprehensive reference source is valuable to all those who give careers advice, as well as to those who seek it. As the task of compiling the book has proved, the only alternative is to set aside several months to search through many hundreds of documents, sort out what is still valid information, resolve inconsistencies and pursue missing details, essential background and unpublished facts.

An important feature of this book – which will not date – is the profiles of over thirty men and women. These profiles capture the real flavour of what the industry offers in terms of job satisfaction, variety of challenge and scope for initiative. Another feature is the extracts from job advertisements, employers' careers literature, and articles which have appeared in *Caterer & Hotelkeeper* and some of the HCIMA's publications. These have been chosen for the interesting detail they provide, and to give a contrast to the main text.

Responsibility for the accuracy of the information in this book and the views it expresses is mine. The book does not necessarily reflect the policy or views of HCTC.

Roy Hayter

Acknowledgements

An undertaking on this scale, at a time when fundamental changes are affecting every aspect of education and training, would not have been possible without the support and patient help of a large number of people. Special thanks are due to:

- Those who provided wordprocessing and secretarial support, in particular Dawn Gilligan, Diana Burton Brown, Diana Beatty and Kate Jennings.

- Colleagues at HCTC for their assistance, in particular Yvonne Barr, Polly Fairburn, Mike Fellowes, Michael Grassis, Paul Hickey, Anne Walker and Claire Wilson.

- Jacquie Shanahan at Butterworth-Heinemann, and John O'Connor, series editor for their encouragement and inspiration.

- Those who helped put Pam Frediani in touch with the people profiled, in particular Peter Davies and Heather Eaglen of Sutcliffe Catering, Adrian Carter of *Caterer & Hotelkeeper*, and David Elton of the Acorn Club.

- Those who supplied information on qualification routes, NVQs and SVQs, in particular Peter Gill and Diana Toolan of BTEC, Christine Keenan of SCOTVEC, Steven Rhodes of TEED, William Blacklock and Veronica Read of City and Guilds, Susan Stevens of ABTANTB.

- At the HCIMA: Lynn Worthington, Bridget Thomas, Rosemary Morrison and Linette Williams in the education department; Tim Knowles, Ann Taylor and Kalpana Amin in the information office; and Ann Share, manager communication services.

- Those who supplied information on career routes, in particular Maggie Tiltman, Commander Brian Purnell, Wing Commander Ted Malone and Captain Philip Sinclair.

- Dee Gasson of Employment Department; Linda Fraser, editor of *Good Food Magazine*; Joanna Trobe, food designer and photographer; Verne George of Merrychef and Jane Hildred of McDougalls.

- *Caterer & Hotelkeeper* for permission to reproduce material, and quote from articles written by Michael Helby, Mel Jones, Kate McDermid, Pam Legate and David Goymour.

- Roddy Watt of Berkeley Scott Personnel Consultants, Mario Bianchin of VIP International, Thomas Hegarty of ITT Sheraton, Grahame Billett and Wendy Holloway of P&O Cruise Fleet Services, and John Jackson for permission to quote from their articles in *HCIMA Reference Book*.

- Those interviewed by Pam Frediani for the profiles: Malcolm Allcock, Travellers Club; Christine Barnes, Catering and Allied Services; Derek Bousfield, Metropolitan Police; Sally Clarke, Clarkes Restaurant; Warrant Officer Lou Hole, Army Catering Corps; Caroline Heagerty, Ritz Carlton; Vivian Higgins, Sutcliffe Catering; Nicholas Jones, Over the Top; Charlotte Kincaid, Sterling Hotel; Alyson Cheyne (née Logan), Lensbury Club; Dee Ludlow, Milton Keynes Forte Crest; Susan Millington, Royal Garden Hotel; Russell Kett, BAHA; Wing Commander Ted Malone, RAF; McCoy Brothers; William MacKinnon, Boy Scouts; Geoff Parkinson, Horwath and Horwath; Commander Brian Purnell MBE, Royal Navy; Sainath Rao, Coburg Hotel; Tina O'Regan, Robin Hood; Margaret Rose, consultant; Sandy Ross, Selfridges; Phillip Ruddock, Ealing Hospital; Captain Philip Sinclair, Army Catering Corps; Jonathan Thompson, Hartwell House; Maggie Tiltman, School Meals Service, Avon; Brian Watts, Bank of England.

1
Getting to know the industry

Almost certainly you already know quite a lot about the industry because you experience its products and services as a customer. This may be for a special treat – a birthday celebration in the local hotel, or a holiday you have saved up for through the year. It may be at quite a modest level – buying a fish and chip take-away, for example. Or it may be through force of circumstances – because you have had to spend time in hospital, for example.

Committing yourself to working in the industry demands a rather better understanding of what hotels, catering and tourism are about. It's an industry that in Britain has not always been recognized for its career opportunities. That this is rapidly changing reflects a more positive public attitude to service. It also reflects the wide acceptance of the importance of hotels, catering and tourism to the economies of Britain, the European Community, and the world as a whole.

For an industry that has always offered good opportunities to travel and work in different countries, this is good news. So too is the industry's healthy growth record in employment opportunities. By the year 2000 tourism will be the world's biggest industry, according to the World Travel and Tourism Council. In 1990 it was worth 5.5 per cent of the world's gross national product – more than \$2.5 trillion.

This book's scope

A huge number of people work in hotels, catering and tourism, in a vast range of jobs and establishments. But because there is no commonly accepted definition of its composition, statistics used to describe its size and scope vary quite considerably.

Of the various alternative names for the industry, 'hospitality' has the advantages of being short and conveying the key element of service. However, it is not yet a recognized term outside the industry – members of the public still think in terms of hotels, pubs, restaurants and so forth, not hospitality establishments. It also seems to ignore the welfare sector of the industry, and inadequately describes industrial and contract catering. Hence the decision to call this book *Careers and Training in Hotels, Catering and Tourism*. Although the book also covers much of leisure, that word has been omitted from the title because no attempt has been made to cover the sport and recreation activities connected with leisure, or the provision of entertainment.

Hotels and catering

Almost one in ten of the UK workforce are now employed in the provision of food, drink, and/or accommodation. The *commercial sector* of the industry includes not just hotels and restaurants, but also holiday camps and leisure centres, pubs, cafés, wine bars, motorway services, roadside restaurants, fish and chip shops, take-away burger and pizza restaurants, entertainment clubs, famous 'gentlemen's' clubs such as the Reform and the Carlton, and contract catering in a huge variety of establishments and settings from livery halls in the City of London, to burger bars and self-service restaurants at sports stadia.

Just over half the industry's workforce of 2.4 million are employed in the commercial sector. The balance – around 1.1 million – provides catering services in other sectors for which catering is not the primary function. The *catering services sector*, as it is known, covers rail, airline and cruise catering, the catering and accommodation services at schools, colleges and universities, nursing homes, hospitals, residential hostels and other establishments for the elderly, ill, and others unable to provide for themselves. It also includes catering in the armed services – the army, navy and air force.

The Hotel and Catering Training Company (HCTC) forecasts employment growth of 5 per cent in the commercial sector over the five years 1990–95, and just under 2 per cent in the catering services sector. Total employment in the industry in 1990 stood at 2,419,000, up 5 per cent on 1987. The industry's recovery from the effects of the Gulf War and the economic recession is expected to lead to a demand for around 683,000 new staff a year from the mid-1990s. A substantial proportion of these will be for skilled, supervisory and managerial staff – equivalent to 3,000 per week.

As in the 1980s, the most dynamic sectors in terms of employment are likely to be restaurants and contract catering. The proportion of jobs in restaurants is expected to rise from 25 per cent in 1990 to over 28 per cent in 1999, making it the largest sector. Pubs and hotels will show steady but slow employment growth. Overall, employment in the commercial sector will increase by 56,000 up to 1995 and by 134,000 up to 1999. Catering services will provide around 12,000 new jobs up to 1999 (excluding domestics and housekeepers who fall within this category).

Tourism

During the 1980s, the number of tourism jobs grew by 25 per cent. Over 1.5 million people are estimated to work in the industry, providing the services and facilities that around 16 to 18 million overseas visitors require each year. They also cater for British people taking holidays, business trips, short breaks and day visits, perhaps to friends or relatives, or to a local visitor attraction. The British take around 135 million tourist trips in Britain, 21 million adults and 7 million children use sports facilities regularly, and over 200 million visitors flock to England's historic houses, wildlife parks and other attractions. In 1990, the most popular tourist attraction in the UK charging admission was Madame Tussaud's with 2.5 million visits. The Tower of London was a close second with 2.3 million visits, and Alton Towers third with 2.1 million.

Many of these tourists require advice on where to go, help with their travel and accommodation arrangements, transport, things to do and see, food and drink and somewhere to stay. So the tourism industry involves:

- Tour operators and travel agents: organizing and selling holidays.

- Marketing, coordinating, planning and research bodies such as: British Tourist Authority, national, regional and local tourist boards, local authority tourist and leisure departments, tourist information offices.

- Tourist attractions: ancient buildings, historical sites, museums, art galleries, stately homes, theme parks, the National Trust.

- Leisure and sports centres, marinas, national parks.

- Accommodation: hotels, motels, guesthouses, caravan parks, camping, self-catering apartments, time-share properties, conference centres, university and college halls of residence.

- Food and drink: restaurants, pubs, snack bars, cafés, mobile catering.

- Carriers and travel operators: scheduled and charter airlines, rail, coach, car hire, cruise ships, ferries.

As this list indicates, there is considerable overlap between the tourism industry and hotels and catering, travel and transport. Some of the jobs in those industries are there because tourists are such an important source of business: consider York, Edinburgh, London, Dover and Stratford upon Avon, for example. In other areas, pubs, restaurants, hotels, leisure centres, bus and rail services and so forth will be used by more local residents than tourists. Nevertheless, tourism provides useful business. Other jobs exist only for tourists, such as couriers, guides and those in travel agencies, tourist information centres and the national and regional tourist boards.

Profile: Christine Barnes

Hotels/restaurants/leisure/contract catering

Although she had worked as a waitress at weekends and during school holidays at a hotel near her home in Wirral, Cheshire, it had not occurred to Christine that she might make her career in the industry. When the head chef pointed out the possibility, and told her of the management course at Blackpool College, there was only a week to go before the start of the 1980/81 academic year. The college promptly sent a prospectus, and by return of post, Christine got her application back. With eight O levels and one A level, she comfortably met the entry requirements, and clearly her attitude was right, after all the owners had left her in charge of the Hotel Victoria restaurant on several occasions.

The three year Higher National Diploma included two six-month periods of industrial experience. For the first, Christine worked as a waitress and commis chef at the three-star Ullswater Hotel, in the Lake District. The following year, she was one of six students selected from 120 to go abroad – in her case, to the Solbad Hotel, Signiswil, Switzerland, to work in the housekeepers department and, for a month, in the food service area.

With her HND and a taste for travel, she set off for Canada in summer 1983. Finding the friend she had gone to join, ill in hospital, Christine got a job as an au pair with a doctor and his family. She also cooked for them, including on their touring holiday of the USA.

Back in the UK six months later, Christine decided she must extend her practical experience in catering. For the next three months she worked in the kitchen and restaurant of Sheldrakes in Lower Heswall, Wirral, a newly opened family run establishment. It was out of season, so she took no salary, except when the owner went away from time to time and she was put in charge.

Then the owner of the Six Jolly Fellowship Porters Restaurant in Chester asked Christine to help refurbish the premises and recruit staff. 'It was his first venture in the industry. I became involved in menu planning, ordering of liquid stock and general running of the restaurant. I became indispensable, but it involved working all hours, with little time off, so I decided I must move on and regard it as another period of learning and practising new skills.'

Back at Sheldrakes, she enjoyed the official title of Restaurant Manager. By November 1984, having run the restaurant while the owners were away, Christine was attracted by an advertisement for chalet girls with Bladon Lines Travel Company in Switzerland. 'I spent five happy months at a top class chalet in the resort of Verbier. Making sure that my twenty guests enjoyed their stay, and were looked after to the

Christine Barnes (*continued*)

standard expected by the company, was hard, but enjoyable work. My duties included menu planning, cooking and presentation of meals within a strict budget. And in my spare time, I learnt to ski.'

Her next challenge, for the Warehouse Clothing Company, was to set up and develop a restaurant at newly acquired retail premises in central Liverpool. This included staff selection, training, menu compilation, cash control and banking.

'Not sure if my future lay in catering, I decided in February 1986 to accept the offer of a place on an eight-day Tour Courier/Tour Manager course, sponsored by the then Manpower Services Commission. It was very comprehensive, with lectures by senior tour managers and tour operators, and three days on tour in the Lake District and Scotland, each delegate acting as tour courier and manager.'

March 1986 saw Christine's past experience and training come together. She was appointed Assistant Manager at the four-star Mollington Banastre Hotel in Chester, and Manager of the Mollington Sportif Leisure Complex. Her love of rowing, sailing, skiing, swimming, and scuba diving, gave a special interest in this new job. Other responsibilities included duty management, ordering and issuing stock, stocktaking, organizing conferences, functions, weddings, and overseeing the general day to day running of the hotel.

Two years later, and only three months after joining contract caterers Catering and Allied Services, Christine's name was successfully put forward for the *Caterer & Hotelkeeper's* Acorn Award (see this chapter). Her first position with the company was Manager of Café des Artistes, in Heals, Tottenham Court Road, London. Recently refurbished to the specifications of Terence Conran, it served around 300 lunches a day. From there, she was transferred to E W Payne in Aldgate, as Deputy Manager, part of a team of four responsible for the running and organization of the 700-seat staff restaurant, 100-seat management dining room and seven directors' dining rooms.

Her promotion to Field Operator came in July 1989. Reporting direct to the Area Manager, Christine is responsible for the day to day running of up to twenty units. This involves close liaison with site managers, monitoring performance, budgeting and taking on specific projects such as the setting up of new sites.

Christine considers 'common sense' a vital quality of her success in the industry. This accords with the Catering and Allied Services policy to recruit managers who have not only the academic background, but practical kitchen skills and experience, plus an enthusiasm for new ideas and the aptitude for working hard to achieve results.

A changing, and increasingly international industry

The hotel and catering industry experienced a series of company takeovers and rationalization programmes during the late 1980s and early 1990s. The twin pressures of high interest rates and reduced spending wiped out a number of companies which had tried to grow too fast, and exposed others to takeover.

Forte Hotels (Trusthouse Forte until 1991) has been the number one UK hotel group for several years, with 338 hotels and 29,530 rooms in 1991 – 8,000 rooms more than in 1990, before the takeover of Crest Hotels. Travelodge, Forte's budget roadside chain, had ninety-two hotels in 1991 with 3,227 rooms. In number two position was Mount Charlotte Thistle (result of the takeover of the Thistle group by Mount Charlotte) with 109 hotels and 14,262 rooms.

UK-owned companies are now major worldwide operators. Holiday Inn Worldwide, owned by the brewery group Bass, was the world's largest hotel chain in the 1991 survey by *Hotels* magazine, with 1,606 hotels and 320,600 bedrooms. Forte was number eleven, Hilton International (owned by Ladbrokes) number fifteen.

European operators starting to break into the UK market include the French companies Accor (twenty-five hotels and 3,639 rooms) and Campanile (twelve hotels and 665 rooms). Scandic Hotel AB had five hotels in 1991 and 1,145 rooms, and CG Hotels six hotels and 872 rooms. Inter-Continental, one of Grand Metropolitan's last hotel interests was sold in 1990 to a Japanese retailing group.

Burger King, still owned by Grand Metropolitan, had increased its number of units to 180 by the end of 1991 and its share of the hamburger market to around 20 per cent. McDonald's is in number one position with 420 outlets and around 40 per cent of the market. Kentucky Fried Chicken, part of Forte, is another key player. Drive-in restaurants are becoming more common in the UK, while the home delivery market has opened up huge expansion opportunities for the pizza chains.

Major mid-price restaurant chains include Harvester, Sweeney Todd's, Prima Pasta and Flanagan's (part of Rank Organization), Beefeater, Pizza Hut and TGI Friday's (part of Whitbread). Expansion into European is important: Whitbreads expect its food chains to account for around 15 per cent of the European market by 1999.

The growth of contract catering is to a large extent the result of privatization. Directly, when for example a local authority places its meals on wheels service, or school meals in the hands of a private contractor. And indirectly, as in the privatization of British Telecom. BT later put its entire catering operation out to tender – worth £60m per year, the largest single catering contract to be placed in the UK (with Compass Services). Civil service catering is another example of direct privatization. Forward Services, the former Civil Service Catering Organization (CISCO) was created in 1991 to prepare for privatization, and produce profits for the first time.

European interests have been reflected by the reforming in 1990 of the Industrial Catering Association under the umbrella of the European Catering Association. In 1991, Forte's contract catering subsidiary Gardner Merchant had 1,200 contracts and 10,000 staff in Germany, Holland, Belgium, France and Ireland, while Forte Airport Services operates the inflight commissaries in Paris, Amsterdam and Portugal.

The tourism scene

The tourism industry is also fiercely competitive. Many people base the decision on where they holiday on price. Tour operators are able to offer attractive deals because they buy airline seats and hotel accommodation in bulk, and work to low profit margins. The critical decision on what price to sell each package has to be taken well before the holidays can be marketed, possibly a year ahead. Even with the best market research, any one of a number of factors can have a severe effect on the careful calculations: sudden increase in oil prices, a terrorism incident or plane hijacking, recession, or even an unfavourable report on the television or in the newspapers.

Often tour operators are linked to airlines, hotels and travel agents. The Thomson Travel Group has major interests in publishing as well as being involved in the travel trade through Lunn Poly. Alton Towers, Chessington World of Adventures, Warwick Castle and Madame Tussaud's share the same owners, the Pearson Group. But strategies change. 1992 saw British Airports Authority withdrawing from the hotel business. And there are major changes in company ownership, and some outright casualties most years.

Quality issues

Quality is an ever-present issue facing the hotel, catering and tourism industry, and one which needs to be continually in the forefront of a successful organization. The quality hallmark – registration under the British Standards Institute's quality assurance recognition scheme, BS5750 – has already been achieved by a catering and leisure complex in Omagh, Northern Ireland, and the in-house catering division of Girobank in Bootle, Merseyside. Other companies well on the route to registration in 1992 included Russell and Brand, Wallsall Catering Service, Gardner Merchant and Sutcliffe Catering. Most major companies are working towards total quality culture – for example, Compass's Quality Assurance Programme.

Training plays a major role in quality and has become accepted as the key to success. Winners of the prestigious National Training Award have included many hotel and catering firms, from the very large such as Whitbread and Sutcliffe Catering, to small, family-run establishments such as Haydon House Hotel in Stoke-on-Trent and the Grapevine Hotel in the Cotswolds. Forte spends over £35m each year on training and developing its staff, has around twenty-five UK training centres and over 5,000 qualified trainers.

Top fifty companies

Rank 1991	Company	Turnover (£m)	Rank 1990	Rank 1991	Company	Turnover (£m)	Rank 1990
1	Trusthouse Forte	2,641	(1)	26	InterCity On Board Services	42.9	(26)
2	Hilton International	780.1	(2)	27	First Leisure Resorts	38.7	(23)
3	Bass Hotels	570	(3)	28	First Leisure Dancing	38.5	(22)
4	Queens Moat Houses	484.5	(4)	29	Greenall Whitley Catering etc	35.6	(-)
5	Rank Holidays & Hotels	437.9	(-)	30	Catering & Allied Services	34	(-)
6	Scottish & Newcastle Leisure	295.1	(6)	31	Vaux Inns	33.1	(-)
7	Scottish & Newcastle Retail	287.8	(-)	32	Friendly Hotels	31.2	(30)
8	Compass Services	264.9	(5)	33	Inn on the Park, London	24.6	(-)
9	Mt Charlotte Investments	241.7	(7)	34	Fairfield Catering	22.9	(40)
10	Rank Leisure	109.7	(-)	35	Allied Leisure	21.8	(34)
11	De Vere Hotels	97.7	(-)	36	Whitegate Leisure	21.7	(49)
12	Boddington Pubs, Hotels & Rests	96.2	(-)	37	My Kinda Town	21	(32)
13	Savoy Hotel plc	92	(11)	38	Letheby & Christopher	19	(-)
14	European Leisure	84.8	(33)	39	Pizza Express	16.7	(39)
15	ARA Services	84.7	(14)	40	Churchill Hotel, London	16.7	(-)
16	Stakis Hotels	83.4	(12)	41	Gleneagles Hotel	16.4	(37)
17	Travellers Fare	78.6	(13)	42	Aberdeen Steak Houses	16	(38)
18	RoadChef	76.6	(15)	43	Brian Smith Catering Services	14	(43)
19	City Centre Restaurants	75.7	(18)	44	Beeton Rumford	13.9	(-)
20	Swallow Hotels	70.4	(16)	45	Scottish Highland Hotels	13.8	(42)
21	Jarvis Hotels	68	(17)	46	National Leisure Catering	13.6	(-)
22	Copthorne Hotels	56.8	(21)	47	Greenfield Holdings	13.1	(-)
23	CCG Catering	55.8	(24)	48	High Table	12.6	(-)
24	Scott's Hotels	54.8	(19)	49	Resort Hotels plc	12.2	(-)
25	SAS Service Partner	44.1	(-)	50	Leisuretime Inns	12	(70)

Source Gaymour, D. (1992) Caterer 100 survey. *Caterer & Hotelkeeper*, 2 January.

Some of the initiatives to improve quality and training

Acorn awards

Sponsored by *Caterer & Hotelkeeper*, for young people who have made a substantial and significant contribution to the industry, in their sector, before they are 30 years old. (See profiles of Christine Barnes, this chapter, and Nicholas Jones, Chapter 6.)

Investors in People

Launched by government in 1990, the aim of the IIP programme is to get as many employers as possible up to a national standard of performance and commitment to their human resource. TECs and lecs manage the programme on a local basis. Underlying the IIP concept are four principles: to make a public commitment from the top to develop all employees to achieve business objectives; to regularly review the training and development needs of employees; to train and develop individuals on recruitment and throughout their employment; to evaluate the investment in training and development to assess achievement and improve future effectiveness. Approved IIP organizations have the right to display the scheme's laurel symbol to indicate their status. Two catering companies were among the first twenty-eight organizations to receive the award: Prospect Foods, which operates Betty's Cafés, and Tulsa Holdings, which operates Great British Burger restaurants, mainly in Wales and the North and invested about 4 per cent of its £2.4m turnover that year in training.

Master Innholder Award

Established in 1978 by the HCIMA with the Worshipful Company of Innholders with a view to extending and giving recognition to professionalism in the industry (see Chapter 11).

National Training Awards (NTA)

Annual scheme introduced in 1987, backed by Employment Department, Channel Four Television, *The Times, Daily Mail*, and Longman Training. *Corporate Awards* are open to employers, for the effective training of all or part of their workforce, and to training providers who have undertaken training for an employer. *Individual Awards* (introduced in 1991) are for individuals who have shown enterprise, initiative and personal commitment to their own development above and beyond their employer's expectations – showing a dedication to their own development that has benefited both them and their employer. In past years successful entries have come from all areas of commerce, industry, leisure and the public sector. Apart from profiting from national publicity, corporate award winners can use the awards logo in recruitment and promotional material. Individual winners receive cash prizes, a training credit and a trophy. Their employer receives a free supply of training materials.

Profile: Jonathan Thompson

Hotels

Jonathan is Director and General Manager of Hartwell House, Aylesbury. 'I feel privileged to be entrusted with the care of this Grade 1 listed building, with its magnificent Jacobean and Georgian facades, its eighty acres of parklands and gardens. I will always be mindful of the very highest standards established by owners Historic House Hotels Limited, and indebted to Richard Broyd, Chairman, for the support and confidence shown me during this challenging part of my career.'

Hartwell House opened in July 1989 with a staff of eighty-five, which includes a large kitchen brigade. There are twenty-nine bedrooms and three suites in the main building, and in 1991 the stable buildings were restored to provide a further sixteen bedrooms and suites.

An astronomical observatory at one time, museum, army billet and girls' finishing and secretarial school at other periods, the history of Hartwell House stretches back a thousand years. Among its famous occupants were William Peveral, the natural son of William the Conqueror, John Earl of Mortaigne, who became King of England in 1199, and Louis XVIII, exiled King of France. Louis leased the house from 1809 to 1814, and it was in the library that he signed the accession papers to the French throne.

'My father was an orthopaedic surgeon, and I always enjoyed meeting and making welcome guests at my parent's cocktail parties, so I worked hard for the O and A levels I needed to get on the Higher National Diploma in Hotel and Catering Administration at Blackpool College from 1972 to 1975.'

Valuable, contrasting experience was provided by two periods of industrial release: in the kitchens and restaurants of Gleneagles Hotel, Perthshire, and undertaking reception, housekeeping and duty management roles in the Abernant Lake Hotel, Llanwrtyd Wells, a small family-run business.

Hearing that 'Student of the Year' winner 1975 had taken up a Management Trainee/Relief Manager post with Centre Hotels, Jonathan decided he should also approach Centre. 'It was a good decision. I received very thorough training in the next three years and lots of good experience.'

From Deputy Manager of the Birmingham Centre Hotel, Jonathan went abroad for his first post as manager. When he took charge of the running of the Palm Beach Hotel in Aquaba, Jordan, the hotel was losing money. But before the year was out, it had become a profitable business and Jonathan's credibility was firmly established.

The Bowater family owned The Compleat Angler in Marlow, Buckinghamshire when Jonathan became its Deputy Manager in 1978. After the hotel's takeover two years later by Trusthouse Forte, Jonathan became General Manager of the Stratton House Hotel in Cirencester. Implementing

Jonathan Thompson (*continued*)

new systems in this twenty-eight bedroom family-owned hotel, pre-pared him for the next challenge, General Manager of Bodysgallen Hall Hotel in Llandudno. A seventeenth century mansion, it was the first property to be restored and opened as a hotel by Historic House Hotels. (Middlethorpe Hall near York followed and, in 1990, the company's fourth venture, The Cadogan Hotel, London, once the home of Lily Langtrey.)

Under Jonathan's management, Bodysgallen Hall received many awards between 1983 and 1989: AA 3 Red Stars; RAC Blue Ribbon; Andre Haperer's Hideaway Report 'Hotel of the Year', 1985–87; Welsh Tourist Board Award for Services to Tourism, 1986; Queen's Award for Export Achievement, 1987; Good Hotel Guide 'Cesar' Award for Out-standing Restoration and First Class Hotel Management, 1988. He worked closely with the Welsh Tourist Board, sat on its Overseas Market-ing Intelligence Committee, and became a Consultative Committee member of Llandrillo College. In 1988 he became a Director of Historic House Hotels.

Within one year of opening Hartwell House, Jonathan's work was rewarded by winning the title 'Buckinghamshire County Restaurant of the Year'. In 1990 the hotel won the Hayer's Trophy, AA 3 Red Stars, RAC Blue Ribbon, and the title 'South of England Newcomer of the Year'. That same year Jonathan was elected a Master Innholder (see earlier in this chapter).

The Hartwell Scholarship scheme is a Thompson initiative. Final year students at Aylesbury College are offered the chance of a year's paid work and training at Hartwell House. Jonathan judges applicants on their personality and dedication, their willingness to learn and work hard. 'They should be able to help our guests enjoy a happy and relaxed stay. We are in the business of providing quality service. And the scheme enables students to absorb an atmosphere where guests' needs are accorded paramount importance. Hopefully, our standards will give some of the industry's future managers a measure of the best that can be achieved.'

Trends by sector

By 1996, UK residents are expected to spend £16.6 billion on overnight domestic tourist trips, 40 per cent up on the present level. During the same period, the number of overseas visitors to the UK is predicted to rise by around 5 per cent per year. The trends behind these encouraging figures include more leisure time, increased disposable incomes, and better transport.

Hotels and guesthouses

There are around 34,600 hotels and guesthouses in the UK (HCTC, 1990). The majority are small – about 19,000 are proprietor or partnership-run, 8,000 employ between one and ten staff, 3,000 between eleven and twenty-four staff, 1,600 between twenty-five and forty-nine staff, and about 1,000 over fifty staff. Hotel employment accounts for one-quarter of the commercial sector. Growth is expected to remain sluggish – through the 1980s it averaged 1 per cent per annum. This reflects the maturity of the industry, as well as a degree of saturation. Although special deals on out-of-season, weekend breaks, conference packages and so forth, provide opportunities in the domestic sector, the principal growth potential lies with foreign visitors. Here the industry is vulnerable to high exchange rates, fears of terrorism, and the economic well-being of key countries such as the USA, Australia and Japan.

Restaurants

There are around 70,200 restaurants, cafés and snackbars in the UK (HCTC, 1990). Over half are proprietor or partnership-run, and less than 300 employ over fifty staff. Marketpower put the number of restaurants in 1991 at 58,700, of which 1,860 belonged to chains.

Generally the move has been away from high-spend gastronomic restaurants. There is greater choice than ever before in the mid-price range: roadside restaurants, bistros, tapas bars, themed restaurants, brasseries, pizza restaurants, and ethnic restaurants representing most of the countries and cultures of the world. Vegetarian dishes have established their place on menus, as have mineral water and a variety of low alcohol and alcohol-free drinks.

The fast food sector has grown the most rapidly. It now accounts for about 25 per cent of the eating-out market, and was worth £3.6 billion in 1991, according to Mintel. All this since 1974, when McDonald's opened its first UK restaurant.

By 1993 there will be sixty service areas on Britain's motorways, used by 200 million people per year. Around 140 million of them will use the restaurants (with 26,000 seats available), fast food or snack units, and 650,000 the low-priced accommodation offered in the adjacent lodges. Since the mid-1980s, meals served in travel-related outlets – including air, rail and motorway services – have risen by 7 per cent a year.

As this success demonstrates, a consistent product, lively atmosphere and affordable prices can attract large numbers of regular customers.

Profile: Tina O'Regan

Licensed trade/hotels

Tina O'Regan's family were in the hotel business in Eire. As a child she would help them out whenever school work allowed. After the death of both parents at quite an early age, the family hotel had to be sold. It seemed only natural that Tina should look to the industry for a job and a career.

There was no question of going to college, so Tina went to work at the Great Southern Hotel in Galway, determined to broaden and build up her skills. Over the next eight years at the grade A four-star hotel, she worked in all departments gaining first-hand experience in the bar, housekeeping, front of house and kitchen.

Marriage followed, and Joey and Tina decided to get work in England. Their application to McMullens Brewery for a management couple post was successful, and in July 1989 they completed the company's training scheme.

Their first post was the White Hart, a 100-year-old public house in the centre of Hertford. Joey looked after the bars and cellar, Tina the forty-seat restaurant and kitchen. Anxious not to lose any of the restaurant's regulars, Tina phased in menu improvements gradually, talking to her regular customers each day to find out what they thought of the new dishes. 'Our prices were slightly higher than usual for public house food, but this reflected the fact that the menu was ambitious. There were at least six fish dishes on my à la carte menu, which changed daily, plus steaks, poultry and so forth. Specials included pasta dishes, the chef's dish of the day and many different salads. On Sundays there was the traditional roast lunch as well as the à la carte menu.'

Joey and Tina's success in building up a good trade was recognized in late 1991. McMullen's put the couple in charge of much larger, recently refurbished premises: the Robin Hood, Botany Bay in Enfield, Middlesex. The twenty-eight-seat, non-smoking restaurant has a very busy lunchtime and evening trade. 'I am again building up my menu, involving my new clientele, and with Joey looking after the bars and cellar, we will make the most of the new challenge.'

Pubs

According to the Brewers' Society there are over 65,000 pubs throughout Britain, employing about half a million people including a large number of part-timers. Around 7,000 of these have restaurants, the vast majority serve food: about 3.5 million pub meals every day. HCTC and the research company Marketpower put the number of public houses somewhat higher, at 73,000 (1990).

The brewers own and operate about 20 per cent of the pubs, the rest are run as freehouses or brewers' tenancies. The industry has been undergoing a major restructuring, caused in part by the Monopolies and Mergers Commission's recommendations that the breweries should control fewer pubs (not more than 2,000 per company).

Most pubs now serve food, many have elegant restaurants offering an extensive menu – the range of beers, spirits, wines, soft drinks and low-alcohol drinks is very wide.

Catering contractors

HCTC estimates the number of contract caterers at 15,360 (1990). The 1991 UK contract catering survey published by the British Hospitality Association, valued the sector at £1.37 billion, a 34 per cent growth on 1990. It accounted for some 8.5 per cent of meals served away from home – nearly 650 million meals. Over half these were in industry and commerce. The next largest sector was independent schools (81 million), followed by the Ministry of Defence (54 million), healthcare (42.3 million), local authority catering (41 million), and catering for the public (in parks and so forth, 50 million). With 10,400 outlets and 91,000 employees in 1991–92, the average number of employees per outlet was 8.7.

The government's privatization programme has opened up an estimated 50,000 additional contacts from the National Health Service, local government, schools, defence and the Civil Service.

Catering service sector

Employment in *education*, which accounts for 25 per cent of the sector, is forecast to increase from 94,000 in 1990 to 104,000 in 1999, according to HCTC. This reflects the expansion in student numbers in further and higher education. Moderate growth is also forecast for the *medical sector*, up from 74,000 in 1990 to 78,000 in 1999. This is mainly as a result of the rise in numbers in residential homes, and growth in meals on wheels and day-centre provision. Improvements in productivity in hospital catering meant that numbers employed declined in the 1980s, despite an increase in the number of patients and a rise in the number of private hospital beds. (According to Marketpower, more than 900,000 patients need to be fed each day in NHS hospitals. Just under 500 million meals were served in 1990 in 2,440 hospitals and clinics and around 5,000 homes.)

Employment in *industrial and office catering*, which accounted for 24 per cent of the sector in 1990, is likely to decrease from 89,000 in 1990 to 73,000 in 1999. This reflects the trend towards using contract caterers. The numbers of catering staff employed in *public administration* are expected to remain steady at around 26,000, or even decline if contracting-out continues apace.

The *retail distribution* sector, which includes both staff and customer catering facilities, is likely to be relatively buoyant in terms of employment: up by 5,000 from 1990 to 49,000 in 1999. This reflects the steady consumer spending growth and a continuing trend towards shopping centres and superstores. Another buoyant sector is *recreation and cultural*, employing 39,000 by 1999, compared to 32,000 in 1990. Rising real incomes, increased leisure time and the widening preoccupation with health and fitness all point to greater investment and participation in this sector in the longer term, and consequently increasing demand for catering services.

Travel sector catering jobs declined in the 1980s as provision, especially on the rail network, was taken over by commercial catering companies. HCTC forecasts marginal growth in the 1990s, with around 20,000 jobs. Two-thirds of these jobs are associated with air travel, a particularly vulnerable sector, as the impact of the Gulf War proved.

Profile: The McCoy Brothers

Chefs/restaurateurs/hoteliers

With the acclaim received for their North Yorkshire restaurant and basement bistro, the McCoy brothers could be forgiven for becoming complacent. This is not the case. The commitment at the Tontine Inn to quality service is, if anything, stronger.

'We were born into the trade', explains Peter McCoy. 'For thirty-eight years my father and mother ran the Masham Hotel in Middlesborough, a pub with a busy food trade. Tom, Eugene and I used to help out when we came home from school. It was a way of life that we naturally slotted into.'

Peter and Tom's involvement in the Masham Hotel increased once they had left school, and for the period immediately following their father's death in 1967, the two brothers ran the hotel – while Eugene sought fame as a rock 'n' roll singer with his own group! Soon it was Peter and Tom's turn to diversify. 'We started a dress boutique over an ice cream parlour, selling clothes by new designers of the day. It was a great success until the opposition undercut our prices.'

John, the eldest of the four brothers, asked Peter and Tom to take over his coffee bar in Middlesbrough – he was leaving to open a country club at Kirklevington, Yorkshire. 'The Purple Onion became the sounding board for the challenges which were to come, with an ever-changing clientele of shop girls, students, hippies, and office workers. After two

The McCoy Brothers (*continued*)

years we had to close to make way for a new shopping centre – but we did get our first mention in Egon Ronay.'

John stepped in again. 'He asked Tom, Eugene and me to take over the catering at Kirklevington. With the help and encouragement of Mara Berni of the San Lorenzo Restaurant in London, Tom and I began to take a serious view of cooking. We started a dining club, Eugene taking charge of the wines and acting as host to club members. It quickly became a great success and in April 1973 we opened the first McCoy's Restaurant as an extra facility at Kirklevington.'

'We had some disasters as we grappled with the problems common to new ventures. But our determination won through. The restaurant established a good reputation, which was recognized by the award of a star in the 1976 Egon Ronay Guide.'

McCoy's Restaurant at the Tontine Inn opened in November 1978. On the A19, not far from Northallerton, the run-down eighteenth century coaching inn was transformed by the brothers. There are six bedrooms, where guests can relax and feel 'at home' with flowery wallpaper, quilts instead of duvets, big white baths and cottage furniture. Downstairs, the first of two large sitting rooms, has large settees and armchairs which envelop you, numerous colourful big cushions and a roaring fire in the winter. Tiger, the hotel cat, often makes an appearance and sits on the back of a chair with a very proprietorial air. The second sitting room, packed with objets d'art, also has the bar. This leads through to the forty-five-seat restaurant, with its Victorian drapings, and giant parasols suspended from the ceiling.

Kevin, Eugene's brother-in-law is Restaurant Manager. Tom cooks 'dishes which have ingredients many customers may not easily find and would not be able to easily produce'. His sauces are renowned.

Downstairs is the bistro, a very popular venue, which exudes an air of laughter and enjoyment. Here the cooking is done by Eugene, who also buys the wines for the business. Peter runs the hotel, generally oversees the business, and takes the role of 'mine host' with enthusiasm and commitment.

The excellent food, service and ambience created at Tontine by the McCoy brothers was recognized from the start. Within its first year the restaurant had been given a star in Egon Ronay's Guide and won his prestigious 'Gold Plate Restaurant of the Year' award. In 1990 it won the 'Catey Restaurant of the Year' award. Celebrities, famous chefs, tourists from home and abroad and dedicated regulars travel miles for the gourmet food and relaxed atmosphere, created by those 'innovative and uncompromising characters, the McCoy brothers'.

Pay and benefits

The HCIMA's 1991 salary survey showed that nearly 36 per cent of respondents earned more than £20,000, compared to 9 per cent in 1987, and 20 per cent earned more than £25,000. In the public house and restaurant sectors, one in four managers earned over £25,000, usually in the form of a profit-related bonus on top of a basic salary. The hospital sector improved dramatically, with 52 per cent of managers earning more than £15,000, compared with 27 per cent in 1990 and only 3 per cent in 1987.

The public house sector, with contract catering, offered the best employee benefits. Overall, 80 per cent of respondents received a pension and almost 60 per cent a sickness benefit over and above the statutory minimum. One in four managers had a company car. Holiday allocations were also increasing with 33 per cent of respondents getting more than twenty-five days holiday a year.

With five years of data available, the HCIMA surveys show a clear trend towards greater parity between women and men. Nevertheless, the proportion of men earning over £20,000 was nearly four times greater than that of women.

The 1990 wages survey conducted by the British Hospitality Association showed the average wage for live-in staff was £126, considerably above the national average for all industries. The average thirty-nine hour week gave a London head chef £361, in the south-west this dropped to £232 and in Scotland it was £240.

A more cautionary message emerged from the 1991 BHA wage survey – average salaries for hotel managers fell by 11 per cent as managers were replaced with younger staff who had lower wage expectations. Restaurants also suffered badly, while wages in the contract catering sector rose slightly, reflecting the greater resistance by contractors to the recession.

A survey conducted in 1990 by *Caterer & Hotelkeeper* found that the average salary for a hotel general manager was £25,000 (£35,000 in London), with £65,000 the highest reported figure. The general manager of a 200-bedroom four-star London hotel could expect to earn between £28,000 and £30,000, plus a car and a bonus scheme of up to 25 per cent of salary.

According to *Caterer* the averages for other positions were: food and beverage manager £16,000, personnel and training manager £14,000, chief engineer (London) £18,000. One exceptional restaurant manager was earning about £30,000 plus £85 a week in tips. However, a more realistic average was £16,000 in London, £14,000 in the provinces. Head housekeepers earned around £12,000, executive housekeepers around £15,500. Front of house managers earned £15,500 on average in London, £11,000 in the provinces. Averages for back of house positions were: financial controller £18,000, food and beverage controller £10,000, night auditor £9,500, payroll supervisor £10,000, store supervisor £8,500 and purchasing manager £10,500.

◆ All team members are provided with a smart costume and enjoy free lunches, free transport from selected areas, nursery facilities, and discounts. *Thorpe Park.*

◆ In return for a track record of real achievement, along with drive and enthusiasm we offer an excellent benefits package, including: private medical insurance, staff discount club, free meals, contributory pension scheme, employee share scheme, free life assurance, long term disability insurance. *Advertisement for assistant general managers, Granada Motorway Services.*

◆ Employment benefits when you join Holiday Inns: attractive and progressive salary that rewards individual responsibility and performance; minimum twenty days' annual holiday per year; free tailored uniform (laundered by the company); free guest-standard meals when on duty; sickness benefit; subsidized staff accommodation (where available). After a qualifying period, you are also entitled to a free 'Weekender' for you and your partner/family at any UK Holiday hotel for each year of service; 50 per cent discount at any Holiday Inn worldwide (subject to availability); anniversary payment. Twenty-five days holiday per year after five years service. *Holiday Inn Recruitment leaflet.*

◆ RoadChef was the first company in the UK to introduce an Employee Share Ownership Plan (ESOP). It enables employees with more than three years service to be given free shares in the company – therefore the more successful the company is, the more you will benefit. *RoadChef recruitment leaflet.*

Profile: Wing Commander Ted Malone

Royal Air Force

Ted Malone's interest in catering developed at a young age. During school holidays he worked at the Midland Hotel, Manchester, then part of the British Transport Hotel group. 'It was hard work over long hours. Fortunately, as a 16-year-old, I could not be expected to work after 10 pm. My last job of an evening was to get two chilled bottles of Jubilee Stout for the Head Waiter.'

Leaving De La Salle Grammar School in 1968 with two A levels, Ted hoped to get a place at the new University of Surrey – then in Battersea, London and one of only two centres to offer a degree in hotel and catering management. He was unlucky, but instead got accepted on the first Higher National Diploma in hotel and catering at Blackpool.

The three year course included two periods of industrial release. These he spent at Gleneagles Hotel in Tayside, probably the most famous British Transport Hotel. Such was his enthusiasm that Ted also spent his summer vacations with BTH, at Gleneagles, at The Station Hotel, Perth and The Old Course Hotel, St Andrews. He worked in the kitchen, butchery and restaurant, on floor service, in purchasing and the front office, and covering various junior management duties.

After gaining his HND, Ted joined British Rail Catering. He was sent on a management course at BR's training centre in Paddington, London. This lead to a Manchester-based post with the Area Manager North West Region. Responsibility for the catering outlets at Euston Station in London and at Liverpool followed, then promotion to Station Catering Manager at Manchester Piccadilly.

'By 1975, I felt it was time to broaden my experience. My fiancée pointed out an advertisement for commissioned catering officers with the Royal Air Force. I attended an interview and found myself on a two-day selection course at Biggin Hill. I was offered a six-year Short Service Commission, and on 22 June 1975, reported to RAF Henlow for the sixteen week officer training course. This pushed me to my mental and physical limits.'

Ted married his fiancée within a week of graduating as Flying Officer, and was sent to RAF Hereford to complete a short induction course on the RAF catering specialization. In April 1976 he took up his first post, as Deputy Catering Officer at RAF Lyneham, Wiltshire, home of the Hercules transport force. Catering had to be provided to over 200 staff in three large messes. There was also an in-flight section and a transit hotel.

After fourteen months Ted was transferred to RAF Leeming, North Yorkshire as Officer in Command of Catering. 'My own boss at last, I was in charge of all aspects of food catering, accounts, production and related

Wing Commander Ted Malone (*continued*)

dining, bar and accommodation services, in five outlets, with around 120 Service and civilian staff.'

After promotion to Flight Lieutenant in 1979, Ted moved as Station Catering Officer to High Wycombe, Buckinghamshire, headquarters of RAF Strike Command. 'There was a stream of high ranking RAF and civilian visitors to look after, and a heavy social function commitment on top of my day-to-day responsibilities.'

Even greater challenges came two years later when Ted was transferred to the RAF's Air Transport Force HQ at Upavon, Wiltshire. With another officer, he was responsible for all aspects of in-flight catering, including forward instructions to suppliers down route and the catering on special flights for VIPs, VVIPs, and government officials. He also had to deal with the particular challenges posed by the Falklands War, with troops being flown thousands of miles to the battle zone and back. 'In January 1983 I was sent to Ascension, the small, almost barren and very remote island in the Atlantic, that is used as a stop-over for flights between the UK and the Falklands. For a six-month unaccompanied tour, I took charge of the three field kitchens. Tents on concrete garage bases housed the simple gas burners on metal frames.'

Having seen the start of the arrival of permanent kitchens, Ted returned to his responsibilities at Upavon and promotion to Squadron Leader. From the end of 1984 to the end of 1987 was spent in Akrotiri, Cyprus as Station Catering Officer. 'With the help of my Flight Lieutenant deputy, we coped with a busy in-flight catering set-up, a hospital, two remote sites on the top of a mountain and three messes providing dining, kitchen, bar, accommodation and function facilities for military and local employees. It was a large station and life was busy!'

Christmas 1987 saw 'the Malone family and sixty boxes, back in the UK in an empty RAF house awaiting the arrival of our furniture from storage and another forty-six boxes. The children really thought Santa had been busy!' Ted had been given his first staff appointment at Ministry of Defence, Stanmore, Middlesex. He was to be responsible for personnel, recruitment and training of Service and civilian staff. In July 1989 Ted was asked to review working practices in RAF messes. Briefing catering officers and mess managers on the new procedures entailed a 'travelling roadshow' visiting all RAF stations.

At less than one week's notice in April 1990, Ted was appointed RAF Assistant Director of Catering and promoted to Wing Commander with responsibility for contract catering, food supplies, plus personnel, training, recruitment, liaising with schools, colleges and trade sponsors. And fifteen months later, he was appointed Regional Commander at the Inspectorate of Recruiting (RAF) East. One of two commanders, this involves the control and supervision of over thirty-one RAF Careers Information Offices, and responsibility for the recruiting of officers and other ranks, for all RAF Trades, from engineer to nurse.

Further information

Careers Service

For your local office, look in the telephone directory.

Careers and Occupational Information Centre (COIC)

- Publishes wide range of careers literature, reference books, videos, software programs and teaching material.
  Rockery Cottages, Sutton-cum-Lound, Retford, Notts DN22 8PJ (publications ordering point, general information on COIC)
  Tel: 0777 705951.
  Room W1108, Moorfoot, Sheffield S1 4PQ (head office and marketing department).
  Tel: 0742 594563/4/9.
  5 Kirk Loan, Corstorphine, Edinburgh EH12 7HD (Scottish office).
  Tel: 031 334-9821.

Careers information

See Chapter 11 for addresses:

- ABTA National Training Board.
- Brewers' Society.
- Hotel, Catering and Institutional Management Association (HCIMA).
- Hotel and Catering Training Company (HCTC).
- Institute of Leisure and Amenity Management (ILAM).

English Tourist Board (ETB)

- Careers in tourism.
  Education and Training Unit, Thames Tower, Black's Road, London W6 9EL
  Tel: 081 846 9000.

Springboard

- One-stop shop, offering careers advice, jobs and training.
  1 Denmark Street, London WC2H 8LP
  Tel: 071 497 8654.

Northern Ireland Tourist Board (NITB)

- Careers in tourism.
  River House, High Street, Belfast BT1 2DS
  Tel: 0232 231221

Scottish Tourist Board (STB)

- Careers in tourism.
  23 Ravelstone Terrace, Edinburgh EH4 3EU
  Tel: 031 332 2433.

Training and Employment Agency

- For Northern Ireland: careers advice, training schemes, open learning, grants.
  Clarendon House, 9–21 Adelaide Street, Belfast BT2 8DJ
  Tel: 0232 244300.

Welsh Tourist Board (WTB)

- Careers in tourism.
  Brunel House, 2 Fitzalan Road, Cardiff CF2 1UY
  Tel: 0222 499909.

2
The main areas of work

There is a good job waiting for you in hotels, catering and tourism. The industry can give this guarantee because it offers opportunities to suit everyone. For your part, you need to decide what you have to offer the industry, and what sort of work will best suit your abilities and character – Chapter 4 returns to this theme. From this chapter you will get a good idea of the main areas of work. Chapter 3 covers the more specialist areas, including marketing, personnel, maintenance, accounting, the armed forces, police, and related areas such as home economics and journalism.

Good craft skills are one of the main driving forces behind any successful hotel, or catering establishment. Customers return to a place where the staff are friendly and good at their job. Businesses staffed by people who know what they are doing, do well. Conrad Hilton's famous saying that the key to success for a hotel was *location, location, location*, has been brought up-to-date by that equally successful hotelier, Charles Forte. Lord Forte puts success down to *good location, good management, good staff.*

If you aspire to a supervisory or management position, you need at the very minimum, to appreciate the skills involved in cooking, waiting, housekeeping, reception, barwork and so forth. Your progress will be even surer if you have a good grounding in those skills.

Food preparation and cooking

Work in the kitchens can be particularly demanding. You will spend most of the working day on your feet in hot conditions. What you are called depends on where you work: 'chef' is more usual in hotels and restaurants, 'cook' in hospitals and schools, 'short order cook' in snack bars and similar operations with a limited menu and the emphasis on a fast turn around.

The pressure is often intense, reaching a peak during service time. Things may even seem chaotic, but well-run kitchens depend on careful planning and preparation, good organization, excellent teamwork and accurate timing. The atmosphere will reflect the style of the head chef: some prefer a calm, low key approach, others a buzzing, noisy environment.

There is great satisfaction to be gained from creating a dish of food that gives enjoyment and pleasure to the person eating it, whether it be a healthy and light meal, vegetarian food and ethnic dishes, or a conventional meal. You will be expected to demonstrate your knowledge of different recipes, styles of preparation and content. Food is not cheap because it comes in bulk, and the equipment costs a lot to buy and operate. This means tight controls at every stage. Hygiene is of the utmost importance and there are very strict rules to be followed, especially when the food is chilled or frozen for reheating immediately before service.

Years of practice – working your way steadily up the ladder – are required to reach the best – and very well paid – positions. You are likely to start as a trainee, apprentice or *commis chef*. If you are in a big kitchen, the next level up, *chef de partie*, means responsibility for one section, for example pastry or the larder. From there you might become second in command, the under or *sous chef*. As deputy to the *head chef* (sometimes called *executive chef* or *maître chef de cuisine*), this will involve you in menu planning, buying supplies, training and supervising staff. Of course, in a small operation, you will be doing almost everything including helping serve customers.

In some kitchens, the menu is limited – for example, to steaks or pizzas – or standardized for the restaurant or hotel chain. In these situations, most of the dishes are bought in ready prepared, chilled or frozen. Many hospitals and schools use cook-chill foods, which have been prepared in a central production unit and transported in refrigerated vehicles.

♦ The kitchen is the creative centre of a Hilton hotel, and the work, although highly demanding, is extremely rewarding. The standard of the food is something guests will remember long after they have left – and will be one of the principal reasons they will return. The food preparation teams work to high professional standards. New recipes and techniques are constantly being developed, making a career in this discipline both challenging and exhilarating. *Hilton Hotels careers leaflet.*

♦ In catering there's no room for sentiment or idealism. I'm happy where I am but eventually I won't want to be cooking this kind of food waiting on tenterhooks every year for the publication of the Michelin guide. It's glamorous for a few but attached to that is a lot of very hard work; you learn more than cooking along the way. *Paul Flynn, sous chef, Chez Nico, London, Acorn Award winner 1991, interviewed by Kate McDermid in* Caterer & Hotelkeeper.

♦ Mine is a long way from a 'normal' kitchen. I have a very casual approach and expect people to work on their own initiative once they've been shown. I could kick their backsides and still not get results. I don't like people living in fear and as a result it's a happy environment and they stay. *Brian Baker, head chef, Hambleton Hall, Oakham, Leicestershire, Acorn Award winner 1991.*

Profile: Sainath Rao

Chef/hotels/restaurants

Sainath Rao's love of cooking began as a child in India. From the age of eight he was given the little kitchen chores. 'I vividly remember being fascinated with the variety of vegetables and how my mother transformed them into various dishes. I tried my hand at preparing a dish when-ever possible, fully aware that I had to eat it, no matter what!'

'A single parent, my mother had to educate herself and bring me up with a little help from grandfather, who was a full-time teacher. My mother passed the three-year Catering and Food Technology course and became a chef. She always told me about what she saw or did. It seemed like lots of action to me!'

At his interview to join the Taj Group of Hotels in 1973, Sainath, who had been brought up a vegetarian, was asked if he could handle meats – he replied yes! Following his induction tour of the enormous kitchens of the Taj Mahal Hotel in Bombay, capable of catering for up to 6,000 guests a day, the Executive Chef asked Sainath which section he would least like to work in. 'Butchery was my quick reply. I am afraid to be with those huge carcasses hanging in there.' That day Sainath had to start in butchery.

'From skinning chickens I graduated to jointing meat and filleting fish. In that first year I worked in eight of the huge glass partitioned sections of the main kitchen, learning the correct usage of different equipment, and the basic planning or *mis-en-place* behind various catering tasks. I also learned the strict protocol for asking questions so you didn't distract the concentration of the chefs. By being helpful over a period of time, I gained their trust and was allowed to watch. At the end of each session I noted everything I had observed in my pocket diary. This helped greatly when I was asked to perform.'

Sainath was sent to Madras for the opening of the 240 bedroom, five-star Taj Coromandel Hotel. 'I joined a team of eight on the first shift in the Coffee Shop and Room Service Kitchen. I managed the Pantry and learnt to cope with the tensions of a busy breakfast and lunch schedule. I always made sure to be well informed of what was to be done and developed the habit of being present an hour before my shift began, to avoid nasty surprises.' Celebrity guests often made impromptu arrivals in the kitchen. 'The cricketers Tony Grieg and Derek Underwood spent many an hour in the kitchen safely away from fans. I learnt to make sure I was always immaculate in my whites and to keep my work area fairly tidy.'

Taj Coromandel sponsored Sainath to join the Catering College in Madras. He attended the classes in the day and worked in the evening at

Sainath Rao (*continued*)

the hotel as usual. Saturday mornings were spent in bakery lessons, for the rest of the weekend he was kept busy at the hotel. After four years Sainath passed first class, exactly ten years after his mother got her certificate.

'When the hotel was awarded the catering contract for the new flight kitchen at Madras Airport, I was sent with a team of six. The disciplines learnt over the years helped me a great deal to organize, to motivate staff without the ranks of supervisors and executives hovering around, and to produce quality meals under the stringent regulations which govern flight catering.'

In his six years at the Taj, Sainath participated in many Food Festivals including Spain, Mexico, Italy, Hungary and Malaysia. 'The lure of learning and trying new areas becoming persistent, I joined Chola Sheraton in Madras. But the demands made by the new job did not satisfy my expectations. I left Madras suddenly, telling my mother to expect me back in New Delhi in two weeks.

'On a visit to the Taj Mahal Hotel in New Delhi, as I walked past the kitchens, I was moved by the planning which had obviously gone into the various departments of the new hotel. I longed to return to activity and I asked to meet the Executive Chef. "When could I start?", he said. "Today" was my reply! I was taken on as a First Commis with a four-figure salary which was substantial. But the euphoria evaporated when I faced a team all physically stronger than me. My first job was to make tea for nearly twenty chefs and cooks, to be served without a break. Rather than run around the unfamiliar kitchen looking for kettles and so forth, I filled a large pan with water and put it on the nearest gas range to boil. The tea took six minutes to serve!'

Working under a group of chefs specializing in regional cuisines, Sainath observed their individual necessities had many ingredients in common which they spent considerable time preparing. 'I came in an hour earlier, and prepared these ingredients in bulk. It helped develop a rapport among the group and I was able to work alongside the chefs from thenceforth without feeling like a stranger.'

Sainath spent two years working behind the scenes for the hotel's various restaurants. Ex-premier Indira Ghandi was a regular guest and Prince Charles dined in the hotel when he visited India.

When the Chairman of the Taj Group needed chefs for his future venture in London, Sainath was one of the twelve chefs selected for interview. He was successful, and after eight months' further training in Bombay, arrived in London with two months to help prepare for the opening of the Gloucester Road Bombay Brasserie. This included time at La Sorbétière in Paris, learning to make sorbets from fruits imported from India.

He spent eight years at the Bombay Brasserie, progressing under the four Executive Chefs over the period, and standing in as relief for all the chefs who went on leave, or left after a transfer. The restaurant was

Sainath Rao (*continued*)

judged as one of the most successful in England, with an average clientele of 250 upwards every day.

'I felt I was beginning to be set in my ways and needed a new challenge. When one of the regular clients invited me to discuss the possibility of opening a new restaurant, I went to see the Coburg Hotel in Bayswater. The building was being renovated and I was ushered into the office of Akbar Verjee, Director of the hotel. I was impressed with the frank discussion which followed and noticed the organized approach and neat analysis of what the Director wished to do, and the attentive listening to what I needed. I worked closely with the architects in the planning of the restaurant and installation of the equipment.'

The Spice Merchant Restaurant opened on 29 November 1990 – Sainath's thirty-fourth birthday, and the eighteenth year of his career. His team included two Senior Chefs, one Assistant Chef and two Kitchen Assistants. Many of the dishes Sainath has collected over the years from various parts of India. 'I changed the menu according to the constant feedback of the appraisals we received. The lunch buffet consisted of fresh vegetables which I picked from the market and the meats were delivered fresh six days a week. Purchasing in a large market requires good communication and negotiation skills, and lots of common-sense.'

Although the restaurant was well received, and enjoyed a regular evening trade, the recession affected lunch time business. Sainath decided that during the day he was wasting his time and his employer's money, so he joined Noon Products, an Indian cook-chill food production company as Executive Chef. From 9am to 5pm he converts his recipes on to computer programs for bulk production, returning to the Spice Merchant for the 6.30pm to midnight shift as Consultant Chef, overseeing the evening trade. Sainath is booked to appear in the BBC *Hot Chefs* programme for one week in October 1992.

'Life is very different to those years in Hyderabad in my mother's kitchen, but I shall always keep the memory of my desire to emulate her cooking skills as a spur to achieving the very best standards.'

Food and drink service

Serving staff play a key role in creating the appropriate atmosphere in which people can enjoy eating and drinking. As the interface between those who prepare the food and those who consume it, you need to know about the food you are serving, its main ingredients and how it is cooked. The way in which you present and serve the food should reflect the care and attention which has been put into its preparation.

The range of food service situations is vast. In roadside and theme restaurants, for example, a friendly, efficient style goes down well. This is also true for the self-service forms of food service: buffets, fast food units, the self-service counters in motorway restaurants, department stores, and employee feeding. In these situations, you are more likely to be called a food service or counter assistant than a waiter or waitress.

Helping set up and keep the counter display looking attractive is an important aspect of the job, since this encourages sales. Depending on where you are stationed on the counter, you will be involved in portioning and serving food, making hot and cold drinks, and taking cash (unless there is a cashier). In carvery restaurants you might have to help with the carving from time to time. If there are vending machines, it's quite likely that you will help clean and refill them. Sometimes you will be involved in some of the cooking – fast food units generally have a rotation system so that staff spend time doing each of the jobs. Other tasks include helping set up the restaurant, filling cruets, filling cutlery trays, preparing tables. During service everything has to be kept looking good, and that may mean clearing and wiping down tables, as well as vacuuming the floor and emptying the bins in which customers have disposed of their food cartons.

Living up to the name 'fast food', means working extremely quickly when the pressure's on. Good teamwork is vital.

In luxury restaurants, the style of service is more formal, with a great deal of protocol. You will have to be able to transfer food from large, often heavy platters or dishes to the customer's plate using a spoon and fork – *silver service*, as it is known. And some or all of the preparations for the final dish may be up to you, positioned by the customer's table, every move watched and smiles of pleasure as you flambé the food with brandy or a liqueur.

Large banquets offer a different challenge again: serving a large number of people quickly, so that everyone gets their food at the right temperature, and the wine when they want it.

In addition to serving customers their food and drinks, you will usually help with laying up tables, polishing glasses and cutlery, greeting customers and showing them to their table, taking orders, and clearing. You may be in charge of particular tables in the restaurant – your *station* – but if you are new to the job you will probably start as a *commis* or junior, clearing tables and fetching orders from the kitchen. In many restaurants it will also be your responsibility to add up the customer's bill, and take payment.

Profile: Alyson Cheyne

Restaurants/clubs

The Lensbury Club, Teddington, Middlesex is a private sports and social club for the employees and pensioners of the Shell Group – and their families. The Club's Restaurant Manager Alyson Cheyne and her staff of around forty-five, run the 110 seat à la carte restaurant, the self-service restaurant (a similar size), a snack bar, and five function rooms which cater for private parties between twelve and 120 people, and are popular for wedding receptions, business meetings and conferences. Catering services are also provided for the Shell Management Training Centre, which forms part of the complex. In her other role as Senior Duty Manager, Alyson deputizes for the House Manager, and also becomes responsible for the kitchens, bars and housekeeping.

Cooking and dietetics were Alyson's favourite subjects at school. But the staff of the Boclair Academy, Glasgow tried to discourage her from considering a career based on these subjects. They were concerned that there would not be enough opportunities. Nevertheless with Food and Nutrition as one of seven Ordinary grade SCE passes and one of three Higher grade passes, Alyson obtained a place on the three-year Home Economics (Food Studies) Diploma course at The Queen's College, Glasgow.

With her diploma and part-time experience waiting and cooking at Wicket's, a small hotel in Glasgow, Alyson was accepted in June 1984 by the Stakis Group as a trainee manager at the Glasgow Steakhouse. The opportunities to progress were slower than she had hoped, so after six months, she moved down the road to the Danish Food Centre, as Assistant Manager and Outside Catering Events Manager.

The restaurant was open for twelve hours daily, employed Danish students, and the Centre sold Danish dairy products. The job was interesting, challenging and very varied, but six months after Alyson had started, the Danish Government withdrew financial support for the project and the Centre was closed.

The new Stakis Area Manager contacted Alyson to persuade her to return to the company as Deputy Manager of the Stirling Steakhouse. From May 1985, she and the manager, also a young woman, worked hard at building up an effective team. Disappointment soon followed. 'I was transferred to the Glasgow Steakhouse and for two months had almost no free time. There was no diversification in my work. In fact I felt blinkered. I tried to approach the situation in a methodical manner, mentally listing all the areas of my work in which I was not satisfied, as well as those I found stretched my capabilities. I then started looking for jobs in those work areas where I could expand my strengths.'

The search led to Alyson's appointment in 1986 as Assistant Manager at the Black Bull Hotel in Milngavie, Glasgow, part of Thistle Hotels. 'This was not the right move either, but it did confirm that I preferred the

Alyson Cheyne (*continued*)

environment of an independent unit, where I had more scope as an individual.'

The ever-changing pattern of her work at the Lensbury Club, where she has been since June 1987, has provided Alyson with plenty of scope to develop her skills. Marriage in May 1991 has not affected her career plans. 'I am really enjoying this job and want to stay on. And in any case Russel's job involves much travelling abroad.'

Alyson is an Affiliate Member of the Hotel Catering and Institutional Management Association.

Bar service

A good memory and good people skills are great assets. Remembering what people have ordered, getting the prices and the change correct. Knowing what you are selling, and being able to suggest alternatives when the brand a customer asks for is not available. A lot of care and attention is behind a good pint of beer, a beautifully presented enticing cocktail, a glass of wine poured to the correct level and served at just the right temperature.

You are also likely to be involved in serving snacks and food, in helping prepare the bar for service, restocking shelves and refrigerators.

The social skills require being friendly to the customers, but not too familiar, and firm when you need to be. Sometimes unpleasant situations can develop when there's alcohol around. Then the right action at the right time can prevent the situation turning unpleasant. Remember that many people come to a pub to enjoy themselves, but not everyone wants to be chatted to.

The bigger pubs have their own *cellar staff*, responsible for looking after the deliveries, making sure the beer is served in the right condition – and for cask conditioned beer that is quite a skill. It will also involve attending to bulk mineral dispensers, sorting out supplies of carbon dioxide gas to give those drinks that should have it, a sparkle, and just the right pressure to get still drinks up to the taps in the bar.

For large events like banquets and conferences, serving staff usually get the drink orders from a dispense bar. This will be behind the scenes somewhere, and the *dispense bar staff* won't have direct contact with the customers.

To work behind a licensed bar, you have to be over 18 years of age.

What the publican/bar manager does

Overall responsibility for a pub means turning your hand to quite a variety of tasks. During opening hours, personal attention to your customers will be important, keeping an eye out to see that your staff are doing their job well, that beer barrels are changed quickly and properly, and that the behaviour of some customers is not allowed to spoil the enjoyment of others, or put you at risk with the law.

At other times, you will be involved in planning work rotas, ordering supplies, helping stock up the bars, stocktaking, doing paperwork, and making sure that customers are attracted to your pub, and spend well when they get there.

♦ Licensees must be able to devise new ways of attracting and retaining customers, must know about licensing and food safety laws, hygiene, information technology, staff training and motivation, cellar management, catering, marketing and advertising, together with budgetary control and effective purchasing with realistic costing of products. *Brewers' Society* Career Opportunities in Licensed Retailing.

Firm self-discipline is required: being surrounded by alcohol and people enjoying themselves can prove a strong temptation. Tact, patience and good humour are also important: you might have to show interest in a story or joke you have been told so often you know it by heart.

The long hours, noise and smoky atmosphere require a lot of stamina. For those running their own pub it can be quite difficult to get any time off. But the close personal involvement with people, and in the success of the business, is very rewarding.

There are basically three categories of licensed house management: where you own and run your own *free house*; where you rent a pub from one of the breweries and operate it as your own business under the terms of a *tenancy* agreement; where you are an employee of the brewery which owns and runs *managed houses*.

Conferences and banqueting

Quite a number of hotels, civic centres, theatres, and leisure centres have facilities which they hire out for conferences, meetings, banquets, exhibitions and similar events for small to large numbers of people. There are also places that specialize in this work, such as the Connaught Rooms in London.

The job of seeing that every aspect of these events runs smoothly, from the provision of sophisticated audio visual equipment, to a note pad and pencil at each place setting, is done by a team led by the conference manager. (In a hotel where the emphasis is on special meals, cocktail parties, dinner/dances and so forth, the person in charge is likely to be known as the banqueting manager.) An eye for detail, excellent communication and supervisory skills, careful planning and coordination are the keys to success. From the first contact with the client, when the emphasis is on establishing exactly what is required – and selling that little extra – to the follow-up after the event, to ensure that everyone is satisfied, and to seek repeat business.

♦ Conference and banqueting is a high profile division. It requires a unique combination of skills, from planning and organization through budget control and creative design to sales, marketing and administration. *Hilton Hotels recruitment leaflet.*

What the catering manager does

Catering manager is the job title used in many industrial and welfare catering establishments for the person in overall charge of the planning and provision of the food and drink service.

Keeping the team functioning at its maximum efficiency, and better than that will be your goal. Budgets have to be agreed and then kept to, pressure on costs is tight. The clients – be they hospital patients, the company's senior management, or the shop floor staff – can be demanding, sometimes even unreasonably so. Suppliers will be cooperative if you are in a tight corner, but the system works best when you and your staff plan ahead carefully, when everyone is well trained and highly motivated. Hygiene and quality standards must never be sacrificed for the sake of cutting corners or because staffing levels are not adequate for the task, or equipment faulty.

♦ The catering supervisor must be over 18 and preferably have catering qualifications. The work involves the preparing and supervizing of main meals and breaks through store operating hours. It also includes coordinating menus, ordering food supplies, controlling costs, organizing and training staff and maintaining hygiene, fire and safety standards. Catering supervisors work five days a week with alternate free Saturdays. In certain locations, some evening work will be necessary. *Marks and Spencer careers leaflet.*

♦ As Operations Manager you will be responsible for a team of forty people producing 60,000 meals each week with a budget in excess of £3m per annum. You must have sound technical and management skills blended with a commitment to furthering public sector enterprise and creativity. A formal food science or catering qualification is essential, together with a track record that will demonstrate your drive and determination. *Oxfordshire Health Authority.*

Profile: Phillip Ruddock

Hospital catering

From Assistant Cook, Royal Victoria Infirmary, Newcastle upon Tyne, 1971, to Director of Site Services at Ealing Hospital in 1990, shows the kind of determination behind Phil Ruddock's career. Six CSE passes got him into Ashington College in Northumberland, and his first clutch of City and Guilds certificates. Later he was to go back to college to gain further C&G certificates, the Licensed Trade Diploma (a side-step that was not pursued), the NEBSS Certificate (Watford College, 1979), NEBSS Diploma (Putteridge-bury College, Luton, 1983), Dietetic Cookery and RIPHH Certificates (Waltham Forest College, 1984), C&G YTS Instructor Certificate (1985), and RIPHH Advanced Food Hygiene Certificate (1989).

The knowledge acquired on these courses contributed to Phil's personal development and steady upward progress through the National Health Service. From Newcastle in July 1976 he moved to Middlesex as Assistant Head Cook, at Hillingdon Hospital, Uxbridge. Phil enjoyed the new challenges, was soon Head Cook, and by December, Kitchen Superintendent at Mount Vernon Hospital in Northwood.

Further experience in production management in a similar post at the very busy St Albans City Hospital gave Phil the confidence to apply for his first management position. In 1982 he was appointed Assistant Catering Manager at Cell Barnes Hospital in St Albans, and within two years he had moved twice up the hospital management hierarchy: Catering Manager II at Hemel Hempstead General Hospital, then back to Hillingdon Hospital as Catering Manager III.

The Conservative Government's privatization programme has brought Phil his most demanding role so far. As Director of Site Services at Ealing Hospital, he took over the catering in April 1990 from contract caterers Gardner Merchant, as well as shared responsibility for transport, security and some of the domestic services. To do this Phil was invited, along with four other colleagues, to set up their own company, Professional Management Team Ltd, which has to work within budgets negotiated with the Health Authority. Phil's staff of over 100 are still employed by the Authority, but this is expected to change.

'Striking out on my own in this way has been quite nerve racking', admits Phil. 'But I have had tremendous support from my staff. I try to be a firm manager, while encouraging a high degree of self-motivation, and giving staff clear responsibilities for maintaining their work areas. Naturally, high hygiene standards are of paramount importance in a cook-chill operation such as we have at Ealing, as they are in hospital catering generally.

Phillip Ruddock (*continued*)

'Food contamination and food poisoning, interest me as subjects. The real challenge is to establish good working practices and raise staff awareness to the level where one can be confident that the product is absolutely safe at the point it is consumed.' Phil has to keep within tight budgets, giving the patients – 'my customers' – food which satisfies their nutritional needs. 'I would hope our patients actually look forward to their meals each day.' One of Phil's main ambitions is that Ealing Hospital should become nationally recognized for its quality and style of food service, and his kitchens noted for their good hygiene practices and level of cleanliness.

Phil has a love of food and all activities connected with it – from growing vegetables and soft fruit to the preparation, cooking, presenting and, of course, the eating!

Housekeeping and accommodation services

The jobs here cover everything from making beds, cleaning bedrooms and public areas, to checking the delivery of the laundry, issuing housekeeping stores, arranging flowers, liaising with reception over the availability of rooms, and with maintenance for repairs. At the more senior levels, you will be involved in helping choose furnishings and fittings.

◆ Housekeeping is very much a team-based department, with each person contributing an essential element . . . The greatest attention must be paid to every conceivable detail, as the smallest considerations can make the biggest difference to the overall impression of the accommodation. *Hilton Hotels recruitment leaflet.*

The *room attendant* (still sometimes called a chambermaid) will have between six and fifteen guest rooms to thoroughly clean and service each day: exactly how many depends on the style of the hotel, and the number of staff on duty. This means starting early, and fitting in your routine around the comings and goings of guests. You will often be on your own, and the work is physically demanding.

Supervising the room attendants will be the *floor housekeeper* or, in smaller hotels, the *assistant* or *head housekeeper*.

◆ Housekeeper/Manager required to manage and run a new high class accommodation establishment at Sandown Park Racecourse and Leisure Complex . . . In addition to breakfast service, occasional other meals will be required at times for racecourse personnel. Cooking and cleaning help will be provided but this is very much a hands-on and lead-by-example role ... Experience of stock, materials, food and cash handling and gross profit realization is essential ... Annual discretionary bonus, private hospital/healthcare scheme, and a spacious self-contained two-bedroomed flat on the premises. *United Racecourses (Holdings) Ltd.*

◆ Housekeeping is a specialized job, like doctors, nurses and the police. A person has to want to do it. It is a career in itself. As a job it has much in common with the film industry. In any one year we can play more roles than Joan Collins and Harrison Ford put together. Whether it be our JR role – trying to get the best from our suppliers – or our Claire Rayner role – playing agony aunt to a very upset executive chef whose Egyptian cotton whites have been lost in the laundry. Believe me, it's constant excitement. The action never stops coming and roles keep rolling. *Deverne Harewood-Sealy, executive housekeeper, Grafton Hotel, London, interviewed in the* Caterer & Hotelkeeper's Career Guide.

Domestic bursars are responsible for the catering and accommodation services of college and university halls of residence. In many establishments this will include looking after conference delegates, holiday-makers, tourists, people on special interest trips and others who use the facilities during vacations. The main concern during term time will be the students, but a number of colleges have purpose-built conference centres that are used by 'outsiders' throughout the year.

◆ As Resident Assistant Domestic Bursar you will be responsible for the day-to-day supervision of a large dining hall and organization of both college and outside functions. The College provides amenities for 500 men and women undergraduates and graduates, and is a venue for conferences in vacations. Applicants must have good experience in all aspects of banqueting and food service and be used to controlling staff. Attractive conditions of service include free board and residence in single accommodation. *St Anne's College, Oxford.*

◆ We are seeking to appoint an outstanding individual to fill the post of Head of Residential and Catering Services (salary up to £30,047 pa). You will be responsible for a budget of £4m pa which includes the management of about 2,200 student residential places, a catering turnover of £1.4m pa and a successful conference centre (100+ bedrooms). It is likely that you will have a degree and/or a professional qualification in a relevant area and the essential requirements for the post are: a thorough understanding of quality management in a complex organization, the capacity to develop and lead an effective and well-motivated team, excellent planning and organization skills, the vision to respond to a rapidly changing environment. *Aston University,* Caterer & Hotelkeeper *7 November, 1991, with the note that previous applicants need not re-apply.*

Reception and front office

A cheerful, friendly personality is certainly an asset, especially when it is combined with good administrative skills. Meeting guests is only one aspect of reception work. There are questions on a whole range of subjects to be answered, bookings to be taken, guests to be registered and allocated rooms, their special requirements to be organized, money to be handled, valuables accepted for sake keeping. Then there are letters to be answered, messages to be taken and passed on. And it's essential to keep housekeeping and other colleagues informed of what is happening.

In all but the smallest hotels a computer will be at the centre of reception systems. These greatly simplify the preparation of guest bills, and the taking of reservations, but do not remove the need for the highest level of accuracy. Other equipment you are likely to be dealing with includes fax and telex machines, the telephone switchboard and word processors.

Receptionist staff have a key role to play in maximizing revenue from accommodation sales. The more senior you get in the team the more pressure you will be under, and the more difficult the choices you have to make. Do you accept a booking now for two nights in the middle of a week, or turn it away because there might be a tour booking tomorrow for the whole week?

♦ You will be called on to do 101 different things, some routine, some unexpected, but all must be handled with complete assurance and professionalism. *Hilton Hotels recruitment leaflet.*

♦ The most important qualities you can offer are your personality, willingness to please and desire to serve our customers well. A high degree of social skills and an exemplary customer care attitude are fundamental to our philosophy. Computerized reception experience is essential and Innsite computer experience is preferable, but full training is always given. *Regency Park Hotel advertisement for head receptionist.*

In a small hotel, the receptionist will have very wide responsibilities, even to the extent of helping in other departments such as the bar and restaurant. The larger hotels divide the work, so that reservations will be looked after by one team, keeping guest accounts by another, and so forth.

The work of porters

Greeting hotel guests and helping them with their luggage, answering their questions about this and that, looking after keys, mail and messages, running errands, making travel and theatre bookings, calling taxis, are some of the activities that keep a porter busy during the day. Those on duty at night will usually have a wider range of duties including checking in later arrivals, dealing with early departures, serving drinks and snacks, distributing the morning newspapers.

For those new to the job, much of the work will be lifting and carrying: guest luggage, laundry, linen, housekeeping supplies, conference equipment, furniture and so forth.

In large hotels these various tasks are divided among the team of *uniformed staff*, as they are often known. The *bell boy* has the job of locating guests and delivering messages. The *doorman* greets guests as they arrive, opening and closing their car doors, calling a *luggage* porter to their assistance, hailing a taxi and so forth. The *hall desk porter* will mostly remain at the porter's desk, to hand over mail, direct guests around the hotel and generally help in whatever way they can. In charge of the team will be the *head porter* or *concierge*.

♦ As well as transporting guests' luggage, porters explain facilities of the rooms such as television and mini-bar, advise on the locations of fire-exits and answer any other questions guests might have. No formal qualifications are required, but a cheerful manner and good spoken English is necessary and knowledge of other European languages desirable. *Hilton Hotels recruitment leaflet.*

♦ The job of head concierge is not well paid, even in a luxury city hotel. But they can benefit from generous tips and perks such as theatre tickets, restaurant meals and sightseeing tours to ensure they are able to make informed recommendations to hotel guests. The best concierges are gifted at guest relations, articulate in several languages, and unquestionably enthusiastic about their work. *Pam Legate writing in* Caterer & Hotelkeeper.

Hotel manager

As manager you are in control. There are certain parameters within which you work – legal, financial and the overall policy of your employer – but the real fabric is up to you. Innovation, initiative – in short, ideas. You need disciplined business skills, and a natural flair for dealing with people. Plenty of energy and enthusiasm are vital, together with lots of common sense and the ability to think, make decisions and take action quickly. Above all, you need to be able to communicate – to have the presence, charisma, style and sheer personality to win the confidence of customers and staff alike.

The demands of the job depend, of course, on the size and sort of operation you are managing. In the small business it will be mostly hands-on work, everything from making beds to serving drinks, while the administrative tasks have to be caught up on when everyone else has gone to bed, and planning is something you might have to leave for the rare day off. In larger organizations, you will be responsible for spending huge sums of money to earn even greater sums. Much of your time will be spent in meetings, at your desk studying masses of financial and statistical data, planning marketing and investment strategies, and dealing with key staff and VIP customers.

◆ For a first appointment, the ideal general manager should be in his or her late 20s, with at least three years as an assistant manager in a good three- or four-star environment. For second and third positions, candidates will probably be between 30 and 40 years of age, and for more senior appointments, have several years' full general managing in a good quality hotel. This experience would probably have been gained in a large company environment ... An average stay of not less than two years with previous companies is expected ... Being a national company, we require managers to be relatively mobile and expect them to move near to their work location. We also prefer managers to live out of the hotel and own their own house. *John Jackson describing the general manager personnel specification of Crest Hotels (now part of Forte), in* HCIMA Reference Book.

Profile: Charlotte Kincaid

Hotels/training

Careers teachers and tutors were encouraging Charlotte to study for an English degree — she had seven O levels and two A levels. But she had enjoyed her school holiday jobs waitressing and helping in the kitchen and was considering a very different option.

'Over lunch in a wine bar, my family asked me directly if a career in hotels and catering was what I really wanted. Without hesitation I replied yes. My teachers at Malvern Girls' College were telephoned to find out about suitable courses. Sheffield City Polytechnic had places available. Following my brother's advice "to get on a train and go there", I was immediately accepted on the three-year Higher National Diploma in Hotel, Catering and Institutional Management.'

The Covenanters Inn, a small hotel in Aberfoyle, Perthshire, was where Charlotte spent her first industrial placement of five months, working in the kitchen, restaurant, bar and reception. For her second placement, she went to Canada, on an exchange arranged by the polytechnic. At the four-star Holiday Inn, London, Ontario, she worked as a receptionist cashier, switchboard operator, reservation clerk, commis chef, and chambermaid.

Before embarking on the next stage of her career, Charlotte decided to fulfil her ambition to visit Australia. She and a college friend back-packed and worked their way around the continent for over six months: 'being forced to become more resourceful, boosted my self-confidence'.

The Intercontinental Hotel, Hyde Park Corner, gave Charlotte her first job in London. In March 1987 she joined the hotel's one-year Training Executive Development Programme, which specialized in front office, sales and marketing, reservations, reception cashier, telephone switch-board, housekeeping, guest relations, personnel and training.

The programme was self-paced. By working hard, Charlotte was able to complete it three months ahead of schedule, and became Assistant Executive Reservation Manager. She gained her Hotel and Catering Training Board Craft Trainer Award during this period.

Front of House Trainer, a new post, at Grosvenor House, London, was Charlotte's next challenge. And after gaining the HCTB Group Trainer Certificate, she was promoted within a year to Training Officer.

Working among portacabins, wearing a 'hard hat' was where Charlotte could be found over the next three months. As Training Officer her task was to set up pre-opening training programmes. Officially opened in December 1990, at a cost of over £50m, the four-star, deluxe, 400 bedroom Sterling Hotel is linked by a covered walkway to Heathrow Terminal 4. The white, five storey parallelogram-shaped building has two end walls made entirely of double glazed glass 2.8 m in depth, which soundproofs everything except Concorde!

Tourism

The *tourist information centre* is often the first port of call of visitors when they arrive in a tourist area. Questions are very wide ranging from what accommodation is available and its cost, car hire, bus and rail travel, tours, theatre and concert tickets, times of church services, sports activities and so forth. It's important for the companies and organizations catering for these visitors that the centre staff are well informed, enthusiastic and friendly, deal with enquiries efficiently, and keep displays of promotional material properly stocked up and looking attractive.

Depending on the area, a good proportion of the visitors may be foreign and speak little or no English, so foreign language skills are a definite plus.

Information centres sell postcards, maps, guides and various other publications, so staff will also be involved in handling cash.

The bigger tourist information centres are operated all year round, usually on every day of the week, and often late into the evening. This means the staff will be on shift duty. Others only open for the summer months, employing temporary staff.

There is a wide range of job opportunities – but the competition is intense – with the various *tourism organizations* responsible for planning, developing, marketing, promotion, administration and general smooth running of tourism facilities and destinations. These include:

- British Tourist Authority (BTA) – helps the tourism industry provide the right facilities at the right time and place. Much of its work is concerned with promoting Britain as a tourist destination through its network of twenty-two overseas offices.

- The four national tourist boards (England, Wales, Scotland and Northern Ireland) – provide a framework of marketing and development support.

- The regional, area and local tourist boards – promote tourism in their region, coordinate the tourist information network, local development strategies, and grading of accommodation.

- The tourism departments of local authorities, and for major towns and cities – marketing the local area, providing a tourist information service, developing tourism ventures to promote a range of leisure and holiday activities for visitors.

Most overseas countries have offices in the UK, some quite large, with a variety of posts open to local British people.

◆ I now work for Blackpool Pleasure Beach as Projects Coordinator. At assistant manager level, my role involves helping the board to investigate the feasibility of new projects and to manage their development. Coordination is vital to ensure that budgets are adhered to, that everyone knows what's happening and that the projects are completed on time. I also become involved in anything from registering trade marks and instructing solicitors, to investigating the availability of government grants and studying ride efficiency. This means working a six-day week as well as attending some evening functions. *Phil Reed, profiled in* Graduate Opportunities in Tourism and Leisure, *published by the English Tourist Board.*

Travel services and tour operations

Some customers come into a *travel agency* without any definite plans. Others know what they want, but it's not actually available and you have to persuade them to settle for more practical arrangements.

Many are coming to buy that very special thing, a holiday. You are selling them an intangible product, a dream. The skill is in offering good value for money and not allowing expectations to be built up unrealistically.

For business travellers making the arrangements can be quite a challenge. They know what they want, but they don't have the time or expertise themselves to sort out complicated airline timetables and fare structures. They certainly don't want to be left hanging around at airports waiting for connecting flights. And they need the freedom to change arrangements if plans alter.

You have to be able to understand accurately and quickly what the customer's requirements are, promptly establish what the airlines, other travel and accommodation companies can offer, and match the two. You may also need to give assistance with travellers cheques and foreign currency, advice about insurance, visas, passports and health precautions. A knowledge of travel geography is important, and you need good selling, administrative, numerical, keyboard and computer skills. Often you will have to do and think about several things at once, for example completing a tour operator's form while waiting for your call to another travel operator to be answered.

Competition among high-street agencies is fierce. Profit margins are slim. This means that public relations, promotions and marketing are increasingly important functions for managers.

Most *tour operators*' staff are office-based, where they plan and cost holidays, negotiate prices with other parties such as airlines and hotels, prepare brochures, plan advertising and direct mail, establish links with travel agents, distribute promotional material, deal with customer enquiries and complaints, and so forth. Tour operators also employ staff overseas: resort representatives to look after holiday-makers' needs, regional and area managers.

Creating holiday packages sounds exciting, glamorous work. And so it is, when the result appeals to a sufficient number of customers to earn a good profit for the operator. But the balance between success and failure is a fine one, and many of the influencing factors are outside the tour operator's control.

Rigorous planning and research skills are therefore as important as marketing skills. The larger tour operators provide opportunities to specialize, for example in training, accountancy or information processing.

♦ When I came to Club 18–30, I was thrown in at the deep end in Pricing and became involved in next season's ski brochure. We had to price the hotels at each resort, look at airport rates, seat rates, and, of course, at our competitors. After that, I jumped across to the Marketing Department, again involved with putting a brochure together. I was meeting designers, buying print, dealing with typesetters and chasing information continuously. Exhausting – but it's a wonderful feeling when you've done it all and it's there, in front of you ... Of course, I've been out to see a lot of the resorts, and though that sounds glamorous, it isn't all the time. You probably end up with massive bags under your eyes because you've only had a few hours sleep – you've been doing photography during the day, and then round checking hotel facilities, going on trips, meeting all the clients ... *Profile of Sandra Mangell in* Graduates in Tourism and Leisure, BTA, 1991.

Guides and couriers

Tourist guides need to have an excellent memory, and a clear voice that is easy and enjoyable to listen to. They should be interested in and enthusiastic about their subjects – whether it is the first or the hundredth tour they are taking around, or it's answering a question they have been asked dozens of times.

Couriers may also act as guides, and alternative job titles are: coach tour manager, airport meet and greet, overseas representative, coach host or hostess, and kiddies rep. The job is about helping other people enjoy themselves. This involves good administrative, organizational and selling skills – assistance with travel and accommodation arrangements, and arranging excursions; a first-class memory and interest in geography, history and local culture – as you entertain your group, pointing out points of interest; and considerable patience and diplomacy – it's down to you to sort out the problems.

Further information

Addresses at end of Chapter 1, unless otherwise stated.

MicroDOORS – interactive occupation information database comprising over 500 records covering about 1,000 job titles. Published by COIC.

Graduate Opportunities in Tourism and Leisure, English Tourist Board. Graduates in Tourism and Leisure, British Tourist Authority, published by Hobsons, Bateman Street, Cambridge CB2 1LZ
Tel: 0223 354551.

Working in Hotels and Catering, Working in Travel and Tourism, Working in Sport and Leisure, COIC.

Occupations – COIC, annual directory.

Graduate Careers Information Booklets – Occupational Series – of the Association of Graduate Careers Advisory Services (AGCAS), distributed by Central Services Unit (CSU), Crawford House, Precinct Centre, Manchester M13 9EP
Tel: 061 273 4233 Fax: 061 273 6657/5255.

3

Specialist areas and sectors

The last chapter dealt with the areas of work and sectors of the industry that people more readily think of in connection with hotels, catering and tourism. This chapter looks behind the scenes at the back-up services. It also looks at catering in the armed forces and police, and briefly at related areas such as home economics, teaching and food journalism.

Maintenance/technical services

With all the coming and going that takes place in hotel, catering and tourism establishments, the pressure on equipment, heating and airconditioning plant, plumbing and other technical services is demanding. A constant programme of maintenance is needed to keep things running smoothly, and the ability to cope quickly and calmly when something does go wrong.

♦ There's plenty going on behind the scenes at every RoadChef site to maintain essential services, such as heating, ventilation, power supplies and to operate our computerized accounting system. People to handle routine maintenance – and even to clean up the car parks. They are all essential to the smooth running of the RoadChef operation. *RoadChef recruitment leaflet.*

Security

In businesses which by their very nature must be open to the public at large, the security of other guests, staff, and property is an ever-present concern. It is now expected that international conference centres should use airport-like security measures and equipment. But hotels and restaurants cannot usually subject their guests to the same scrutiny. Instead, they have to rely on everyone's vigilance, perhaps on the use of uniformed security staff at staff and delivery entrances, and the discrete supervision of guest areas by other security staff, possibly in plain clothes, or using closed-circuit television.

In many cases, security will be contracted out to a specialist firm, who will provide the staffing. However, some hotels employ their own security staff.

Accounting/finance

Efficient financial control is the backbone of a successful operation. Keeping track of every financial transaction, checking and re-checking. Knowing what has been spent on what, how much is owed to suppliers, how much customers owe the business, calculating wages and salaries, dealing with VAT, and so forth. You need to enjoy working with figures, and to maintain the highest standards of accuracy even when dealing with large amounts of quite boring information.

Many make their way into well-paid positions from line management, having proved they have the necessary administrative and financial skills, but moving to another company or another industry in order to get further advancement can be very difficult without accountancy qualifications. (See profile of Russell Kett, Chapter 5.)

♦ A career in finance with Hilton offers the chance to gain experience in a complex multi-site operation. It is recommended that candidates gain experience in another aspect of the hotel business before specializing in finance, as the knowledge gained will prove invaluable in understanding the hotel finance procedures. Joining as a trainee you will learn all the basic accounting functions such as auditing, bought and sales ledger, costing and controlling and credit procedures, and there are many opportunities to move up the organization. *Hilton Hotels recruitment leaflet.*

Marketing/sales/public relations

Attracting new business and more business from existing customers is vital in the competitive world of hospitality and tourism. To be successful in marketing and selling, you should enjoy taking a high profile. As part of your job you might have to make many phone and personal sales calls. This means being confident in your product, and able to sound convincing. There will also be the rather monotonous jobs like building up mailing lists, and personalizing thousands of letters for a big direct mail campaign. There are lots of creative challenges, like getting a new brochure produced, and you will have your share of the burden (!) of dining and wining.

Planning and executing successful strategies require inspiration as well as a thorough understanding of the principles and techniques of marketing. (See profile of Maggie Tiltman, Chapter 6.)

Profile: Caroline Mary Heagerty

Public relations/sales/cooking/teaching

'Father insisted on telling the assembled family about the origin and characteristics of each wine served at our meals. Sometimes his knowledge and enthusiasm was rather lost on us, but in later years we all had reason to be grateful for what was a wonderful education in wine appreciation.'

Caroline also remembers joining family friend Bet Cox, a teacher at The Cordon Bleu Cookery School, London, in her home kitchen in Sussex. 'As a 12-year-old I had great fun learning new cooking skills under Bet's expert eye.'

Cookery was her strength, Caroline decided, 'I was not academic.' Nevertheless, six O levels and Bet's tuition put her at an advantage and she gained her Cordon Bleu Diploma in July 1982. The following summer was spent cooking on a fifty-foot luxury yacht as it sailed around the south coast of France. 'It was a most agreeable way of earning a living, and I couldn't wait to repeat the experience the following summer.' In the meantime, Caroline had an opportunity to learn typing and to pursue another interest, interior design. A three-month course at the Inchbald School of Design in London, was followed by three wonderful months as a student of history and fine arts in Venice, Florence and Rome.

Selling sandwiches to shops and offices in Kensington and Chelsea – sandwiches made by her own business, was Caroline's next venture. She then spent a more settled eighteen months on the teaching staff of The Cordon Bleu Cookery School. Teaching a range of courses, from beginners through to advanced, and demonstrating various cooking techniques was a challenge and demanded many new skills. 'It helped develop my self confidence, and gave me my first experience of public relations work, when I got involved in preparing food to be photographed for the school's brochures and a book on cookery.'

But the PR world was to be kept waiting for a while. After a month cooking for a family in Val D'Isere, France, Caroline set up another business in London in May 1985. Her company 'Shaken not stirred' specialized in food for cocktail parties. By September she had become an employee again – this time as a personal assistant to the managing director of Badenock and Clark, City-based financial recruitment specialists. Feeling once more the 'call of the sea', Caroline left the British winter for the West Indies and USA, where she cooked and crewed on luxury sailing yachts for nine months. Then followed two years in Hong Kong with Remy Nicholas Fine Wines and Spirits. As Sales Development Executive, Caroline was responsible for both the trade and corporate accounts.

Caroline Mary Heagerty (*continued*)

She organized wine tastings, special functions for the press and leading clients, and magazine promotions.

From Hong Kong to Grosvenor House, London in September 1988 and the designation Sales Promotions and Public Relations Executive. Caroline became responsible for writing and distributing press releases and follow ups, preparing and organizing various marketing ventures for the hotel, and working alongside other PR staff in Forte's exclusive hotel division on the development of joint promotions and marketing strategies. Special responsibility for the development and management of the Ninety Park Lane Dining Club, meant arranging events and special offers throughout the year, and she was involved in the pre-launch and launch PR activities for the new business floor, 86 Park Lane.

The Ritz Carlton Hotel Company appointed Caroline their Public Relations Manager in March 1990. Specializing in elegant, exclusive hotels, the group has properties in America, Australia, Hawaii and Europe. The launch of the company's Quality Vision scheme throughout its hotels has fully involved Caroline, and meant regular visits to the group's US headquarters to liaise on methods of implementation. On one of these trips Marketing and Sales Director David Elton, over a cup of tea, surprised Caroline with the news that she had been appointed Public Relations Director for London and Europe. Her brief is to establish the name Ritz Carlton within the European market.

Personnel and training

Good management realize they need good staff, and that means putting a lot of effort into recruiting the right people, training them, and looking after them. It is not uncommon for capable managers to have a period as training officers and, after two to four years, have the option of following this profession through to corporate level (and getting specialist qualifications), or reverting back to line management at a more senior level, or going into an associated area such as sales or consultancy.

A good working knowledge of often complex employment laws is important, as well as company procedures on such matters as discipline and grievances. (See profiles of Charlotte Kincaid, Chapter 2, Susan Millington, Chapter 4, Margaret Rose and Maggie Tiltman, Chapter 6.)

◆ Each hotel has a person responsible for the recruitment, welfare, training and development of the employees, and to become one of these human resources managers you must be an excellent communicator, able to get on with people at all levels, have a knack of putting people at ease and be able to win the trust and respect of the staff you represent. *Hilton Hotels, recruitment leaflet.*

Army

Length and type of training depends on point of entry:

- *Apprentice trades (chef)*: reach satisfactory standard in selection tests; age range: 16 to 17½ years; two-year scheme of cookery instruction, military, physical, adventurous and sporting training. (See also profile of Warrant Officer Lou Hole in Chapter 8.)

- *Officer (ACC)*: five GCSEs including English language; BTEC/SCOT-VEC National or Higher National; pass ACC, Regular Commission Board, and Medical Board selection tests; age range: 18 to 29 years; twelve-month standard military course at Royal Military Academy, Sandhurst.

Officers are also recruited through the Army Undergraduate Cadetship Scheme (for Regular Commissions), and Army Undergraduate Bursaries (for Short Service Commissions). The schemes provide financial assistance to candidates reading for appropriate degrees in return for an engagement for service. For the Cadetship, the minimum requirement is five years after graduation. Cadets are commissioned as a probationary Second Lieutenant, paid an officer's salary while at university, tuition fees are paid, and a Regular Commission granted on graduation. The student with a Bursary remains a civilian at university, is paid a grant, gets a Short Service Commission on graduation, and is required to serve for three years.

Government announced in autumn 1991 that the Army Catering Corps will cease to exist as a separate body. Its functions will be combined with those of the Royal Corps of Transport, Royal Army Ordnance Corps and Royal Pioneer Corps, to form a new logistics corps. Catering will be just one of the functions of the new corps. The reorganization will bring together the procurement, supply, cooking and service functions of catering. It is also likely to mean that stewards will become part of the catering function – until now they have been regimental.

- When you join the ACC you're a soldier first and foremost, and in an emergency it's only a short distance from the kitchen to where the action is, and from your 'whites' to your combat dress and equipment. Your military training will teach you self-confidence and self-reliance, and these qualities, combined with your craft and management skills, will benefit you not only in your Army career but also afterwards in the civilian catering industry. *Army Catering Corps recruitment leaflet.*

Profile: Captain Philip Sinclair

Army Catering Corps

An HND graduate from Westminster College, Philip was told at an interview with a contract catering company that he would be ideally suited as an Army Officer and should consider making a career in the Army Catering Corps. This advice helped make up Philip's mind. It was one of the options he had been considering, and he knew the Corps offered professional training and career development, much respected by the civilian sector of the industry.

Passing out of the Royal Military Academy, Sandhurst, in September 1985, Philip began his career as a Platoon Commander, in the rank of Second Lieutenant. During this first eighteen-months tour, Philip, also took the appointment of Training Officer. This meant time on adventure as well as military training, and gave him the opportunity to pursue to the full his interest in sailing and skiing.

Philip was able to develop his catering management skills on the ACC Young Officers Course which he completed in August 1987. He was soon promoted to Lieutenant, and posted to the British Army of the Rhine (BAOR) as Specialist Catering Officer for the Third Armoured Division Headquarters and the Signals Regiment. With a staff of forty military cooks and civilians, Philip was responsible for all the usual catering duties, and special requirements like feeding hundreds of soldiers and officers in the field, or running a VIP tent.

Promoted to Captain ten months later, Philip completed his tour as Area Catering Officer for Soest, West Germany. In overall charge of the catering for the ten units that comprised the Sixth Armoured Brigade, he had twenty-six catering outlets to look after, with a feeding strength of up to 5,000.

After completing the Army's Junior Command and Staff Course in December 1989, Philip spent six months as the Forces Catering Advisor in Belize. Here there were many varied and interesting problems to overcome, including supply, real estate, responsibility for RAF catering, and the planning of new kitchens for the British Forces, Belize.

In August 1990, Philip Sinclair was appointed to SO3 (Recruiting), a Captain's post, to coordinate all recruiting matters for the Army Catering Corps. A year later he moved to SO3 (G3) with responsibilities for operations, home defence and security, and in June 1992 to Cyprus to take up the post of Officer Commanding Central Catering for the British forces on the island.

Royal Navy

No formal educational qualifications are required, but candidates must pass some basic tests in general knowledge, numeracy and mechanical aptitude. Those with two GCSEs (or SCEs), including English language, may become Warrant Officers. Those with four GCSEs may be considered as commissioned officers.

All specialist courses are preceded by seven weeks basic Naval training at HMS Raleigh, near Plymouth. *Stewards* stay on to attend a five-week professional course at the Royal Navy Supply School. This covers bar and food service, valeting and cabin work. Before going to sea, four to eight months are spent at a Naval shore establishment working under a Senior Steward.

Cooks spend eight weeks at the Royal Navy Cookery School in Aldershot, followed by six weeks back at HMS Raleigh. Here four weeks on catering accounting is followed by some field cookery and practical experience in cooking for large numbers. Up to a year is spent at a shore establishment before going to sea.

♦ The number of *cooks* that can be carried in ships is strictly limited, so each person needs to know something of all aspects of food preparation, cooking, presentation, including cakes and bread, with particular emphasis on hygiene and logical *mise-en-place* within a confined area. Skilful presentation plays a big part in the morale of a ship's company.

♦ The work of *Chief Petty Officer Caterer* requires qualities of leadership, cooperation, tact and imagination coupled with a thorough grasp of the details of catering management under all conditions, ashore and afloat.

♦ The standard of personal service required for Naval Officers is equivalent to that expected in a good hotel or club; an even higher standard is required for Senior Officers, who have extensive official entertaining responsibilities, particularly in foreign ports; this service is provided by the *Steward Branch*. Stewards are trained in all aspects of bar service, accounting and management, waiting, pantry and accommodation service, food service and care and control of tableware, catering and personal hygiene, elementary cooking and valeting. *Extracts from Royal Navy job descriptions.*

Profile: Commander Brian Purnell MBE

Royal Navy

The son of a close-knit, Welsh speaking, Metho-
dist family, Brian found it difficult to settle down
to the academic side of school life at Llangefni.
'With the support of Mr Davies, my headmaster
and a great man, I volunteered to be the first boy
to take part in the cookery class. My ears still
burn when I remember what my fellow boy
pupils had to say!' Those lads would eat their
words, if they knew that the young Purnell's interest in cooking would
lead in less than thirty years to his appointment as Naval Catering
Advisor, at the rank of Commander in the Royal Navy, the first cook/
caterer to ever do so.

Failing to gain any certificates at school, Brian decided at 15-years-old
to take a full-time job with Dewhurst Ltd — he'd already got some
butchery experience. 'Seafaring was in my mother's family, so I thought
why not use my skills as a butcher in the Merchant Navy and see the
world! But with no vacancies at either Cunard or Blue Funnel Lines, I had
to stay on with Dewhursts. Then they transferred me to the Holyhead
branch which meant cycling twenty-eight miles to and from home each
day. My father suggested I join the Royal Navy, if I still wanted to go to
sea, but as an engineer not a cook.

'I had to face my father's wrath when I got home from the RN
recruiting office at Wrexham, where I told them of my experience and
interest in butchery. This would be useful for the job of ship's cook, they
said and five weeks later I had to report for a medical in Liverpool. I was
eighteen and this was my first journey outside Wales. Liverpool seemed
vast and noisy.'

Six weeks square bashing at the Supply Secretariat School at Chatham
was followed by thirteen weeks training at the Cookery School of the
RNSS (Royal Naval Supply School). 'Although it was hard work, I enjoyed
every minute. After covering the basic skills we had to produce the dishes
for a weekly menu. In the final, very intensive practical test, I was
awarded 78 per cent and given special dispensation to be paid as a Cook
(S) Ships' Company Cook, in ten months instead of the usual twelve.
Back home that Christmas, I felt so proud of my uniform. As I walked up
the street in Bangor, ladies asked to touch my dickey collar for luck! But
when the time came to report to HMS Goldcrest at the Fleet Air Arm
establishment in Haverfordwest, my mother was heart-broken. My older
brother left soon after to join the Army, and I think she blamed me for
splitting up the family.'

On his first ship, a Manxman Class Minelayer, Brian got used to
sleeping in a hammock. 'It was slung from two hooks in the mine tunnels

Commander Brian Purnell (*continued*)

aft. Each morning I had to roll up my hammock and carry it the full length of the ship, back to my mess deck, before reporting for duty in the ship's galley. Life on HMS Apollo was disciplined with leisure time spent carrying out hobbies such as rug-making and picture framing.'

Five months in the galley of HMS Vernon, Portsmouth, was followed by service on HMS Brighton as she sailed to the Far East. On return Brian met his wife to be, Anne, a Sunderland girl.

After passing the examination Brian became a Leading Cook in July 1964 and was drafted to HMS Collingwood (Training Establishment). Here he competed in his first Hotelympia Salon Culinaire and passed the Petty Officer Cook examination.

With no formal educational qualifications, Brian had to spend some of his early days of married life, studying for O level English Language and the General Paper, which he passed in November 1966. 'The Navy was establishing the catering branch so I decided that it was time to specialize and attended what was then the Long Catering Course at HMS Pembroke. After promotion to Petty Officer Caterer I continued my training on HMS Caledonia at Inverkeithing, Dunfermline. My first ship as a Senior Rate Caterer was the Frigate HMS Llandaff, which I joined in September 1967 at Singapore. The operation of two galleys feeding 240 ratings and twenty officers respectively, plus functions, was a challenge to my newly learnt management skills.' Illness cut short this experience, and back in Scotland, Brian was appointed Ship's Caterer, with complete responsibility for the financial and management control of the catering organization at HMS Lockinvar, South Queensferry.

After two years at sea on HMS Dundas, where he was involved in the last traditional issue of 'pussers' rum, Brian was sent to HMS Osprey at Portland, as Petty Officer Caterer responsible for the Ship's company dining halls. Promotion soon followed and in 1972 he became Staff Chief Caterer to Flag Officer Sea Training (FOST). 'My job was to inspect and monitor standards of cookery, galley and personal hygiene, safety and catering accounts on all the Royal Navy and other NATO ships which came to Portland for operational sea training. I also taught galley fire fighting techniques to the cooks, and how to build and use field kitchens ... without doubt, one of the most enjoyable jobs of my career.'

O levels in History and Geography gave Brian the four GCEs he needed to be considered for officer training at Dartmouth – and just before he reached the upper age limit of thirty-four. Two pre-qualifying weeks were followed by one term as an SD Officer Candidate at St George Division, Dartmouth. 'Among other things I learnt leadership, public speaking and managerial techniques. It was a very proud day in March 1965 when I passed out as an Acting Sub-Lieutenant.' After six weeks at Greenwich learning the divisional and personnel administration skills required of a naval officer, Brian joined HMS Sultan at Gosport. As Acting Sub-Lieutenant Supply Officer Catering, he was responsible for the overall catering for the Ship's company galley, senior ratings' galley and the officers' wardroom galley, with 990 personnel eating 3,600 meals

Commander Brian Purnell (*continued*)

daily. Highlight of the many special functions was a visit from the Queen Mother in 1976, 'Her Majesty ate heartily and praised me on the choice of menu when I was presented to her after lunch.'

Two years at sea followed. As Sub-Lieutenant and then as Lieutenant Supply Officer Catering, he was responsible for the welfare of 950 officers and men on board the cruiser-helicopter carrier HMS Blake. 'I was personally responsible for compiling the Wardroom menus, including those for official receptions. And there were lots of those when the ship was deployed as Flag Ship in South and North American waters.'

In 1979, Brian returned to FOST at Portland. 'During this period I wrote reports galore and occasionally deputized for the Deputy Staff Supply Officer in his absence, often reporting direct to the Admiral.'

Responsibility for training followed – as Officer in charge of the Caterers and Stewards Training School at the Royal Navy Supply School. Regular extraneous duties included leading a team of stewards and cooks for special catering functions in London on behalf of the Admiralty Board. 'Attended by Royalty, government ministers and Senior Service Officers, everything – sometimes even the water – had to be assembled and transported from HMS Pembroke in Chatham to London.'

At the outbreak of the Falklands campaign, Brian was sent to Ascension in the South Atlantic as the Combined Services Catering Officer, responsible for the day-to-day feeding and other domestic requirements of all service personnel on the island. 'There was two weeks to organize a catering operation to feed 2,000 people using as much fresh provisions as possible. I had a mixed team of Royal Navy, Royal Air Force and Army Cooks, stewards and caterers. We had three separate field kitchens, with one of them open for twenty-four hours a day. I also had to organize their accommodation, provide for those transiting the island, including VIPs, prisoners of war, and the survivors of ships sunk, and supervise the provisioning of warships en-route.'

Back at Chatham, he learned of his MBE for services during the Falklands campaign. 'I feel very proud to have received such an honour for doing what I was trained to do as a professional caterer.'

To reinforce this training, Brian gained in 1982–3 his HCTB Trainer Skills Two, NEBSM Certificate in Supervisory Studies, City and Guilds 717 Alcoholic Beverages and 707–1 Food and Beverage Service. He also attended the RN Lieutenants' Course at the Naval College at Greenwich. In late 1983, he joined the Directorate of Fleet Supply Duties (DFSD) at the Ministry of Defence, London, as the Ship Galley Design and Catering Equipment Adviser. 'My boss was Captain Mike Pearey who featured in Roy Hayter's first book *A Career in Catering*, published in 1980. For the next thirty months I often had to travel 1,000 miles a week to inspect the catering facilities of newly built RN warships. I am sure I aged in this job!

Now a Lieutenant Commander he attended the Supply Charge Course at HMS Raleigh from September to December 1986. 'One month later I went to sea as the Supply Officer of HMS Argonaut, a Leander Class Frigate. This meant I had sole responsibility for all logistical support,

Commander Brian Purnell (*continued*)

including naval, air and technical, general ship spares, pay and cash, secretarial and catering. I was also legal adviser to the Captain when called on. The highlight of this happy and most enjoyable period was being involved in the rescue of Richard Branson, when his balloon ditched into the Irish Sea during his attempt to cross the Atlantic.'

Promoted in 1989 to Deputy Base Supply Officer at HMS Osprey, Portland, a 2,500-strong Naval Air Station gave Brian a chance to combine his administrative responsibilities with his own particular style of management. He regularly took groups of his staff on adventure training which included sailing, walking and hill climbing in Snowdonia. 'I wanted my young staff to realize that nothing is impossible if you set your mind to it. If you are dedicated, single minded and determined to pursue a career course, the rewards are there waiting to be taken, no matter how modest your background. And particularly so in the Royal Navy – as I hope my experience shows.'

In October 1991 Brian was promoted to Commander. His next appointment was that of Naval Catering Adviser, stationed in London at the Ministry of Defence. The lad who joined the Service as an Assistant Cook in August 1959, aged $17\frac{1}{2}$, had made it to the most senior catering appointment available in the Royal Navy.

Royal Air Force (RAF)

The RAF offers a variety of training schemes to suit a wide range of entrants. Chefs, steward/mess managers and clerk caterers fall within the Catering Trade Group. Those selected (no specific entry requirements) enter the RAF as aircraftmen/women and after recruit training, receive basic trade training at the RAF School of Catering.

For *officer* training a degree, professional qualification, HND, OND and five GCSEs, or civilian managerial experience in catering or allied trades and five GCSEs is required. An eighteen-week Initial Officer Training course at RAF College Cranwell is followed by six weeks' specialist training at the RAF School of Catering, Aldershot. This leads to a first posting, probably as a station Catering Officer.

Part of your career will be spent on a station, where you're likely to be the only Catering Officer, taking care of accommodation, restaurants, reception areas, bars and lounges, as well as special functions. The station may also have a hospital, an in-flight catering section, an airfield buffet or a field catering unit. (See profile in Chapter 1 of Wing Commander Ted Malone.)

Police catering

The field of operation varies enormously, from locations where all the food and equipment has to be taken alongside the other paraphernalia of a military or police operation, to beautiful dining halls and well-equipped permanent facilities. Recruitment and training schemes depend on the authority concerned.

♦ Police catering is a major operation which provides a service twenty-four hours a day, 365 days a year. The catering department is responsible for all catering arrangements at police premises and outside catering on occasions when there are demonstrations, state visits, sporting fixtures and other major events and emergencies. In other words, from delicious fish and chips to a Royal banquet. *Metropolitan Police recruitment leaflet.*

The Merchant Navy

There are opportunities (but relatively few) for a catering career in the Merchant Navy. For example, you can join the Royal Fleet Auxiliary Service as a junior catering rating. Your duties will include cleaning officers' cabins and the main public rooms, serving at tables and assisting at official receptions and functions. You will be given instruction in cookery techniques and galley maintenance and will assist in the loading and storage of stores. On attaining adult grade (normally at age 18), you will be assessed as to your suitability for steward or cook duties.

Profile: Derek Bousfield

Police catering/Merchant Navy/hotels

Success in gaining City and Guilds 150 and 151 (forerunners of General Catering 705 and Cookery for the Catering Industry 706–1) encouraged Derek to stay on at college. In 1968 he passed the Intermediate membership examination of the HCI (now HCIMA).

To have a break from his studies at Llandrillo College, and gain experience, Derek spent the next year with Thistle Hotels. He worked in Scotland, at the Stuart Hotel, East Kilbride, then for his father, the manager of another Thistle Hotel, before returning to study for the HCI Final membership.

An interview with the Merchant Navy led to an immediate job offer as an assistant purser/chief steward. After an anxious period of waiting, he was suddenly told to fly out to Durban in South Africa, and report to his ship. 'I will never forget. It was 3am and the ship looked gigantic in the dark. It all seemed very threatening. I had had no special training, so it was hard not to panic and shout out aloud "Help! What am I doing here?" Once on board, however, I was pleasantly surprised by my oak-panelled quarters. That first voyage was certainly full of experience – perhaps the worst was meeting a tidal wave at sea off the Indian coast.'

Returning to college in 1971, this time to Ealing Hotel School, Derek re-took the subjects he needed to gain his HCIMA Final Membership. He spent the summer working with his father, before joining Thistle Hotels as a Trainee Assistant Manager at the Midland Hotel, in Morecambe.

During his four years with Thistle, Derek was for a time Assistant Food and Beverage Manager at Liverpool Airport – Thistle held the concession for the catering services, duty free shop and the bonded stores. 'The managers took it in turns to be on call, and so it was me who got the news at 3am one morning that a jumbo jet had been diverted to Liverpool. We should expect 450 hungry passengers for breakfast in half an hour! Needless to say my staff rose to the occasion – from their beds – and rushed in to help prepare the food.'

A career blow followed. Derek left Thistle to become manager of the Oakley Arms Hotel in Maentwrog, North Wales. But the appointment was to last only three months. The owners unexpectedly sold up.

From managing various catering outlets in the Mecca group, including nightclubs, bowling alleys and large banqueting suites Derek joined the London Metropolitan Police Catering Department in 1980. For seven years he was involved in the operational side of the service, before being promoted to Higher Catering Officer and moving on to Technical Services, concerned with kitchen design. 'I then became involved with recruitment and special projects – our aim is to present catering as an essential part of the Metropolitan Police support services, with an important contribution to make to the force's overall efficiency.'

Derek Bousfield (*continued*)

In 1991, Derek moved to the Police Training College at Hendon, where he is responsible for serving 40,000 meals per week. 'I have a good team, with two catering officers, eleven managers and 120 staff, dealing with anything from day to day feeding to VIP and Royal banquets.'

Cruise ships

The cruise line industry is one of the fastest growing sectors of the world's leisure industry. Travellers can choose from small yachts sailing among the Greek islands, to 'fantasy palaces' providing non-stop entertainment and luxury accommodation to upwards of 2,500 passengers as they cruise the Caribbean. The USA market is particularly buoyant, while many European-based operators are aiming at the more adventurous traveller who wishes to explore the lakes of Russia, or the coast of Scotland, for example.

At least half the staff on a typical cruise ship are employed in the food, bar and purser's departments. On the SS *Canberra*, for example, part of the P&O fleet, the food department is responsible for preparing and serving 7,500 meals a day to passengers and crew. Key roles include that of provision master, running the storerooms. The purser's department is responsible for the accommodation aboard ship and passenger comfort, and is the administrative centre of the operation. Crews may be recruited from as many as forty different countries.

♦ To enjoy life at sea you must be able to work as part of a team: not only within your own department, but also with the rest of the ship's company. You must be able to work within a disciplined, structured society. You must be able to commit yourself totally to the job. At sea the complete hotel operation is self contained,the materials for each job are carried with you and when things go wrong, only the facilities, the ingenuity and flexibility of those aboard are available to find the answer. *Grahame Billett and Wendy Holloway of P&O Cruise Fleet Services writing in* HCIMA Reference Book.

Consultancy

Even the very largest companies call on external consultants from time to time, to get impartial advice and specialist expertise. This means that consultants do have to concentrate on a particular area, be it finance, feasibility studies, design and equipment, public relations, marketing, training, employment matters, small businesses, or whatever. Many of the leading UK consultants are attached to large accountancy firms such as Stoy Hayward and Touche Ross. Others operate independently, relying on personal contacts and entries in directories published by the HCIMA, for example. (See also profile of Russell Kett, Chapter 5.)

Profile: Geoff Parkinson

Hotel, tourism and leisure consultant/account-ant

With good A levels in Mathematics, Physics and Chemistry, everyone believed Geoff Parkinson should study Mathematics for his degree. 'Call me an angry young man, or a rebel if you like, but I decided to do what I thought would interest me. I applied to the two places you could do a degree in hotel management at the time – the Scottish Hotel School, now part of the University of Strathclyde, and Battersea College, which became the University of Surrey.'

He was accepted at Surrey and spent his industrial release year at the Skyway Hotel, Heathrow, then an independently owned hotel. 'I discovered why all casual waiters have a *nom de plume* – or is it *nom de spoon*? I also learned the taxman has a keen interest in the banqueting payroll – a discovery which stands me in good stead as an accountant today!'

His decision to enter the industry had been opposed. And now that he had obtained his hotel and catering degree, Geoff decided that 'line management in the industry was not for me. My interview with the careers officer at the university came to an end after only two minutes, when I announced I wanted to qualify as a chartered accountant.'

As an articled clerk the pay was very low, but Geoff persevered, worked and studied hard for the next three years, and re-sat the notoriously difficult exams once only. In 1974 he joined Horwath & Horwath UK, consultants to the hotel, tourism and leisure industry. H&H was then a division of Hesketh Hardy Hersfield, and is now part of Stoy Hayward, the leading firm of accountants, business advisers and liquidators.

A director of Horwath & Horwath from 1977, and a partner in Stoy Hayward from 1982, Geoff's main responsibilities lie in market analysis and investment appraisal, assisted by his team of thirty-two consultants. 'My working life is really enjoyable. There is no set routine. Every project is different. In 1978, for example, I made twelve trips to Egypt in eight months. In the early 1980s I got to know well the then undeveloped tourist areas of Portugal, Spain and Turkey. In 1991 it has been Central and Eastern Europe, and China. There is also a stimulating contrast between the concentration required for a single assignment setting up a new venture, and running the London office, where there are several assignments going at any one time.'

Geoff feels he was completely justified in turning aside from the career path which was originally thought best for him. Nor does he regret any of his subsequent decisions. Life cannot be dull when, from one week to the next you could be:

Geoff Parkinson (*continued*)

- examining the possibilities of a golf course in Dubai to be watered by its own desalination plant,
- assessing the future development opportunities for the premier golf resort at Gleneagles Hotel, Perthshire,
- advising on the development of the 1992 Barcelona Olympic Village,
- planning a harmonized hotel grading system for the European Commission,
- appraising for the City of Stockholm, its hotel development over the next decade,
- assessing the existing and potential human resources requirements of the hotel and tourism industry in Zimbabwe.

Geoff Parkinson became a Fellow of the Hotel Catering and Institutional Management Association in 1982.

Food service adviser to a catering supplier

Behind the expanding range of convenience products available to caterers are teams of people developing recipes, carrying out research into customer preferences, testing and tasting products, advising on nutrition content, preparing food for photography, giving demonstrations, and writing instructions so the end-user will store and prepare the product for consumption correctly.

Catering equipment also has to be extensively tested before it is manufactured in quantity. New equipment may mean adjustments to traditional recipes – certainly the case with microwave ovens, and the more complex processes of cook-chill, cook-freeze and vacuum cooking.

Then the equipment has to be demonstrated. At most catering exhibitions a large proportion of the floor area is taken over by displays of catering equipment, and a popular way of attracting interest is by mounting non-stop cooking demonstrations.

Home economist/consumer adviser

The work of food service adviser is quite often carried out by a home economist with catering experience. Home economics – and this is the reason it is now frequently referred to as consumer studies – covers a wide range of subjects including materials and equipment used in the home, care of clothes and textiles, design and dress, planning and budgeting, relationships in the family and community. (The degree courses in consumer sciences at Robert

Gordon and Northumbria universities changed their name from home economics to reflect this breadth of subjects.) The range of career opportunities is correspondingly wide – including retailing, marketing and advertising, publishing and journalism, appliance and equipment, textiles and design.

Food design and photography

Food designers prepare food for photography. This is a very creative and challenging job, demanding great patience. Making food look really delicious in a photograph also of course relies on the skills and understanding of the photographer. Good lighting is a must, but the heat of the lights will soon play havoc with the food, so careful planning and good coordination are essential.

Training as a home economist would help provide the technical background for treatment of foods. Training in cookery is an advantage, particularly for achieving the high standards of presentation that are required.

Food journalist

Cooking, eating, and drinking make good TV, newspaper and magazine stories. And naturally the best stories are written by people who have a good understanding of their subject.

Environmental health officer

While many EHOs pursue a general career and give advice on a wide range of functions, others become specialists in such fields as food hygiene, and health and safety at work.

The job of protecting the public from the dangers associated with consuming food which is unfit or has been exposed to contamination, requires a detailed knowledge of food processing procedures, and of microbiology related to food-borne diseases. It also requires firmness and tact in dealing with caterers and others who are not coming up to the appropriate standard. In severe cases, the offending premises can be closed down immediately by the EHO, and the people responsible imprisoned for up to two years.

The laws on health and safety are equally strict. They are there to protect employees, contractors and members of the public from the hazards caused by unsafe working practices, inadequately maintained equipment and build-ings, lack of training of personnel using cutting, mixing and similarly danger-ous equipment. EHOs are required to make sure that employers draw up and abide by a safety policy, and provide adequate first aid, washing and sanitary facilities for staff.

Toastmaster

The job of a toastmaster calls for a strong, clear voice, a very good memory, organizing ability, unlimited patience and tact, power of command, un-flappability and a sense of occasion.

Butler training

The art of service is something best learnt from another master of the art. Books on etiquette and household management will help, but there is much more that relies on personal experience and highly individualized expertise.

Profile: Leslie Bartlett

Butler/teacher

After leaving school, much to everybody's amazement, Leslie Bartlett won a scholarship to attend the then Westminster Technical Institute of Cookery and Waiting. 'At that time the world's only food school and still the finest one of its kind. I was there in 1925–6 and entered the world of catering as a *commis* and later *chef de rang* at, among other places, the Grosvenor Victoria, and Trocadero restaurant.'

In 1931 Leslie entered the world of private service. Starting as a second footman, he rose to become a butler. Since that time he has served the cream of the land, including members of the Royal Family.

'Unsettled after the 1939 war, I joined the Merchant Navy and during the next twelve years circumnavigated the earth five times, made twenty-nine assays through the Suez and nine through the Panama canals. I visited forty-three countries and one day went back to school and learnt to be a teacher.

'Fourteen years ago I founded my school and since then have achieved some success with ex-students in many parts of the world. In recent years I have been invited to far away places to impart my knowledge to others: Honolulu to teach Polynesians, and then to another paradise island, the world's smallest republic of Sao Tome e Principe to teach Filipinos and the native Creoles. I soon hope to be going to South Korea and Japan. At the age of 80 I do find these adventures very much to my liking. When I stop only the good Lord knows and until that time arrives, I will be like that appalling commercial on the tale of Ariston, I will go on, and on and on.'

Franchising

A franchise might enable you to get involved in your own business almost immediately. You are buying into an already proven and established operation, which is well known in the marketplace – a Pizza Hut, for instance. It is easier to borrow money. You will get training, marketing and other assistance from the franchisor in return for an initial fee and an on-going fee. In return you commit yourself to certain standards, and are committed to the standards of others – which if they are lower, is not such a good thing.

Your own business

If you have the ambition to run your own business, there are a great many opportunities for starting up a restaurant, hotel, pub or catering business. Indeed if you are considering entering the industry as a career change, it can be the best way to get in. It won't be easy, and the risk of failure is high. A modest first step puts you at the least risk: a sandwich bar, café or guesthouse, for example. (See profile of Nicholas Jones, Chapter 6.)

Teaching in further education

Good, up-to-date experience in the industry is important. Generally you will be expected to hold at least the equivalent to the qualification you propose teaching. If you then wish your teaching career to advance, studying for higher level qualifications is very desirable. To get an entry into the profession, or to get a taste of what the work is like, consider taking a part-time position.

A teaching qualification is not essential, but the majority of lecturers either obtain one on a full-time basis in the early stages of their teaching career, or take a part-time course.

A one year full-time course leading to the Certificate in Education (Further Education) is offered by Bolton Institute, Huddersfield University, Wolverhampton University and University of Greenwich, London. You must be between 24 and 50 years of age, with industrial experience and qualifications appropriate to your proposed study area (these include hotel and catering, travel and tourism). If you are under the age of 24, you may be accepted with a degree. The Scottish equivalent, Teaching Qualification in Further Education, is offered at Jordanhill College of Education in Glasgow (address details in Chapter 12).

The part-time option, available over one year at a large number of colleges, leads to the City and Guilds 730 Further and Adult Education Teacher's Certificate. This is equivalent to the first two stages of the Certificate in Education, and it is then possible to take a short bridging course for the CertEd(FE).

Further information

- See also end Chapters 1 and 2.
- *Working in series* – COIC.
- *Occupations* – annual reference book, COIC.
- *Graduate Careers Information Booklets* – published by the Association of Graduate Careers Advisory Services. Available through CSU (see end Chapter 2).

Professional bodies and other organizations

Addresses in Chapter 11
- British Association for Commercial and Industrial Education (BACIE).
- British Association of Hotel Accountants (BAHA).
- British Dietetic Association (BDA).
- British Nutrition Foundation (BNF).
- Chartered Institute of Marketing (CIM).
- Club Secretaries and Managers Association (CMSA).
- Hotel and Catering Personnel and Training Association (HCPTA).
- Institution of Environmental Health Officers (IEHO).
- Society of Catering and Hotel Management Consultants (SCHMC).
- Wine and Spirit Education Trust (WSET).

Specialist careers

Army Catering corps

Army Careers Information Office (see phone book under 'Army'), or write to: Recruiting Officer Headquarters, Army Catering Corps Training Centre, St Omer Barracks, Aldershot, Hants GU11 2BN.

Royal Navy

Royal Navy and Royal Marines Careers Information Office (see phone book under 'Naval establishments'), or write to: The Director, Naval Careers Service, Old Admiralty Building, London SW1A 2BE.

Royal Air Force

Royal Air Force Careers Information Office (see phone book), or write to: RAF Office Careers, Stanmore, Middlesex HA7 4PZ.

Co-ordinating Agent, Merchant Navy Officer Training

30/32 St Mary Axe, London EC3A 8ET
Tel: 071 283 2922 Fax: 071 626 8135.

British Dietetic Association (BDA)

- Professional association: membership open to those with degrees or certain postgraduate qualifications in dietetics.
  7th Floor, Elizabeth House, 22 Suffolk Street, Queensway, Birmingham B1 1LS
  Tel: 021 643 5483.

British Nutrition Foundation (BNF)

- Education, research and information-providing organization on nutrition and related health matters, with the objective of helping individuals to understand how they may best match their diet with their lifestyle.
  15 Belgrave Square, London SW1X 8PG
  Tel: 071 235 4904 Fax: 071 235 5336.

Guild of Professional Toastmasters

- Aims to maintain the highest professional standards at all types of functions worldwide.
  Ivor Spencer, President, 12 Little Bornes, Dulwich, London SE21 8SE
  Tel: 081 670 5585/8424   Fax: 081 670 0055.

Institute of Home Economics (IHE)

- Professional body for home economists: distributes careers information about the increasing variety of areas in which home economists work.
  Aldwych House, 71–91 Aldwych, London WC2B 4HN
  Tel: 071 404 5532.

Institute of Public Relations (IPR)

- Prescribes standards of professional and ethical conduct for the PR industry; runs courses, provides education and training support.
  The Old Trading House, 15 Northburgh Street, London EC1V OPR
  Tel: 071 253 5151 Fax: 071 490 0588.

Institute of Purchasing and Supply (IPS)

- Sets, tests and assesses professional standards and arranges supporting education and training facilities, offers wide range of courses, seminars and publications.
  Easton House, Easton on the Hill, Stamford, Lincolnshire PE9 3NZ
  Tel: 0780 56777 Fax: 0780 51610.

Institute of Training and Development (ITD)

- Represents training and the interests of the professional trainer; qualification schemes include the Certificate in Training and Development and the Diploma in Training Management.
  Marlow House, Institute Road, Marlow, Bucks SL7 1BN
  Tel: 0628 890123 Fax: 0628 890208.

Ivor Spencer International School for British Butler Administrators

- Owner and principal, Ivor Spencer.
  12 Little Bornes, Dulwich, London SE21 8SE
  Tel: 081 670 5585.

The London School of British Butlers

- Owner and principal, Leslie Bartlett.
  32 Teeswater Court, Mangold Way, Erith, Kent DH18 4DG
  Tel: 081 310 9274.

National Council for the Training of Journalists

- Offers a range of short courses included *Writing for a Market*; run over three weekends this programme is designed to equip students to research and write news stories, feature articles and press releases, and to 'sell' them to their own employers, or to market them as a freelance.
  Carlton House, Hemnall Street, Epping, Essex CM16 4NL
  Tel: 0378 72395 Fax: 0378 560586.

Scottish Association of Master Bakers

- Professional and training body.
  4 Torpichen Street, Edinburgh EH3 8JQ
  Tel: 031 229 1401.

Toastmasters and Masters of Ceremonies Federation

- Brings together professional toastmasters and masters of ceremonies, encouraging them to further and expand their knowledge, while upholding the principles and traditions of the profession.
  Peter Frost, Hon General Secretary, 44 Trinity Avenue, Enfield, Middlesex EN1 1HS
  Tel: 081 363 3099.

Small businesses

Advice and training to help small businesses is available at almost every stage of their development. Your local TEC or lec, the Small Firms Service run by the Employment Department, the HCTC and your bank are good starting points.

Business opportunities are advertised in the *Caterer & Hotelkeeper* and *Dalton's Weekly*, and many estate agents specialize in hotel and catering properties.

Through the HCIMA book service and your local bookshops and libraries, you can choose from the considerable number of books and guides published on starting up your own business.

British Franchise Association

Franchise Chambers, Thames View, Newtown Road, Henley-on-Thames RG9 1HG
Tel: 0491 578050.

Youth Business Trust

- Offers help to 18–25 year olds who want to start their own business.
  Prince's Youth Business Trust, 5 The Pavement, Clapham, London SW4 0HY
  Tel: 071 321 6500.
  Prince's Scottish Youth Business Trust, 6th Floor Mercantile Chambers, 53 Bothwell Street, Glasgow G2 6TS
  Tel: 041 248 4999.

Rural Development Commission

- Provides help and advice for businesses setting up or operating outside main towns
141 Castle Street, Salisbury, Wilts SP1 3TP
Tel: 0722 336255.
Also many local offices (see telephone book).

Business in the Community

- Gives details of Local Enterprise Agencies which will give advice and information to people setting up or with small businesses (see Chapter 11).

4

Planning your career, qualifications and training

Some people settle on the hotel, catering and tourism industry as their career choice quickly. Geoff Parkinson, profiled in Chapter 3, was undeterred by the opposition he got to his decision – either initially, when he decided to study for a hotel and catering management degree, or four years later when he was about to graduate and cut short his interview with the careers adviser by stating he wanted to be a chartered accountant.

Others, like Charlotte Kincaid in Chapter 2 are drawn to the industry as a result of a holiday job. Tina O'Regan (Chapter 1), Sally Clarke (this chapter), the McCoy brothers (Chapter 1), and Vivian Higgins (Chapter 7), were among those introduced to a love of food and cooking as children.

For some it is a more difficult choice, or like William MacKinnon (this chapter) not the first choice. There is no harm in that. No matter how certain or uncertain you feel, it will be a useful exercise to analyse the pros and cons carefully:

1 Your strong points, and what you like doing.
2 Your not-so-strong and your weak points, and what you do not like doing.
3 Your goals for the short-, medium- and long-term future.
4 What is essential to achieve those goals: this will certainly include appropriate experience, and quite probably some qualifications. For some jobs qualifications are now a necessity – for example, if you want to go on a particular company's training scheme, or you want to enter the catering service of the armed forces at a certain level.
5 What you think will make achieving those goals more likely: particular type of experience, a higher level qualification and so forth. If at some stage, you want to work in Europe or elsewhere abroad, language skills are very important.

Finding what suits you best

One of the greatest attractions of the industry is the ease of mobility – particularly during the early stages of your career – from one area of work to another, from one type of business to another. This gives you a chance to find out what sector of the industry and type of work you like best, before moving up the management ladder (when it becomes more difficult to make radical changes).

Christine Barnes, profiled in Chapter 1, gained experience of hotels, restaurants and leisure before settling with great success in the contract catering sector. Alyson Cheyne (Chapter 2) took a while to find what she really enjoyed doing.

However, for those aspiring to management, mid-career moves do require careful thought. If you have specialized in a particular sector, it may not be easy or wise to move to a better position in another sector. Jonathan Thompson (Chapter 1), and Dee Ludlow (Chapter 5), have remained in hotels throughout their successful careers. Philip Ruddock (Chapter 2) has remained in hospital catering, Brian Watts (this chapter) has kept to the two closely related sectors, employee feeding and education catering.

Malcolm Allcock, on the other hand (also in this chapter), has moved between hotels and clubs a number of times. Within a short time of reaching his ambition of becoming a general manager in London's west end, his hotel was sold to developers and Malcolm made redundant. Happily the next move, back to clubs, worked out very well.

♦ I moved from district management into public relations, but stayed with the same company, Charringtons. I'm still in the licensed trade so it was not exactly a quantum leap. But I was unprepared for the incredibly fragmented nature of this job. I never imagined anything so frenetic and stimulating. And it had other plus points – after a few months, my wife remarked that the phone wasn't ringing in the night any more. A PR man is always available, but in my previous job I had an average two calls every evening from managers with problems. *Bob Humphries, interviewed in* Hospitality.

The career of Sandy Ross (Chapter 8) has been interrupted five times by company take-overs.

♦ In general, most people become fairly typecast. If their background is in hotels they tend to stay in hotels; if it's in contract catering, that is where they stay. There is more border-crossing in disciplines like sales and marketing, with hotel sales people moving into other areas. Line operations people rarely change. *Roddy Watt, partner at Berkeley Scott, recruitment advisers, interviewed in* Hospitality.

And not everyone has the success Nicholas Jones has enjoyed (Chapter 6) in setting up their own business.

◆ Of every five industry managers setting up their own business, two pull out in the first year through lack of backing or under-capitalization; another two are not convinced they made a wise move and keep an ear to the ground in case a better opportunity comes along. Only one mover in five is likely to make an unqualified success of his or her own venture. *David Coubrough, managing director of Portfolio, recruitment advisers, interviewed in* Hospitality.

Getting to know yourself

It may seem simplistic, but a useful exercise for many people is to ask themselves 'Do I like ...':

- dealing with people?
- early responsibility?
- travelling?
- wearing uniforms?

- dealing with detail?
- working unusual hours?

- working as part of a team?
- the freedom to change jobs?
- working for myself?
- working for a big company/organization?
- the excitement of noise and crowds?
- variety?

Draw up a checklist of what you like and don't like. Find out how the industry matches up to your requirements. Have a look again at your checklist. Perhaps some things are emerging as more important now that you have found out more. Or maybe you thought working at weekends would be a definite turn off, but overlooked the advantages of having time off in the week when other people have to be at work running the shops and businesses you need or want to use.

◆ ... the ingredients have to be right and only you can supply them. That means stamina, initiative, ambition, hard work and commitment in equal proportions. We haven't said it's easy – but we will say that with these attributes there's no limit to your career potential. *Burger King (part of Grand Metropolitan).*

◆ What sort of people get the most from working in a hotel? Well, people who like variety, and would hate the same routine day in, day out. People who like working with people, and who get a 'buzz' out of helping others. Teamwork people. People who take pride in themselves and in their own achievements. People who can have fun: work hard, play hard. It's not often you find hotel people who don't have a good social life. *Forte Hotels.*

Do spend some time planning where you want to go in your life and thinking, discussing and investigating how you might get there.

Observe. Talk to as many people as possible. Ask questions. Ask more questions. Read as much as you can. Visit hotel, catering and tourism establishments. Ask the staff what it's like working there – you will be surprised to find how many people jump at the chance to talk about their job and themselves – it helps to be a bit of an egoist in the industry's front-line jobs. Take any chance that comes your way to try it out for yourself.

Career guidance services

Get the most from your local Careers Service, TEC or lec. Young people are entitled by law to free access to the comprehensive help and guidance that the Careers Service offers.

From 1993 many adults in work will be offered credits which they can use to buy the guidance and assessment services of their choice:

- Information about occupations and the local jobs market (if appropriate).

- Advice about education and training.

- Assessment and guidance to help plan their future development on the basis of their existing capabilities and potential.

- Counselling and advice about how to obtain qualifications, or credits towards them on the basis of skills and knowledge that they already have (accreditation of prior learning).

The scheme, announced in the February 1992 White Paper *People Jobs and Opportunity*, will operate on a pilot basis for two years, involving fifteen TECs/lecs.

Some recruitment specialists offer a careers guidance service (for which they are likely to charge). The HCIMA provides a similar service to its members. There are also professional careers guidance companies.

If you're not ready to commit yourself

At the end of this exercise you may not be ready to commit yourself, and would prefer to keep your options open, with the freedom to make a decision when you are ready. There is certainly nothing wrong in this:

- Choose the sort of job where you will get a good insight into as many different types of work as possible, or at least be able to move on from easily, and without disadvantage (see Chapter 6).

- Choose a course which gives you the maximum amount of freedom – as

Some of the schemes and initiatives for school/college/industry links

Compacts

An agreement between employers, schools and colleges, and young people in the 14–18 age range, whereby each party makes a commitment to achieve certain agreed goals. The aim is to improve the achievements of young people in school/college and to demonstrate the link between this achievement and the ability to secure a worthwhile job – participation in the scheme guarantees young people a job with training, or training leading to a job. Initially confined to inner city areas, and nationwide from 1991, Compacts are usually integrated into Education Business Partnerships.

Education Business Partnerships (EBPs)
A formal agreement and joint venture, under the overall management of the TEC/lec, between a community's educators and employers, committing them to work together to improve education and employment opportunities in their local area. The aim is to raise the aspirations and achievements of individual learners, to allow them to maximize their potential and to enable them to become part of a skilled and adaptable workforce. Example activities include: careers guidance, involvement in the curriculum, providing work experience, bursaries to support further education and training, teacher placements in industry, seconding employees to work in schools and colleges, sharing resources and equipment, and providing company-based project centres for local schools and colleges.

Pickup
Professional, Industrial and Commercial Updating Programme: a vocational education and training service provided through a partnership of employers and colleges to meet the updating and training needs of those who have been in work for some time, usually in a professional or managerial capacity, and are looking to revive, or change direction in, their careers. The programme does not pay directly for courses or training. Instead it supports initiatives such as the development of training packages, short courses or distance learning materials which will give adults access to more and better training. The *PICKUP Training Directory*, which holds records of nationwide short courses in a variety of subjects, can be accessed via TAP points and Prestel. It is also available on disk and in a printed set from Macmillan, London.

TVEI
Technical and Vocational Education Initiative: programme involving local authorities, schools and colleges. TVEI is designed to prepare young people (aged 14–18) for the world of work by making sure what they learn at school, and the way in which they learn it, is more relevant and better adapted to their future employment.

you will see from Chapter 5, many college programmes are now modular in structure so it is quite easy to pick and mix, and to move from one programme to another.

- If you do not feel ready to start a course, consider taking a year's break after school to get some work experience – most colleges will accept a deferred entry application.

- Avoid taking jobs or courses which are strongly biased to a certain route. If you are not absolutely certain you want to be a hotel accountant, it would be foolish to start your articles. If you think you are interested in cooking, but not sure how you will feel about working in a hot, noisy kitchen, it would be better to take a general catering course which includes some cooking.

Overcoming prejudice

One of the beneficiaries of the Charles Forte Foundation (see Chapter 11) has been John Dever. John has been confined to a wheelchair all his life, but he has never allowed this to come in the way of his goals. With the Forte award John has been able to embark on a research degree for a PhD at the Scottish Hotel School, University of Strathclyde. He has investigated the possibilities of employing more disabled people within the industry and looked at ways of providing more accessible facilities for disabled guests and employees.

After a seven year break to raise a family, Maggie Tiltman (profiled in Chapter 6) put a lot of hard work into ensuring that her career moved on quickly again. Well before the Sex Discrimination Act, she also stood up for her rights when she found that a man reporting to her was earning more than she was, simply because he was a man.

Dee Ludlow, first hotel manager in London's Park Lane (profiled in Chapter 5), gives this advice to women joining the industry: 'You will have to work much harder than your male counterparts to prove your-self, and to achieve a senior management position.'

In a *Caterer & Hotelkeeper* report on women managers in the hotel and catering industry (Mel Jones, 9 January 1992) Janet Gray, head of human resources at Jarvis Hotels, gave similar advice to readers: 'I was conscious of having to try harder than my male colleagues and that I had to be seen to be better than them to merit promotion.' This is how individual companies fared in the snapshot survey of women managers which formed part of *Caterer*'s report:

- *Queens Moat Houses* – six out of 103 general managers, with many female deputies.

- *Hilton UK* – one board member, three out of thirty-five general managers, between 30 and 40 per cent of middle management.

- *Swallow* – three out of thirty-two general managers, eight out of twenty-six deputy general managers, seven out of ten head office managers.

- *Stakis* – two out of twenty-nine general managers, sales force and computing/systems staff predominantly female.
- *Jarvis* – one board member, three out of thirty-eight general managers, 30 per cent deputy general managers.
- *Mount Charlotte Hotels* – seventeen out of 107 general managers, fourteen out of thirty-one deputy managers.
- *Scott's Hotels (CHIC)* – one out of fourteen general managers, ten out of eleven sales managers, 60 per cent of front of house managers.
- *Holiday Inn Worldwide (UK)* – two out of seven on UK management committee, two deputy general managers, six head office managers.
- *Hidden Hotels* – joint managing director, five in senior managerial positions in sales, marketing, promotions, personnel and training.
- *Forte* – 1 woman on board, 53 per cent of managers, 26 per cent of senior management.
- *Pelican Group* – managing director, director of development, three restaurant managers.

The 1991 Commission for Racial Equality report *Working in Hotels* found that ethnic minority employees were disproportionately concentrated in the unskilled grades and in hotels in London and Heathrow. Among the Commission's recommendations was that hotel groups should actively seek to attract more ethnic minority applications for jobs in the industry. This could be done by building links with local community organizations, getting involved in work experience programmes, and introducing positive action programmes such as targeting training opportunities towards ethnic minority employees who have either expressed interest in promotion to supervisory posts, or who have been identified through staff appraisals as having career potential.

Profile: Brian Watts

Employee feeding/accommodation services/ education catering

After studying at what is now Waltham Forest College, Brian Watts joined the Army Catering Corps in 1955 under the National Service scheme. The experience he gained in management skills was invaluable in the post of Assistant Catering Manager of the British & Commonwealth Shipping Company, which he took up in 1957. Responsible for feeding City of London office staff and the shore staff at the Royal Group of Docks, Brian was soon promoted to Catering Manager. In 1963 he joined J Lyons & Company, in charge of staff catering on the main production site.

His next appointment was with Ford Motor Company. As Deputy Food Services Manager, Brian was responsible for contract caterers serving 64,000 meals per day throughout the UK. It was a seven-day-week, twenty-four-hour operation.

At Ford, and then as a consultant for the King Edward VII Hospital Fund for London, he helped set up a number of the UK's first cook-freeze systems. At King Edward, he was also involved in surveying and modernizing several large hospital kitchens.

Brian's next move, in 1971, was to the University of Essex as Catering and Accommodation Services Manager. As well as a full range of catering facilities, bars and shops, there were 1,800 single study bedrooms and accommodation facilities for another 1,000 students off campus. The job also involved developing conference and summer school trade at the University, including the opening of a forty-bed purpose-built conference centre.

In 1978 he joined the catering department of the Bank of England. Within four years he was appointed a director of B E Services Ltd, which had been set up as a wholly owned subsidiary to provide catering services to employees of the Bank of England in the City, at the Bank's printing works, and at its sports complex. Two years later he was made Managing Director of B E Services.

Outside visitors cannot fail to be impressed by the diversity of facilities offered at the main unit in the City of London, a building dedicated entirely to catering for Bank staff. With a bar, wine bar and self-service coffee shop providing a wide range of drinks, snacks and light meals, there are also grill bars, carveries and self-service restaurants offering a full menu. The function room can accommodate different numbers of people 'at the touch of a button', allowing great flexibility of use and making the most efficient use of staff.

All washing up is centralized with highly automated equipment. The

Brian Watts (*continued*)

kitchens are designed to maintain the high standards of hygiene, safety and food preparation demanded in such a large operation.

Brian is convinced that profit is quality driven. This means employing good staff and looking after them. He has introduced effective financial control systems, many of which are computerized so increasing take-up of the services by Bank staff and reducing turnover and absenteeism among his own staff. Indeed he has transformed the image of industrial catering in the eyes of both customers and staff.

Recognition of this came in 1978, when Brian received the prestigious Catey award 'Industrial Caterer of the Year'. As Director of the European Catering Association, a member of the Confrérie des Chevaliers du Tastevin and the Reunion des Gastronomes, he continues to set the pace for the employee feeding sector of the industry. A regular speaker at seminars and courses organized by the Industrial Society, he is also a partner in the management and design consultancy, Food Services Associates (Henley) Ltd.

Getting experience and training

The favoured combination in employers' eyes is a suitable qualification and experience in the industry. Certainly people have made very successful careers in hotels and catering without the benefit of formal qualifications, but employers are becoming more demanding and your chances of a good job that will lead to a successful career are much improved by appropriate qualifications.

There is no doubt too, that the considerable success of those people who have joined the industry with an appropriate qualification have raised the level of expectation that aspiring craftspeople, supervisors and managers in the future must themselves have such a qualification – or at least its modern-day equivalent.

On the other hand, there is a huge imbalance between the industry's demand for qualified staff, and the output from college and industry training schemes. HCTC estimates that college output provides only 27 per cent of the annual replacement needs for all skilled personnel in the industry. The shortfall is most severe at management level, where the college output is only 7 per cent of the replacement needs.

What comes first?

If you are already working in industry you will want to choose a course, training scheme or distance learning package that can help you get qualifications without totally disrupting your life. Academic entry requirements no longer represent the barrier they once did. Colleges have much greater flexibility in deciding whether you are likely to benefit from and successfully complete a particular programme of study. The process of *accreditation of prior learning* (APL) will enable your previous achievements to be taken into account (described in Chapter 5, where the entry requirements for various levels of college-based course are also detailed).

If you are planning what to do when you leave school, one way of avoiding the chicken and egg situation of which comes first, qualifications or experience, is to choose a full-time course that includes periods of experience. The length of this experience can vary from a few days or weeks to around twelve months. Many students top-up this by working in the industry during their holidays from college, and some students also get weekend jobs. Indeed you may find it useful to get a taste of what the industry is like by finding a part-time job for the next school holidays.

And whether or not a full-time course seems the best choice, you should spend a little time thinking about the other options. These include:

- Finding a job straight away where your employer will give you time off to attend a day release course at the local college, and/or training on the job which will help you gain National (or Scottish) Vocational Qualifications – NVQs or SVQs – through demonstration of your skills and ability in the workplace. A distance learning package, possibly in combination with short courses, may be a more suitable way of developing your knowledge.

- Working for a year or so, then, with the benefit of knowing more about the industry and the sort of work you enjoy, going to a college to gain a qualification.

- Getting a place on a Youth or Employment Training programme.

- However well qualified you are, you won't walk straight into a senior job on your first day. You will be working at all operational levels, learning what it is like to belong to a team that takes a real pride in the job. You'll soon find it's a team that's going somewhere knowing its contribution to the organization is appreciated and recognized. *Rank Hotels and Catering (a division of the Rank Organization plc).*

- Without our investment in training, we wouldn't survive in the marketplace. Our success depends on the excellence of the staff we employ – at every level in the organization. We rely on them to sell and operate a wide range of catering and related services, each one tailored to a particular need. This means our standards have to match those of our clients – many of whom are household names in industry, commerce and the public sector. *Sutcliffe Catering*

Profile: Susan Millington

Personnel/hotels/housekeeping/store catering

Susan often helped with the cooking at home – she can remember making custard at the age of two. At school she did well at Domestic Science and was regularly asked to demonstrate at open days. The careers teacher tried to put her off hotel work, yet the local radio found her ambitions of such interest they interviewed her. And her father had no wish for her to follow in his footsteps as a banker.

With three O levels and two CSE passes Susan applied in 1975 to three colleges to do the two-year Ordinary National Diploma in hotel and catering. 'I wanted to go to Westminster College and was delighted when they accepted me. I was one of the youngest in my class and although I was successful on the course, it was not easy to find a job. The gulf between studying and the real world was frightening.'

As Trainee Housekeeper at the Marble Arch Holiday Inn she had a difficult start. 'Although the scheme provided for set periods covering different jobs, this did not materialize. After ten weeks as chambermaid I thought "enough is enough" and asked to be put back on to the training programme. After four months I was made Floor Housekeeper, transferred for two weeks to Swiss Cottage, and two months later to Plymouth. I was pleased to be working in a provincial hotel. When I got back to Marble Arch I was put through the in-house trainer scheme and made responsible for the training of all new housekeepers.'

Susan moved to the Holiday Inn Bristol in 1979. 'I was nine months as Floor Housekeeper and loved every minute of it. But it was a bitter disappointment to be told that, at 21, I was too young for promotion!'

Taking matters into her own hands Susan took up the Deputy Head Housekeeper post at the 152 bedroom, Oaklands Park Hotel in Weybridge, Surrey. Her responsibilities included the care and welfare of fifty residential elderly guests. 'It was quite traumatic. If any of the residents needed medical help I was immediately involved.'

Susan returned to London and became Coffee Shop Supervisor at a prestigious departmental store in Regent Street. 'But living at home again did not work out. A close personal relationship failed, I missed the hotel environment and felt there was no future in the job.'

As Cocktail Bar Supervisor at the 340 bedroom Westmoreland Hotel opposite Lords Cricket Ground, London (now a Hilton), she was one of three supervisors responsible for twenty staff in the bar, restaurant and kitchen areas, plus the ordering and stock control of liquor and food. 'I loved the hectic life, especially when the cricket season started!'

Tragedy struck in August 1982. One week after passing her driving

Susan Millington (continued)

test, Susan was admitted to hospital with a suspect lump on her foot. 'After an anxious week I learned I had a very rare cancer in the bone tissue of my foot. The consultant surgeon gave me all the facts and recommended amputating my left leg just below the knee.

'Two weeks after the operation my first prosthesis was fitted and with physiotherapy I slowly learned to walk again using crutches. Of course my future employment was a worry, but Brian Zealey the General Manager and Hans Pffeifer Food and Beverage Manager, told me to concentrate on getting fit: they would find a job when I was ready.'

Susan kept busy typing, reading, revising her accounts skills. She joined a disabled swimming club, won many medals and became the Ladies' Champion. 'I went water skiing, horse-riding and gliding to prove to myself and others that I was able to take part in a normal life. The stigma of being disabled was tremendously frustrating – too fit to get any help, but not 100 per cent able to cope with all the events of life.'

The Westmoreland lived up to its word, and Susan started work again in a job which suited her changed lifestyle, Breakfast Restaurant Cashier. 'I got up at 5 am, drove to work for the 7 am to 11 am shift, then returned home to my physiotherapy session. Slowly my walking was improving. Music helped with the rhythm. But as soon as I looked up I would lose my sense of balance. This was a difficult skill to learn, but I couldn't spend the rest of my life looking down at the ground.'

As her strength grew, Susan worked as a Relief Evening Cashier, and then, at Mr Pffeifer's suggestion, as Reservations Clerk. She held this post until February 1985, when it was back to hospital for an operation to adjust the stump. 'I had a lot of new legs during this period. It's a bit like shoes – they wear out of shape and become uncomfortable to wear.'

A period of difficult self-analysis followed. 'I sat down and thought out what I wanted to do, and where I wanted to go. I had to face the facts and change my career pattern. I could take each day as it came, but trying to plan for a new future in the industry was terribly frustrating. So much more so that I once sat and wept with rage and threw my false leg at the wall! That gave me the "kick" to get up and move forward!'

Over her anger, Susan applied for internal promotion and was appointed Head Housekeeper/Administration at the Westmoreland. Responsible for the day-to-day running of the department with seventy staff, her work involved dealing with guests' requests and queries, interviewing and employing housekeeping staff, compiling worksheets, controlling and ordering stock, monitoring costs, liaising with Company representatives, and chairing departmental meetings.

Further promotion followed quickly when Susan became Personnel Assistant/Wages working under the Personnel Manager Sue Hale. Encouraged by Sue to expand her knowledge of the personnel side she became involved in maintaining the payroll for 150 staff, selection and recruitment of staff, training, disciplinary procedures, typing, meetings and general administrative duties. After Sue Hale left to become Personnel Manager at the Royal Garden Hotel in Kensington Susan joined her as

Susan Millington (*continued*)

Personnel Assistant in 1987 in a team of six. Two years later she was to take over from Sue.

'James Brown, the General Manager suggested I apply. Although Head Office held up my acceptance pending medical reports, fortunately there was no problem. With the support of a Personnel Assistant, Training and Personnel Officer and Occupational Health Nurse, I am responsible for the welfare of 350 staff, attending group meetings of executive personnel within Rank Hotels, liaising with shop stewards and advising heads of departments on recruitment, discipline and general staff problems.'

In August 1991 Susan married Sandro Mazzola. Sandro, who was Restaurant Manager of the Royal Chase Hotel, Enfield until made redundant, plans to open his own restaurant one day, and Susan wants to be part of that. In the meantime, with the Royal Garden likely to change ownership, uncertainty surrounds her own job. 'Whatever happens, I would like to keep my interest in personnel and training.'

Pam Frediani, who interviewed Susan at the suggestion of Peter Davies, Group Personnel Director of Sutcliffe Catering writes: 'Susan has achieved all the goals she set, despite adversity. She is a brave, unflinching example to anyone faced with similar problems.'

The evolving qualification and training scene

The first hotel school in the UK was opened (at what is now Westminster College) in 1910. The first cookery and waiting qualifications were introduced in 1944/7. The first management qualification was introduced by the Institutional Management Association (predecessor of the HCIMA) in 1947. That same year, the Scottish Hotel School for the first time offered a Diploma in Hotel and Catering Management. This became a degree course in 1966 with the creation of the University of Strathclyde, one year after Battersea College's diploma obtained degree status with the creation of the University of Surrey.

Until the 1970s, catering education lagged behind that for other industries. The creation of the Technician Education Council (TEC) and Scottish Technical Education Council (SCOTEC) – forerunners of BTEC and SCOTVEC – meant that catering at least kept abreast with developments in vocational education. Now, in the 1990s, it has moved firmly to the forefront, being one of the first industries to gain provisional and then full accreditation for National Vocational Qualifications and Scottish Vocational Qualifications, NVQs and SVQs.

At the same time, far-reaching and fundamental changes are affecting the structure and funding of further and higher education establishments, the general provision of training opportunities, and the careers service.

The new NVQ/SVQ system (described in detail in Chapter 7) covers all activities carried out in the industry, from cooking and serving food and drink, to managing a large hotel, and all jobs from luggage porter to reception manager, room attendant to housekeeper. At craft level, NVQs and SVQs have had an immediate impact, replacing from 1992 such well-established schemes as City and Guilds 706 series, Cookery for the Catering Industry, and Caterbase, HCTC's modular work-based qualification scheme.

European initiatives

European Diploma

Initiative taken by a group of sixty colleges from all EC member states offering hotel and catering courses. The qualification is intended as an addition to existing provision, and to be recognized throughout the EC. HCIMA was represented on the group, but in 1991 the Association decided to concentrate on working with EFAH for the accreditation of existing qualifications (see Chapter 11).

Euroqualification
A joint EC programme intended to lead to more harmonized training courses, better adapted to the new qualifications arising from European development. UK contact point: Qualifications and Standards Branch, Employment Department (address at end of Chapter 6).

EUROTECNET
EC programme to explore the impact of technological change on vocational qualifications and training systems, and to identify new skill needs in the workforce.

FORCE
EC programme concerned with the development of continuing education and training in firms.

IRIS
EC programme to promote exchanges and links between women-only training schemes.

LINGUA
EC programme to promote the knowledge of foreign languages within the Community. Contact point is ERASMUS (address in Chapter 5).

PETRA
EC programme focusing on the initial vocational training of young people and their preparation for adult and working life.

TEMPUS
EC programme to mobilize Community further and higher education to support the growth of market economies in Eastern and Central Europe.

Being work-based, NVQs and SVQs will present a more viable route to qualifications for those who are unable to attend a college or training centre, or who can only do so on an occasional or part-time basis. The take-up of part-time programmes leading to BTEC and SCOTVEC National and Higher National awards has never been significant, so NVQs and SVQs are expected to fill a long-felt need.

A parallel development, which will affect full-time supervisory and management courses, is the introduction of General NVQs and General SVQs. The first schemes in leisure and tourism were being piloted in 1992/93.

Training schemes

Depending on your age and circumstances, you may be eligible to join a *Youth Training (YT)* or *Employment Training (ET)* scheme. (If you are in Northern Ireland, the equivalent schemes are the *Youth Training Programme*, and *Job Training Programme*.) These provide a programme tailor-made in length and content to suit your needs, and which leads, as a minimum, to a National or Scottish Vocational Qualification (NVQ or SVQ) at level 2.

You have a YT place *guaranteed* if you're:

- aged 16 or 17, haven't found a job yet, and not in full-time education,
- older than this, but haven't been able to start training because of disability, ill health, pregnancy, language problems, custodial sentence/remand, care order.

ET schemes are intended for those aged between eighteen and fifty-nine, who have been unemployed for six months or more. You may also be eligible if you:

- have been receiving certain kinds of benefits,
- have been out of the labour market for more than two years, looking after a family or relative,
- have a disability,
- have just left the Armed Forces or been affected by large-scale redundancy,
- have a first language other than English, and need to improve your English in order to get a job or train,
- want to train to start your own business,
- have been in custody,
- want to train in a skill shortage occupation,
- need special literacy or numeracy training.

Trainees are paid an allowance, or wage, or both throughout the scheme –

not a lot, but probably better than you would get if you were looking for a job off your own back, with no qualifications to show. Workplace on-job training is undertaken by qualified trainers, and you also spend time at a training centre or college, where you join up with the rest in your group and learn other new skills.

How this off-job training is organized will depend on your needs and how the scheme is organized. The idea is to cause least disruption to you and to your job. You might therefore spend most of the week with the employer, and one day at the training centre, or longer periods at work and two or three days at the training centre. Another method used is for a block of twelve weeks or so at work, followed by four weeks at college – and so on, for the duration of the scheme (not usually longer than two years for YT). Or distance learning may play an important role.

All schemes are managed under contract with the Training and Enterprise Council (TEC), or, in Scotland the local enterprise company. Some YT schemes are employer-led. That means the employer engages you as an employee and arranges for your off-job training to be provided. Other schemes are arranged by an umbrella organization – this may be the HCTC, ABTANTB, or a consortium of local employers and a college or other training provider, for example CATEC (Catering and Training Education Consortium) which involves Guildford College. The umbrella organization provides the off-job training, makes arrangements with employers for you to get work experience, handles the paperwork and payment arrangements, and is responsible for quality control.

High Technology National Training (HTNT) is part of ET. Courses supported are all full-time (up to a maximum of twelve months), at Higher National Certificate level or above and include a period of employer placement. Tourism is one of the specialist management areas covered, with support given to more than 200 places on fourteen tourism and leisure management courses throughout Britain in 1991/2.

Course fees are paid in full by the Employment Department, and you receive a training allowance. To be eligible you must intend to work on completion of the course in Great Britain or elsewhere in the EC, in a job which uses your new skills. When the course starts you must be unemployed, aged between eighteen and fifty-nine, normally resident and allowed to work in Britain.

Self-study

Not an easy option, but it does mean you can study and work at your own pace, when it suits you, and get better qualifications – an opportunity you might not have otherwise.

Self-study comes under various names. 'Distance learning' is the description adopted in this book to identify those qualifications which can be studied in this way. Other names used are 'open learning' and 'flexistudy' – hence the Open College and the Open University.

In its simplest form, self-study means buying text books, audio tapes, videos and so forth which relate to the subject area you are studying. Much more helpful, however, are the purpose-made distance learning packages, such as NEBSM *Super Series* (published by Pergamon Open Learning, Oxford). These involve you working through the text, exercises, and assignments. For some programmes, such as the HCIMA Professional Certificate and Diploma, you have access to a tutor for expert guidance and counselling, and attend tutorials or short courses from time to time.

In its White Paper *People, Jobs and Opportunity* (February 1992), the Government announced its plans to give all TECs and lecs, in partnership with local library services, the chance to make suitable learning materials and back-up services available in local libraries over the next three years.

Recording your qualifications and experience

Three national systems have been introduced in recent years for encouraging individuals, and young people in particular, to build up a systematic record of their qualifications, experience and career aims.

National Record of Achievement (NRA)

Launched by Government in February 1991, the NRA is intended to be the key part of an individualized personal database which will accompany people throughout their careers. Over two million were issued in the first year, mainly to 16-year-olds. In early 1992, Government asked NCVQ and SCOT-VEC to take over development and marketing of the NRA, working in partnership with TECs, lecs and others to promote its use throughout working life.

The information collected in the NRA will provide a curriculum vitae (CV) for the individual, with the advantage over the conventional cv that what goes into the file is the result of an agreement with the teacher or trainer. There are five sections:

- Summary of school achievements – which describes the curriculum undertaken, the National Curriculum statutory assessments, overall comments on performance and achievements, and attendance records.

- Summary of qualifications and credits – cumulative list of GCSE and A levels (or Scottish equivalents), NVQs and other professional qualifications and credits.

- Summary of other achievements and experiences – for example, sporting and voluntary activities, performance in communications, numeracy, information technology and other core skills.

- Personal statement – a chance for the individual to record his/her progress to date, including any relevant information not mentioned elsewhere.

- Employment history – details listed in the standard way.

National Record of Vocational Achievement

The system used prior to 1992 by NCVQ in England, Wales and Northern Ireland for recording an individual's achievement through all stages of her/his education, training and working life. The National Record consists of four sections:

- Personal record – gives information on achievements in educating, training, work and leisure time.

- Action plan – includes long-term career aims, medium range qualification goals, immediate achievement targets and a statement of training and assessment arrangements.

- Assessment record – charts the progress made towards the achievement targets set out in the action plan.

- Certificates – show credits or achievements within the system.

The essential features will be incorporated in the enhanced NRA system.

Record of Education and Training (RET)

SCOTVEC's system for documenting career-long achievement. It records each success in a SCOTVEC National Certificate module, Higher National unit, Workplace-assessed unit, or group award (such as SVQ or HND), and recognition of the qualification by professional bodies and others.

Profile: Malcolm Steel Allcock

Hotels/clubs

Malcolm is Secretary of the Travellers' Club, which was founded in 1819, 'to provide a point of reunion for gentlemen who have travelled abroad, to which they could invite members of foreign missions and travellers of distinction, as visitors'.

The Club's facilities include twenty bedrooms and several impressive public rooms, two of which are strictly 'out of bounds' to members' wives and other female visitors: the Library, with its priceless collection of travel books and maps, and the Smoking Room with its huge and very comfortable leather chairs and settees. Protocol and tradition abound, so in the Coffee Room – never referred to as a restaurant – one long narrow table is reserved for members who wish to dine alone, perhaps to read a book over their meal, but certainly not to talk, while another table is kept for members who wish to join other members not entertaining visitors that day, and enjoy a conversation.

With ambitions to be a theatrical director, Malcolm left Alfreton High School in Derbyshire in 1956 with two A levels and three O levels, to do his one year's National Service. He spent the period with the Army Catering Corps at Aldershot, and decided to make a career in the hotel industry. He was accepted on a four-year Trust House management training programme, which included kitchen, restaurant, hall porter, cellar and bar, reception, night management and accounts duties. 'I was lucky. There were very few training schemes available in 1957, not many college courses either, and I wanted to start earning money straight away.' At The New Bath Hotel, Matlock Bath, Derbyshire, Malcolm's general manager was John McDonald. 'John and his wife Connie gave me a disciplined approach to cash and stock controls, which was to be a valuable skill for the future.'

John took Malcolm with him, first to The Great White Horse Hotel in Ipswich and then, in August 1961, to the Flying Horse in Nottingham, a four-star hotel with eighty bedrooms. Here he completed his training scheme and was promoted to Assistant Manager, with control of the food and beverage departments, housekeeping, furnishings and equipment. 'I even learnt how to mature Stilton, one of the hotel's specialities.'

Cliff Richard was an occasional visitor to the Flying Horse, and in Malcolm's next job as Deputy Manager of the luxury forty bedroom, privately owned, Mitre Hotel in Oxford he met Elizabeth Taylor, Richard Burton and other famous guests.

A sharp contrast was to follow. As Food and Beverage Manager of the 250 bedroom, three-star Shaftesbury Hotel in London, from September 1963, a regular ninety-hour week was spent organizing large functions, deputizing for the General Manager, and providing relief management at other establishmer s in the Associated Hotels group.

Malcolm Steel Allcock (*continued*)

A year of this was enough. Moving to a new environment, Malcolm became Assistant Manager of the Royal Over-Seas League in St James's, where he was to spend eight years. He was soon promoted to House Manager with 125 staff, responsible for personnel, front of house (the club has 120 bedrooms), and banqueting (for up to 400 people). 'There were wonderful characters such as Lady Wavell, wife of Lord Wavell who was Viceroy of India during the second world war. She treated the Club as if it was the Vice Regal mansion!'

At the Royal Air Force Club in Piccadilly, as House Manager from October 1972, Malcolm was responsible for the daily running of the Club. Similar to a small luxury hotel, it had seventy bedrooms and an equal number of staff. A year later he returned to the hotel scene as Assistant General Manager at the Ritz. 'It must have been one of the shortest interviews ever – after about two minutes, Geoffery Graham, the General Manager offered me the position.'

Paul Getty, Jackie Kennedy, Barbara Cartland, Judy Garland, Dame Margot Fonteyn and the Rolling Stones were some of the legendary names Malcolm recalls from this period. Following the hotel's takeover in March 1976, he was promoted to Deputy General Manager, responsible for the daily administration of the hotel, and its 282 staff. One of the functions he recalls helping organize was Prince Philip's sixtieth birthday party in 1981. 'The housekeeper, on entering the private suite to check everything was in order, found the Queen standing on the settee in her stockinged feet, trying to obtain a good view of Buckingham Palace.'

'And when King Carl Gustav of Sweden was staying at The Ritz during its massive renovation programme, the waiter wheeling the trolley laden with His Majesty's breakfast, disappeared under the dust and debris of a collapsed corridor wall!'

Sometimes the guests caused havoc. Betty Davis had a difficult reputation among the staff at Malcolm's next hotel, Forte's exclusive Hyde Park Hotel. As Room Division Manager from June 1982, he was responsible for all front of house departments, including housekeeping. As well as preparing and administering the budget and maintaining staffing levels for the front of house, it was his job to maximize occupancy of the hotel's 160 bedrooms and twenty suites.

Occupancies rose to their highest level during the boom years of 1983–4. The hotel was the scene of much Government hospitality – famous guests included the Prime Minister of Japan and film stars Richard Gere and Ava Gardner. 'One guest – who shall be nameless – insisted on covering the floor of her suite with freshly laundered white bath towels each day.'

'While the experience at the Hyde Park was useful, in some respects my career had taken a step down. I considered leaving London to find a general manager appointment, but once out of the West End it can prove extremely difficult to return. All the recruitment agencies told me they were doing their best, but how difficult it was etcetera, etcetera. Then I

Malcolm Steel Allcock (*continued*)

saw an advertisement for the position of General Manager at 7 Down Street, a small, exclusive hotel in Mayfair, London.'

Malcolm had achieved a long-held ambition: general manager of a top class hotel. But the small, all-suite hotel, with its rooms decorated individually in Indian, Japanese and other styles, and bathrooms fitted with jacuzzis, was sold after less than a year to property developers. Malcolm was made redundant and found himself at forty-nine out of a job.

'The next few months were very difficult. Thankfully, I had remained in touch with some of the club secretaries, and this led to a temporary appointment at The Travellers' Club, after the previous incumbent had left quite suddenly.' Malcolm quickly started on sorting out the rather chaotic state of affairs. His appointment was made permanent and at the following annual general meeting, the Chairman paid a generous tribute to the transformation Malcolm had brought about.

Membership has started to increase after many years of decline, the Club's facilities are being improved as quickly as resources allow, and in 1990 for the third year, the Queen Mother's private Christmas party hosted by Her Majesty's Household was held at the Club. A gracious hand-written note of thanks from Her Majesty's Private Secretary was delivered at 8 a.m. 'It made all the effort put in by my staff worthwhile, and certainly provided a divergence from the correspondence taking place in the members' comments book at that time about the new potatoes the Chef was serving. Was it right to serve them out of season? Why were they peeled and so forth!'

Paying for your training

Most people – but by no means everyone – living in the UK are entitled to have, at least once in their life, a substantial element of their education and training expenses paid for by:

- their local education authority (LEA) – England and Wales,
- Scottish Office Education Department (SED) Scotland,
- Education and Library Board (ELB) – Northern Ireland,
- Training and Enterprise Council (TEC) – England and Wales,
- local enterprise company – Scotland,
- Training and Employment Agency – Northern Ireland.

Those not in this situation may be fortunate to get sponsorship by an employer.

Many students on full-time courses will qualify for some support from the

LEA, ELB or the SED – the system of grants and student loans is explained in Chapter 5.

Tax relief on vocational training

From April 1992 tax relief has been given on payments made by individuals for training leading to NVQs and SVQs up to and including level 4. You are entitled to deduct a sum equivalent to the basic rate of tax (25 per cent in 1991/92) from the study, examination or assessment fees paid to training organizations, including the VAT element (if any) on those fees. Effectively this means you pay the training organization only 75 per cent of the amount of the fees due (assuming 1992 tax rates). The training organization then claims the remainder from the Inland Revenue. To qualify for tax relief, you must:

- Be resident in the UK, or resident in the UK for six months or more in the tax year, or visit the UK regularly each year for substantial periods.

- Not be receiving or entitled to receive financial assistance from any public body in respect of the course.

- Not be entitled to claim any other tax relief in respect of the payment.

To pay the lower fees, you have simply to complete a declaration that you are entitled to tax relief.

If your employer gives you some payment towards the cost of the course, you still get tax relief on the amount you pay the training provider. However, the amount you receive from your employer counts as pay, and will be subject to PAYE.

Tax relief is not available on travel costs to attend the course, equipment, or text books. Only printed material, audio-, video- or computer-based materials which are integral to the training being undertaken will qualify.

Career Development Loans

Loans are available for between £300 and up to 80 per cent of the course fees, plus books and materials and, in some cases if you are on a full-time course, living expenses, up to an overall maximum of £5,000 (1992 figures). You can apply for a career development loan if:

- You are over 18 and not receiving other support for training and education.

- You will work in the UK or elsewhere in the EC after the course.

- The course is suitable for the work you want to do and lasts between one week and one year – any mode of study is acceptable including distance learning.

Career development loans are sponsored by the Employment Department in partnership with Barclays Bank, Clydesdale Bank and the Co-operative Bank.

The Government pays the interest on the loan for the duration of the course and for up to three months afterwards. Then it will be up to you to repay the loan, plus any further interest in instalments. The loan repayment period is agreed with the bank when you take out the loan.

Training credits

Training credits were successfully piloted in 1991 by a number of TECs and lecs, and are being progressively phased in. The Government's aim is that by 1996 every young person aged sixteen to seventeen leaving full-time education will have the offer of a training credit. In some areas, some 18-year-olds may get credits too. One of the main aims is to give young people greater choice and control of their vocational education and training.

The credit may have a local name and may look like a cheque book, a credit card or a bond, with a typical value of at least £1,000 – individual values in the pilot schemes were often much higher than this. With the voucher you will be able to 'buy' approved training relevant to your employment and career aspirations. The choice of training may be very wide, for example: in-house training by your employer, attendance on a full- or part-time college course, joining a training scheme such as those offered by HCTC and ABTANTB, going to evening classes, or following a distance learning scheme.

You will be given help and advice over the choices that are available, and in drawing up a personal action plan. There are certain rules to safeguard the quality of the training you receive, which will be explained to you. For example, the training provided must be delivered by an Approved Training Organization and to at least NVQ/SVQ level 2.

Employer sponsorship

Employer sponsorship usually takes the form of support while you study on a part-time, block release or distance learning course, or – still quite rare in hotels and catering – help with your living expenses while studying on a full-time course. When sponsorship takes the form of a supplement to your local education authority grant, the size of your grant may be reduced (see Chapter 5).

In return for your employer's help, you are likely to be expected to make certain, quite reasonable commitments, such as working for the employer during periods of industrial release and the vacations. There is no legal obligation for a sponsored student to remain with the employer after completing the course – or indeed to complete the course. However, there is a recognized moral obligation to stay with the sponsoring employer for at least a year or two before moving on to other employment.

Some examples of sponsorship

The European Catering Association of Great Britain (see Chapter 11) offers a sponsorship scheme through its London branch members, and a group of colleges in the area. The purpose is to encourage young people to enter the industrial and contract catering sector of the industry.

The scheme can provide for payment while working (in vacations for full-time students), college and examination fees, travel costs, essential books, uniform, knives and uniform laundry allowance. Participating employers set their own particular conditions and at what level they operate the scheme. For example:

- Providing on-job training to young people wanting to start work straight away, leading to NVQs at levels 1 and 2.

- Releasing trainees to attend college on a full- or part-time course.

- Providing BTEC National Diploma students with a year experience, re-lease to attend the one-year full-time HCIMA Professional Diploma course, followed by a one-year fixed-term contract as an assistant manager.

- Offering a one-year trainee management scheme for HND or degree holders, leading to a job with the company.

The four-year Specialized Chefs Course run by Bournemouth and Poole College in association with members of the Academie Culinaire de France operates on a block release basis: six months in college, nine months in industry. All trainees are paid a training allowance during college periods. Uniforms, knives, textbooks, examination fees and so forth are also pro-vided. Sponsoring employers include the Savoy, Roux Restaurants, The Meridien, The Connaught, Claridge's, Langan's and Chewton Glen.

Students on the HCIMA Professional Certificate course are generally spon-sored by their employer, with paid time off to attend the local college on a day-release basis. An example of a particularly convenient arrangement is that pioneered in 1990 by Thames Valley University (TVU). Students from hotels in the Savoy Group, the Swallow International and the Westbury attend the Savoy Training Centre, instead of travelling the much greater distance to Slough.

Students applying for a full-time place on the HCIMA Professional Di-ploma at TVU are eligible to enter the Booker Fitch Food Services compe-tition. The winner receives a bursary.

Gardner Merchant, the contract-catering division of Forte plc, has a joint arrangement with Blackpool and The Fylde College, and Highbury College to offer a two-year BTEC Higher National Diploma. In addition to the college-based programme at Portsmouth or Blackpool, training and experience is offered at Gardner Merchant's residential training centre at Kenley, Surrey, and at one or more of the company's many units throughout the UK. Total time in the industry is thirty-six weeks. On successful completion of the course, students are offered a position on the Gardner Merchant Young Managers Programme.

Butlin's Holiday Worlds and Hotels offer a number of bursaries to students on full-time courses at HND level or above. The scheme involves working at a Butlin's Holiday World for at least one placement from college, and subsequently for a period of three months after final exams. A place may then be offered on the company's management trainee scheme.

The McDonald's Scholarship Programme is open to students who have been accepted on a recognized course (HND, or degree, for example) in business studies or any other related discipline. The award (£2,250 in 1992) is spread equally over the three years of study. Students must be available to work for at least eighty hours per term either during the vacation and/or term time, when they are paid at the standard hourly crew rate. Students follow a McDonald's training programme and have the opportunity to spend time working in a department of their choice for a short period during their second year summer vacation. They may also be offered the opportunity to complete any industrial placement period with McDonald's.

The postgraduate diploma/MSc programme at Oxford Brookes University, which is organized on a block-release basis (see Chapter 10), requires the applicant's employer to assume financial responsibility and to provide the necessary support for work-based learning and project work.

Concord Hotels, a training and recruitment consortium of privately owned and individually managed hotels, offer a two-year graduate scholarship scheme for management trainees leading to the HCIMA Professional Diploma. The trainees, most of whom have already completed Concord's in-house two-year management training scheme, remain on the payroll of hotels within the Concord group. The scheme begins with one term at Oxford Brookes University (September to December). Three terms working in sponsor hotels (January to December) follow. The final two terms are based at the University (January to July).

The postgraduate programme at Manchester Metropolitan University has also built up a strong partnership with a number of employers, and some places on the scheme are usually sponsored.

Profile: Sally Clarke

Chef proprietor

'Family holidays were often spent in France, and the many meals we enjoyed in small village restaurants were a particularly special experience for me. Then, at the age of thirteen, an introduction by Mother led to a part-time job during school holidays with outside caterers Jean Alexander Ltd of Guildford, Surrey.'

School finished, the next step was to study at Croydon College for two years, on the Ordinary National Diploma (OND) course in Hotel and Catering Operations (the forerunner of today's BTEC National Diploma). Then it was back to France in 1973 to learn the secrets behind those wonderful meals Sally had enjoyed as a child.

Her first three months were spent on a course at the Cordon Bleu School in Paris, and the next year working as an apprentice in three restaurants, 'chopping vegetables and observing'. With only her meals provided at the restaurant, Sally took a job with a French family. In return for cooking their evening meals from Monday to Friday, she was given free board and lodging.

London, 1975. Advice sought from experts Pru Leith, Elizabeth David and Margaret Costa leads to a job with Pru Leith's outside catering company. This valuable experience and, with the task of revamping the menu of a City wine bar, the opportunity to be innovative, led to Sally's appointment in 1977 as head teacher and demonstrator at the Pru Leith School of Cookery.

A year later, a Californian she had met while in Paris, asks Sally to help set up a restaurant in his home state. She spends four years in the USA, mostly in Los Angeles, before returning to the UK in 1983, with the sole aim of setting up her own business.

Clarke's Restaurant, in Kensington Church Street, London opened its doors for the first time in December 1984. The area abounds in antique shops, ideal for the top quality food Sally offers.

Such was the success Sally made of her business, that within three years she had purchased the property next door to the restaurant. This she operates as a speciality bread, wine and cheese shop. Sixteen different types of bread are sold, hand-baked in a small industrial unit in Ladbroke Grove, Kensington, by her baker and one assistant. Over 1,200 loaves a day are produced in addition to pastry goods for the restaurant and shop. The bakery also supplies other restaurants, hotels and speciality shops in central London. The staff complement for the shop and restaurant is thirty-five.

Clarke's Restaurant specializes in what Sally describes quite simply as 'good food'. The menu is changed daily for lunch and dinner. For lunch you could be eating:

Sally Clarke (*continued*)

Thinly sliced prosciutto ham served with ginger fruits

x x x x x x

Grilled corn-fed chicken filled with sun dried tomato, served with herb purée

x x x x x x

Warm blood orange pudding

x x x x x x

British cheeses with homemade oatmeal biscuits

To become a successful restaurateur, Sally believes, you need to have a love of food and be prepared to travel to learn the trade.

Keeping your career plan up-to-date

Having decided where you want to get to, and what experience, training and qualifications will help you get there, you must keep this plan up-to-date.

The best thought-out plans won't always work. The profiles throughout this book give plenty of examples of how matters can be taken out of your hands – the business closes or is taken over by another company, or you simply find you don't enjoy a particular aspect of the work. Use unplanned events as a reason for reassessing progress towards your long-term aims, not an excuse to give up. Take a positive role in securing the personal development, experience and training you need to reach your goals.

Determination can see you through unimaginably difficult times. Hard work and ambition will also serve you well. Sue Millington's story earlier in this chapter shows what remarkable courage she needed. Brian Purnell (Chapter 3) is the first cook in the Royal Navy to have risen to the rank of Commander. Sainath Rao (Chapter 2) made his mark on his seniors by coming into work an hour earlier each day, to make their job easier. You might think you could get taken advantage of – but as Sainath so vividly describes, extra effort at the right time in the right situation can bring eventual reward far beyond the initial inconvenience and risk of exploitation.

If you have an overall plan in mind and keep adjusting it to meet changing circumstances, you can avoid drifting about, or stagnating doing something that's not quite right. And here is some further advice from Roddy Watt of Berkeley Scott Personnel Consultants (adapted from his articles in *HCIMA Reference Book*):

♦ Before accepting a highly paid, glamorous position overseas, consider the future. Getting back on to the career ladder at home can prove difficult. Certainly, do not expect to earn more than before you left.

♦ Never leave a job voluntarily before arranging another job. Potential employers will see this as a reflection on your temperament and lack of forethought. And it's far more difficult to find a new job if you are unemployed.

♦ It is essential to achieve a solid track-record and this means sticking out the first few jobs for at least a year each, even if you find them dreary. The exception is if you move in an upward direction within the same company. The other exception is the real disaster: if you have clearly made the wrong move there is no point sitting it out for the sake of it. Most employers will allow you one of these, but no more.

♦ Do not drop a category to attract a title and money when, at the end of the day, you can be successful in your chosen stratum and be better off. It is easy to descend the ladder but it is difficult to reverse the process.

♦ If you are a small company and there is no way ahead – move.

♦ Unexpected promotion may speed up the process you have already planned. It may change your aspirations, in which case you should adjust your overall plan. Or it may be a false lead, made because your employer is desperate to fill a particular position. You're tempted with more money and an attractive job title, but consider honestly how well you will be able to do the job, and what the experience will count for when and if you get back on to your main career path.

♦ Once you have decided on your chosen field or strata of the industry, stick to it. Do not expect to get an interview with a contract catering company, for example, if your last relevant experience was five years previously. It is easier to move from a five- to a four-star hotel, than it is from four- to five-star, and from a hotel in London's West End to the country, than from the country back into the city.

♦ All organizations are political: the larger they are, the more intense the politics become and great caution should be exercised. The personality conflict is more often than not the result of unpleasant political dealings.

Profile: William MacKinnon

Hostels/accommodation management

Born into an Army family, William was educated in Army schools in various parts of the world, and then at the University of Swansea, from which he graduated in 1976 with a BSc in Economics and Material Science. His first job was with British Leyland as a buyer at the Longridge Plant, Birmingham. But there were many divisive elements among the large workforce at the time, and after three years William left to join a small business producing partitioning and ceilings.

'Although the work was varied – estimating, drawing, ordering materials and controlling labour teams – I very much wanted to be involved in "man management", rather than "production management" and decided to take a year away from work to sort out my future career.' The change in career direction was not easy. His next post offered a combination of managing materials and a small staff, then in 1981 a position arose with the Boy Scouts Movement at Rowland House in Stepney, London as Duty Warden in charge of maintenance.

Rowland House closed in 1982 and William was appointed Duty Warden at Baden Powell House in Queen's Gate, where he was later promoted to Hostel Manager.

Baden Powell House, which opened in 1961 and was architecturally advanced for its time, has thirty-eight bedrooms, providing accommodation for 112 people. William has fifteen staff, including an Assistant Hostel Manager, receptionist, clerical staff, plus a housekeeper with two assistants and three cleaners. He is also responsible for liaising with the contract caterers to ensure the standards required by the Boy Scout's Movement are maintained.

Throughout the year, except for Christmas Day, Baden Powell House provides hospitality to members of the movement visiting London from other parts of the UK and the rest of the world. 'I aim to run a very high standard hostel, with efficient work systems to ensure that costs are covered – it is a non-profit-making charity, and Scouts pay a nominal sum for their accommodation. I try and maintain a disciplined, but friendly atmosphere, so that our young visitors enjoy their stay.'

With the growing inter-communication between European Scouting Associations, an increase in the numbers of European visitors to Baden Power House is likely, which could extend the work of the Hostel Manager. 'Good staff relations are essential to this aim. I have tried to create a strong team spirit. Training has to be mainly on the job, as external courses would prove too costly. When recruiting I look for staff who already have the necessary qualifications and, just as important, I look for people who can make decisions. I want them to be able to face the challenge of dealing with a small operating unit.'

Further information

See also end of Chapter 5.

Educational Guidance Services for Adults (EGSAs)

- Offers free, independent advice, not all areas have a service, but your local library will be able to tell you if one exists near you.

Women's Returners' Network

- Specializes in giving advice and information to women who want to get back into work.
  81–103 Euston Street, London NW1 2ET
  Tel: 071 388 3111
- If you think you have been a victim of *race* or *sex discrimination*, contact your local Jobcentre or Citizen's Advice Bureau in the first instance.

Commission for Racial Equality

Elliot House, 10–12 Allington Street, London SW1 5EH
Tel: 071 828 7022

Equal Opportunities Commission

Overseas House, Quay Street, Manchester M3 3HN
Tel: 061 833 9244

Disablement resettlement officers

- At Jobcentres, give specialist occupational counselling to people who have problems in finding and keeping work or training due to illness, injury or disability.

Databases

- National Database of Vocational Qualifications – information on NVQs and other vocational qualifications: description, structure, component parts, details of units required to obtain the qualification. Also the organizations and awarding bodies associated with them.

- Training Access Point (TAP) – computerized network of training courses available locally. A TAP terminal is based at Springboard in London (see end Chapter 1).

Financial support

Training Credits

The Training Credits Enquiry Point, Training Credits Branch, Employment Department, Block A, Floor 3, Porterbrook House, c/o Moorfoot, Sheffield S1 4PQ
Tel: 0742 597626

Career Development Loans

Freepost Career Development, PO Box 99, Sudbury, Suffolk CO10 6BR
Freephone: 0800 585 505
or enquire from branches of the three participating banks: Barclays Bank, Clydesdale Bank, The Co-operative Bank

Training and Employment Agency

- For Northern Ireland:
  Clarendon House, 9–21 Adelaide Street, Belfast BT2 8DJ
  Tel: 0232 244300

Central contact point for local enterprise companies

Scottish Enterprise, 120 Bothwell Street, Glasgow G2 7PG
Tel: 041 248 2700 Fax: 041 221 3217

Central contact for Training and Enterprise Councils

The TEC Development Branch, TEED, Moorfoot, Sheffield S1 4PQ
Tel: 0742 753275
A list of TECs and lecs is also available from Business in Community (see Chapter 11).

Youth and employment training programmes

Your TEC or lec (see above), local Careers Office and Jobcentre (see telephone book), HCTC and ABTANTB (see end Chapter 1). An information pack on High Technology National Training (HTNT) is available by calling Freephone 0800 444245.

Youth Training Programme (Northern Ireland)

YTP Customer Information Officer, Netherleigh, Massey Avenue, Belfast BT4 2JP
Tel: 0232 763244

Job Training Programme (Northern Ireland)

JTP Customer Information Officer, Gloucester House, Chichester Street, Belfast BT1 4RA
Tel: 0232 235211

NVQ/SVQ awarding/validating bodies

Further information in Chapter 11 (see end Chapter 7 for list of lead bodies):

- Association of British Travel Agents National Training Board (ABTANTB).
- British Institute of Innkeeping (BII).
- Business and Technology Education Council (BTEC).
- City and Guilds (C&G).
- Hotel Catering and Institutional Management Association (HCIMA).
- Hotel and Catering Training Company (HCTC).
- National Council for Vocational Qualifications (NCVQ).
- National Examining Board for Supervisory Management (NEBSM).
- Scottish Vocational Education Council (SCOTVEC).

Other providers of distance/open learning material

Addresses in Chapter 12.

Open College

- Titles include: *Focus on Clean Food* (leading to IEHO Basic Food Hygiene Certificate, RIPHH Primary Certificate in Hygiene for Food Handlers), *Introduction to Supervision* (leading to NEBSM Introductory Award), *Effective Supervision* (leading to NEBSM Certificate in Supervisory Management), and *Firm Start II Starting The Business.*

Open University

- Established in 1969 with the particular purpose of providing a readily accessible, highly flexible, distance learning route to degrees and other qualifications; on many courses, subject choices can be made from year to year, while building up credit towards a full degree (see also Chapter 10).

5
Choosing a college course

Choosing a college course is an important decision, so the clearer you are at the outset about your overall aims, the more likely your decision will be the right one. As you start to examine the options – and there are a great many – pay particular attention to:

1 What level the qualification falls at.
2 How the course will contribute to your overall career aims.
3 Entry requirements.
4 Subjects that will be studied.
5 How long the programme of study will be.
6 Where the course is available.

None of these issues is exclusive:

- Sometimes the choice of courses is restricted to those offered by colleges in your area (see Chapter 12).

- Given the decision to study for a particular qualification, you may have no choice over the length of the course.

- While many qualifications are designed for a particular career, other career routes within the hotel, catering, leisure and tourism industry are not automatically closed off. Nor do they limit the possibility of studying for more appropriate qualifications at a later career stage.

- Colleges and awarding bodies will usually accept alternative entry qualifications, especially from those who have gained appropriate experience.

- Where there is strong competition for entry to the course – which tends to be the case at degree level, and with popular colleges – applicants who only satisfy the minimum entry requirements are unlikely to be successful in getting a place.

Profile: Dee Ludlow

Hotels

From the age of four Dee was included in Sunday luncheon parties at The Bull at Wrotham, Kent, an occasional family treat. In later years she would invariably absent herself from the table as soon as lunch was over, to visit the kitchen. 'I loved the busy atmosphere, and was often allowed to help out, chopping or stirring under the supervision of the chef.'

Realizing that Dee's heart was fast becoming set on a catering career, her father decided to expand her insight into the trade. From the age of ten she joined him occasionally in busy, smart restaurants and, by way of complete contrast, on visits to a transport cafe on the A2!

At a career interview at school, she described her burning ambition to become a hotel manager. But the careers officer brushed these thoughts aside with assurances that Dee could easily become a teacher or a nurse. 'So my father wrote to Charles Forte to get the advice that I should find a good catering college and study hard.'

'After considering Westminster College, which I could commute to from home, I chose Brighton College, as it meant I would have to live away from home, which I felt was right at this stage in my life.'

For her industrial release after the first year at college, she worked at the London Metropole. Dee made a good impression and was given special release from college to continue working at the Metropole for an extra few months, as Acting Personnel Manager.

She did such a good job, that soon after returning to college she was asked to work at the Brighton Metropole. She was able to gain useful experience as a conference and banqueting supervisor, breakfast supervisor and evening housekeeper, but some weeks she logged up forty hours at the Metropole, on top of college lectures and homework! Careful not to let her studies suffer, Dee graduated in June 1976 with a Higher National Diploma in Hotel and Catering Administration. She immediately took up work on a full-time basis at the Brighton Metropole as supervisor and then as deputy manager in the coffee shop.

Further promotion quickly followed, to Assistant Food and Beverage Manager, which included conference and banqueting, and then to Personnel Manager. She also became Careers Adviser for Sussex, and Deputy Chairman of the local Hotel and Catering Industry Training Board Regional Advisory Committee. Her book *Working in a Hotel* was published in 1982, and is now in its 7th edition. Aimed at fourth year secondary school students, it filled the information gap that Dee found when considering her career choice.

In March 1982 she helped open The Pembroke Hotel, Blackpool, as House/Personnel Manager. She was promoted to Deputy General Manager in July 1986, and in December took up the same position at the London Metropole. At the time this four-star hotel had 571 bedrooms,

Dee Ludlow (*continued*)

two restaurants, banqueting rooms for up to 250 people, 24-hour room service and a staff of over 260. Dee could certainly feel proud of her progress in the ten years since she left college.

But it was not time to rest on her laurels. She set about earning a reputation for being a troubleshooter manager, who could quickly ident-ify and solve problems. This led to her appointment as Acting General Manager at the Metropole, and then, in February 1990, as General Manager of The Chelsea Hotel, Knightsbridge, a 225 room, four-star deluxe hotel, and Sarova Hotel Group's biggest London property. Her success brought acclaim in a special report 'Women at the Top' in the magazine *Meeting in London*.

Following a big 'head-hunting' exercise, the Brent Walker group ap-pointed Dee General Manager of The Londonderry Hotel in March 1991. 'When as a child my father drove me along Park Lane to see its large hotels, I made up my mind to work in one of them one day. I know that he would feel proud that I have more than achieved that aim by becoming the first woman hotel general manager in Park Lane.' (Dee's advice to women joining the industry was quoted in Chapter 4.)

Sadly this appointment was short-lived. After six months organizing the multi-million pound refurbishment, Dee and all her staff were made redundant. Brent Walker's financial crisis meant the indefinite post-ponement of the hotel's reopening. Dee has since joined Forte as General Manager of the Forte Crest in Milton Keynes.

Qualification level

NVQs and SVQs, General NVQs and SVQs are structured in levels, level 1 being the simplest, level 5 the most advanced.

Other clues to level of qualification, are the use of the words Certificate, Diploma, Higher and Masters. By convention, a Diploma is generally higher in level than a Certificate. A Higher Diploma or Higher Certificate is generally higher in level than a Diploma or Certificate. A Masters degree (MSc or MA) is above a first degree (BSc or BA).

While it is important to be as clear as possible about the relative standing of a qualification, you should also find out what the arrangements are for taking steps up the qualification ladder as your studies and career progress. If you find you get on really well, and would like more of a challenge, can you transfer on to a higher level course?

The answer in more and more situations is yes – see also *upward pro-gression* below. The NVQ and SVQ system (see Chapter 7) has no barriers whatsoever to upwards progression. There are a great many units to choose from, and each has a value in its own right, as well as contributing to a particular qualification. You don't have to achieve a certain unit or qualifi-cation within a certain number of years. You don't have to start all over again if you have a particular difficulty at some stage.

Individual subject passes have a value in their own right, so if it is necessary to change programmes, or leave off your studies for a period, you will generally earn credit towards a qualification. The BTEC Certificate of Achievement operates on this principle: it is not a qualification in its own right, but will count towards a Continuing Education Certificate or Diploma.

Should you have to change college for some reason, it is becoming easier to get credit at the second establishment for the work you have already done at the first. Some colleges organize the subjects studied on degree courses into three standard levels to make such transfers simpler.

Career aims

Courses are developed with a specific aim in mind – for example, to prepare for a supervisory position in the hotel and catering industry following an appropriate period of experience. At the foot of the hierarchy (NVQ/SVQ levels 1 and 2) are the foundation courses, such as BTEC First and SCOTVEC National, and those designed to provide basic operative and craft skills. Levels 3 and 4 (which includes BTEC and SCOTVEC National and Higher National awards) correspond broadly with advanced craft, supervisory and junior management jobs. Level 5 corresponds with middle management.

Entry requirements

The trend is certainly towards fewer and more flexible entry requirements. The main concern of colleges and awarding bodies is that you will be able to benefit from the course, and with due effort will be successful in obtaining the qualification you seek.

Applicants are often invited to visit the college for an interview with course tutors and admission staff, and possibly to complete a short entry test.

- The 1991 Government White Paper *Education and Training for the 21st Century* announced the proposal to award the Advanced Diploma to those gaining two A levels at grades C or above, an equivalent combination of A and AS, equivalent vocational qualifications, or a combination of A level, AS and vocational qualifications; and the Ordinary Diploma to those who have gained four or five GCSEs at National Curriculum levels 7 to 10, equivalent vocational qualifications, or any combination of these.

Profile: Russell Kett

Hotel, tourism and leisure consultant/hotel accountant/computer consultant

Russell was encouraged by his family to consider a career in the medical profession. Unimpressive A levels in Chemistry, Physics and Biology led him to reconsider his career plans. 'I had thoroughly enjoyed working as a waiter and kitchen assistant in a Blackpool snack bar, in the school holidays, and I was enthusiastic when my careers teacher suggested I might consider a future in hotel management.'

Blackpool College offered him a place from September 1971 on the three-year HND. 'My first industrial release was at the Blue Boar, Cambridge. I was supposed to be in the kitchen and the restaurant, but Bob Palmer, the General Manager had other ideas. I was "deep ended" as the hotel's general assistant, working in all departments as required, and deputizing for the assistant manager on occasions.'

Early responsibility was also a feature in his second industrial release, spent at the Prince of Wales Hotel, Grasmere. After a week as general assistant, Sandy Cowan, the General Manager asked him to take over the vacated post of Assistant Manager for the next six months. 'It was a real compliment when towards the end of this time he put me in charge of the hotel during his holiday.' Russell continued to work the occasional weekend during term time at college.

Finance was one of his final year options at college. 'I revelled in the financial aspects and decided to specialize in that side of the industry.' Russell gained his HND in Hotel and Catering Administration in 1974, and the accolade 'Student with the most management potential'. He was attracted to the idea of hotel consultancy but decided to first get experience and formal exposure to a large hotel company.

As an internal auditor with Strand Hotels, then part of J Lyons & Co, he conducted assignments and investigations throughout the company. David Bryan, his boss, realizing Russell's aptitude, encouraged him to expand his knowledge of computerized accounting systems. He was seconded to the Electronic Data Processing department. Strand Hotels was at the forefront in hotel computerization in the early 1970s. After two years, he was promoted to Assistant Financial Controller at the Cumberland Hotel, the group's 900 room London flagship, which gave him the opportunity to acquire real 'hands-on' experience of the accounting side of the industry.

Trusthouse Forte (now Forte) had acquired Strand Hotels and Russell decided to see if he was ready for consultancy. He was attracted to an advertisement for a junior consultant with Horwath & Horwath UK, the

Russell Kett (*continued*)

hotel, tourism and leisure consultants. Selected from among ninety applicants, he joined the company in 1977 to gain considerable experience of hotel, market and financial feasibility studies, take part in assignments involving the provision of accounting systems, catering facility appraisals, and to gain promotion to senior consultant.

Jonathan Bodlender, then Manager Director of Horwath & Horwath and Chairman of the British Association of Hotel Accountants (BAHA), asked Russell to assist him in the running of the Association. 'My interest in BAHA grew. I became Secretary in 1978 and, thanks to the active encouragement of H&H, who provided secretarial support, and released some of my time, we were able to increase membership significantly.'

All this over a period when Russell was spending two evenings a week and the occasional weekend for three years, at the then Ealing College studying for a Diploma in Management Studies.

As Marketing Manager for ADP Hotel Services (now Innsite) from 1983, Russell played a large part in the company's rapid growth to become the UK market leader in the provision of hotel and catering computer systems. As well as marketing, he advised clients on their accounting systems, budgeting and financial modelling applications. He found time to continue as Secretary to BAHA and in 1986 was awarded Fellowship of the Association. That same year he was made a Fellow of the Hotel Catering and Institutional Management Association.

Then providence stepped in. 'At a chance meeting one evening at traffic lights in London's Finchley Road, Geoff Parkinson, a director of Horwath & Horwath, encouraged me to consider rejoining the company. I had enjoyed hotel consultancy work and realistically my role within ADP was partly a consultancy one. At the age of thirty-one I returned in December 1984 to H&H as a managing consultant.'

To Project Director, Greene Belfield-Smith, Europe's largest hotel and catering consultancy was Russell's next move, in mid-1987. Further consultancy experience in the UK, USA, Europe and the Middle East followed. 'It was a varied and exciting period, when I might be carrying out an assessment and valuation for the privatization of a group of Greek hotels one week and, in complete contrast, advising the YMCA on accommodation and catering reorganization the next.'

BAHA activities continue to keep him busy. Chairman since 1988, he plays a key role at the Association's conferences. He has addressed international delegates in Cyprus, Malta, and in 1990, was in Washington to address delegates at the annual convention of the International Association of Hospitality Accountants on the 'Impact of the EC Single Market on the hotel industry'.

As an Associate of Touche Ross (which GBS merged with in 1987), Russell has reached 'the last leg before Partnership. I hope I'll make it, but whatever the outcome I will have thoroughly enjoyed the experience and the achievements I have gained. I just hope I can have as much fun going to work in the future.'

Entry requirements for school leavers

If you are planning to move straight from school to college, then GCSEs, SCEs, A and AS levels remain the principal measurement of whether you are up to the demands of the course. Where GCSEs are specified, the acceptable grades are A, B or C. Where SCE Standard grades are specified, these should be at credit level 1 or 2, or at general level 3.

Pre-vocational, foundation and craft level   Generally no specific entry qualifications are laid down, however for particular courses some colleges will look for evidence of a standard of English, and a subject testing numeracy.

Supervisory level   For the BTEC National Diploma or Certificate, or a two-year programme of study leading to a similar combination of modules for the SCOTVEC National Certificate, the general entry requirement is four GCSEs or four SCEs. Colleges may look for subjects demonstrating general literacy and numeracy skills. Other desirable subjects include travel and tourism, economics, a science or a language.

Junior management   Applications for the BTEC Higher National Diploma or Certificate are generally expected to have at least one A level, plus appropriate supporting GCSEs. The minimum entry requirement for the SCOTVEC HND is usually two SCE Higher grade passes and three Standard grades. For the SCOTVEC Higher National Certificate it is usually one H grade and three other S grades. Generally it is useful to have subjects which demonstrate literacy (ideally English), numeracy (ideally mathematics, or a science), and an interest in the area (ideally travel and tourism). What colleges look for will depend on the emphasis of their particular programme.

Degree   The minimum entry requirement is two A levels and three GCSEs, or five SCE passes of which three are at the Higher grade. Many students admitted have three or more A levels, or four SCE Highers. Some establishments specify subjects – generally English and mathematics, and a science subject. Students with three A level passes should have a pass in one other subject at GCSE. Two AS level passes at grades A to E are normally accepted in place of each A level pass, but the college may insist that applicants have reached the equivalent of A level in at least one specific subject. Some colleges will not count the same subject at more than one level.

Postgraduate   A first degree, or in some circumstances a HND is the normal entry requirement for a postgraduate diploma. For entry to a masters degree an honours degree is usually required, or success on the earlier postgraduate stage.

Other acceptable qualifications

In place of GCSEs: GCE O levels at grades A. B or C; CSE grade 1.
In place of SCE Standards: SCE Ordinary or O grades 1, 2 or 3 (A, B or C until 1985).
For entry to a supervisory programme: a good CPVE or Diploma of Vocational Education at Foundation level, with an appropriate profile.
For entry to HND: C&G Technological Baccalaureate with credit.
For entry to a degree programme:

- C&G Technological Baccalaureate with distinction.

- Irish Leaving Certificate with passes at grade C or better in at least four approved subjects, including English, at the Higher level at one sitting. Some colleges specify three passes at Higher/Honours level, plus the equivalent of two at standard/ordinary level.

- International Baccalaureate (minimum of twenty-four points).

- European Baccalaureate (with at least 60 per cent overall).

- Most European Matriculation certificates.

- The SCE Higher grade is likely to be replaced by a three year, 10-subject Scottish Baccalaureate.

Guide to some of the abbreviations
A level   Advanced level GCE
AS   Advanced Supplementary level of GCE, first examined in 1989: accepted as equivalent to half an A level
CPVE   Certificate of Pre-Vocational Education: 1 year, full-time scheme designed for young people aged sixteen and over, including those in sixth form, to help them make the transition from school to adulthood, and provide a route to higher level qualifications; replaced in 1991/92 by the Diploma of Vocational Education (see Chapter 8)
CSE   Certificate of Secondary Education
GCE   General Certificate of Education
GCSE   General Certificate of Secondary Education
SCE   Scottish Certificate of Education

Upwards progression

Appropriate vocational qualifications are accepted alternatives to the academic requirements. In this way, the BTEC First gives entry to the BTEC National, and the BTEC National to the BTEC Higher National. The relevant group of SCOTVEC National Certificate modules gives entry to the

SCOTVEC Higher National. City and Guilds certificates can give entry to the HCIMA Professional Certificate, which in turn gives entry to the HCIMA Professional Diploma. A good BTEC National Diploma or SCOTVEC National Certificate can meet the entry requirements for a degree course.

Qualifications such as a BTEC Higher National Diploma and HCIMA Professional Diploma (or Part B, the Diploma's predecessor), generally give exemption from at least the first year of degree courses. A number of HNC, HND and degree courses are designed to allow progression from HNC to HND, and/or from HND to degree.

Entry requirements for mature students

Awarding bodies and colleges make special provision for accepting mature applicants who do not have the appropriate academic entry qualifications. Three factors will be taken into account:

- age of applicant (a minimum age of twenty, twenty-one or twenty-five is often specified),

- number of years experience in the industry, and at what level,

- ability to succeed on the course.

Relevant prior qualifications and experience may give exemption from certain parts of the course.

Access courses are offered by groups of colleges in different parts of the UK, designed for adults without standard entry qualifications who want study experience before going on to apply for a place on an HND or degree programme.

An example is the one-year preparation programme offered by Shrewsbury College, to give entry to the HND course at Birmingham College of Food, Tourism and Creative Studies. Two options are offered: fifteen hours per week at Shrewsbury College will give access to year 1 of the HND, twenty-five hours per week access to year 2. The programme, which provides an introduction to the subjects covered on the HND, leads to BTEC Certificate of Achievements.

In Scotland, a similar example is the access course offered by Telford College, Edinburgh. The compulsory element includes SCOTVEC National Certificate modules in hospitality studies, tourism, communications, behaviourial science, computing and mathematics, and economics. Modern languages and food studies may also be studied. *SWAP*, the Scottish Wider Access Programme operates in the same way.

Some colleges offer an *associate student scheme*. Under this arrangement, students can study units selected from any course. For those over twenty-one no formal entry qualifications are required. There is usually a limit placed on the number of hours attendance per week. Besides providing a taste of higher education to those who may wish to take a full- or part-time course in years to come, the scheme is popular with people who wish to update their skills and knowledge for career development, or simply to pursue education for personal enjoyment.

Accreditation of prior learning (APL)

APL is a process for gaining credit for what you already know and can do – whether this is through work experience, leisure pursuits, training, short courses, or whatever – but don't have a paper qualification to prove. APL takes the frustration out of the situation many people have found themselves in – well able to do a job, with excellent experience and unquestionable ability, but perhaps because they had no opportunity to go to a college, are regarded as unqualified.

The APL process is being adopted by more and more awarding bodies, including most of those you will encounter in this book. It is a strong feature of the NVQ and SVQ system.

To ensure the APL process is fair, you will be expected to spend some time collecting details of the learning you wish to demonstrate. The usual process is to speak to an adviser first, to get an initial idea of the qualification level it is practical for you to aim at, and establish the learning outcomes demanded by that qualification which you are likely to be able to meet. The person advising you – called an assessor or mentor – will have the authority of the awarding body involved.

You then compile what is known as a portfolio of evidence. What this contains will depend on the sort of work you have done, but it might include a detailed job description, samples of work, photographs of work you have done, a learning diary, and so forth. In some cases other forms of assessment may be required such as an interview, or the assessor observing you performing a task.

This portfolio is then presented to the awarding body for your claim to be assessed, and the appropriate credit or certificate issued. In the case of City and Guilds and SCOTVEC, for example, the assessment process is delegated to approved centres and trained verifiers, subject to quality assurance checks. The HCIMA mentors are Fellows of the Association, and the recommendation for credit goes to the Board of Fellows. Many colleges, training organizations, TECs and lecs, provide APL services.

The *Credit Accumulation and Transfer Scheme* (CATS) developed by the CNAA, works on similar lines. Students are given a credit rating on their previous qualifications and work experience. This speeds up the admission process to degree and postgraduate programmes, and indicates what exemption, if any, can be given to parts of the programme. It can also enable the student to build up an award from courses at different institutions. In-company training can be included in the scheme.

A variation of CATS is the *Credit Accumulation Modular Scheme* (CAMS). Awards are achieved through the accumulation of credit points gained by successful completion of course modules, with transfer possible between programmes with like-value modules.

Guide to minimum ages

- *At least twenty-five* – some Masters degrees/Postgraduate diplomas

- *At least twenty-one* – NEBSM Diploma, DMS

- *At least seventeen in Scotland, eighteen elsewhere* – Higher National Diploma/Certificate,
  Degree

- *At least eighteen* – NEBSM Certificate (for those working in hotels, catering, tourism and leisure; in some industries the minimum age is twenty-one)

- *At least sixteen* – most other courses

Subjects studied

Clearly, the choice of subjects will reflect the qualification route. Here you might decide for something quite specific: hotel reception, for example. Or you could consider a more general qualification that will keep your options open: leisure studies, for example.

For most qualifications, at most levels, there is a core of common subjects that will be similar no matter what college you go to. At degree and postgraduate level, however, the core subjects will vary from programme to programme, even if the award title is the same.

The greatest variation will occur in the range of optional subjects available. These can give you the opportunity to pursue a particular interest, even to specialize in that area, for example vegetarian cookery.

A number of colleges give their students the chance to gain more than one qualification. For example, a two year Professional Chefs course may include NVQs at levels 1 and 2 in Food Preparation and Cooking, as well as Wine and Spirit Education Trust Certificate, City and Guilds Communications Skills 361, Food Hygiene Certificate, and First Aid Certificate.

Students on the BTEC National Diploma in Leisure Studies at Guildford College of Technology have the opportunity of gaining at least one nationally recognized coaching award in a sport of their choice, advanced First Aid certificate, Bronze Medallion in Life-Saving, Pitman or RSA Word Processing certificate. An Outward Bound expedition to assess students to develop leadership and communications skills is an integral part of the BTEC First Diploma in Hotel and Travel offered by the college.

Where courses lead to a number of different qualifications, the college may also award its own diploma or certificate. One well known example is

Westminster College's Professional Chef Diploma, indicating all-round competence on this three-year full-time course which includes various NVQ awards up to level 3, and a BTEC First Diploma.

Other examples include the Diploma in Professional Catering, awarded by Bournemouth and Poole College of Further Education to those who successfully complete the two-year full-time course, and Highbury College's Diploma in Catering Operations (two-year full-time course) and Diploma in Professional Cookery (three-year full-time course).

On the one-year, full-time Diploma in Advanced Catering offered by Canterbury College, there is another unusual element. After one term of advanced practical work in cookery and restaurant service at Canterbury, and conversation French, students travel to France to spend a term at the Lycee Professionel Rheims (where accommodation is provided with local families), followed by a term spent working in hotels and restaurants in and around Rheims.

Length of study

There are four principal categories of college-based course:

- Full-time – students expected to be available (that is, not in employment) to attend lectures, seminars or other college-based learning activities, except (normally) during weekends or vacations.

- Full time (sandwich) – some of the term time (and also, in many cases, some of the vacation) is spent gaining experience in the industry.

- Part-time – college-based learning activities are timetabled on a particular day, afternoon, and or evening (or a combination), so that students in employment have to spend the minimum time away from their workplace.

- Block release – students attend college-based learning activities for blocks at a time, usually a minimum of a week and not more than four weeks or so. A programme of study may consist of several such blocks spread over a year or two years. The arrangement is intended to allow students to gain experience at the same time, in paid employment. (Belfast Institute offers the HCIMA Professional Certificate course on a block release basis. Students spend three days a week in college, two in industry. There is continuous employment throughout the two years, with sponsorship by the Training and Employment Agency in year one, and by the employer in year two.)

Full-time courses are generally organized in multiples of one academic year (from September or October through to June or July of the following year). Some level 1 and 2 courses do not require a year of full-time study, but tend to be offered by colleges in combination with other courses, so that attractive one- and two-year programmes are created.

Where courses are organized on a modular basis, you may have great flexibility to study individual subjects, or construct a programme that suits your particular abilities and needs – both in terms of subject content, and in terms of level of qualification. You may be able to study different parts of the course at different colleges in the UK and abroad. You may not be tied to the traditional academic year. (Highlands College in Jersey, for example, accepts students on part-time courses all through the year, examinations to be taken when the student is ready.)

Guide to length of college-based courses

BTEC First Diploma – generally one year full-time, or two years part-time. A period of industrial experience is likely to be included. This may be in a block, of three weeks for example, or on a one-day-per-week basis in the second half of the year.

BTEC First Certificate – generally one year part-time.

BTEC National Diploma courses and equivalent SCOTVEC National Certificate programmes – two years full-time. Industrial experience is usually arranged, in one or two periods, sometimes during the vacation. At some colleges, industrial experience is arranged on a one-day-a-week basis during term time.

BTEC National Certificate – generally two years part-time.

HCIMA Professional Certificate – two years part-time.

SCOTVEC Higher National Certificate – generally one year full-time.

SCOTVEC Higher National Diploma – two years full-time: twelve weeks industrial experience is usually included between year 1 and year 2.

BTEC Higher National Diploma – two years for entrants with a National Diploma, including a minimum of twenty-six weeks industrial experience. Until recently, A level entrants had to follow a three-year course with a rather longer period of industrial experience – typically a year, but a number of colleges now offer a standard two-year HND, for A level and National Diploma entrants.

BTEC Higher National Certificate – generally two years part-time.

HCIMA Professional Diploma – on a full-time basis takes one year, two years as a sandwich course (which includes a period of industrial experience), and three years as a part-time course.

Degrees – three or four years, depending on whether it is a pass or honours degree, also the length of industrial experience and entry qualifications.

Postgraduate diplomas and taught masters degrees – generally one year full-time, two or more years part-time.

Where to study

Changes in the funding of further and higher education have given students a much wider choice of where to study. A relatively new development is the option offered by some colleges of spending time in Europe or North

America. The alternative – of qualifying in a hotel school abroad – will continue to be favoured by some of those with the means to afford it.

The size and location of the college should be considered – whether it is in a city or the country. What learning resources are available – library, media resources, language laboratories, training restaurant and kitchens, bar, reception and housekeeping areas, science laboratories, seminar and lecture rooms and so forth? If you are married, with a young child, are nursery facilities available at the college, or nearby?

What sort of reputation has the college got? What do people who have studied there have to say? How does the course you plan to study rate in overall importance at the college? If you are one of only a few HND students in a large college where everyone else seems to be on a degree course, you may regard yourself and your course less positively. (Colleges tend to specialize in certain courses of similar level. A number offer mostly levels 1 to 3 courses. Others also offer Higher National Diplomas, while some only offer Higher National Diploma and degree, or only degree and postgraduate diploma. As the list of colleges in Chapter 12 indicates, a few colleges offer almost the full range.)

Leisure and student facilities should be considered – those available at the college and in its vicinity. What about transport connections for getting to and from the college, and travelling home during vacations? Is suitable accommodation available – either in college-maintained properties: student flats and halls of residence, or in the private sector – bed-sits, flats and houses let to students at an economical rent? What catering facilities are available at the college for snacks and main meals?

College of the year

1991 saw the launch of the College of the Year Awards by *Caterer & Hotelkeeper* and sponsor Innsite Hotel Services:

Category/winner	*Shortlisted*
Craft: NVQ/SVQ level 2	
Birmingham College of Food, Tourism and Creative Studies	Omagh College Norwich City College North Nottinghamshire College, Worksop
Supervisory: NVQ/SVQ level 3	
Highbury College, Portsmouth	Belfast Institute Thames Valley College (now Thames Valley University)
Management: NVQ/SVQ levels 3/4	
Manchester Polytechnic (now Manchester Metropolitan University)	
	Oxford Polytechnic (now Oxford Brookes University) Ealing College (now Thames Valley University)

Paying for your education and training

Student loans, training credits and other forms of financial support are increasingly important, and you should read those sections in Chapter 4. This chapter deals with grant support.

Education authority/department grants

The whole system of grants and awards is enormously complicated, and subject to change. For up-to-date details you should ask your grant awarding authority for a copy of its guidance booklet (addresses at end of chapter).

The regulations make a distinction between: *award* – both the fee element, and a maintenance element; and *grant* – only the maintenance element. However, it is more usual to use the term grant – as it is in this book – to cover both the:

- *Fee element* – tuition and other course-related fees for which you are liable, normally paid direct to the college by the grant-making authority. Students who have attained the age of twelve, but not the age of eighteen on 1 September of the year their course is due to begin, are entitled to have some or all of their fees paid by their local authority or region. Some authorities pay the fees for full-time students up to the age of nineteen or twenty, provided they are resident in the area, and will be studying at a college in the area.

- *Maintenance element* – towards your personal expenses during term time and the Christmas and Easter vacations (standard rates are set, depending on where you are living during term time and where you are studying) *less* any income of your own, and any assessed contributions from your parents or your spouse, based on their income. This element is normally paid in termly instalments.

There are two basic types of grant:

- *Mandatory* – the grant-making authority is required by law to pay, and

- *Discretionary* – it is up to the authority whether it pays or not, and, for many courses, how much it pays.

If you are under nineteen, and in difficult financial circumstances, a small grant may be available towards your living expenses. If you want to attend a college outside your local authority area or region, you should contact your grant department to find out what help you will get towards tuition fees.

Basic mandatory grant rates

Living at home: £1,795 (England and Wales); £1,660 (Scotland)
Living away from home: £2,265 (England and Wales); £2,200 (Scotland)
Living away from home in London: £2,845; £2,780 (Scottish students)

The Government's policy has been to freeze basic grant rates at these levels (set in 1990–91). Any increase in support will be provided as a student loan (see below), not grant. The maximum loan will be increased annually by an amount reflecting inflation rate, until the loan facility and the grant each provide approximately half the total support (year 2007 or so). From then on, grants and loans are expected to be index-linked.

Studying elsewhere in the EC

Local authority/education department grants are not presently available for full-time courses in other EC countries. British nationals, who choose to attend a European institution, may be entitled to an award from the EC country in which they study.

If you wish to include a European element in your course, a more practical option may be to get on a course in this country which gives you the opportunity to undertake part of your studies abroad (more details later in this chapter).

What courses qualify for grants?

Mandatory grants are available for *designated* courses. In almost all cases these are full-time or sandwich courses, which lead to:

- Degree

- Diploma of Higher Education

- Higher National Diploma and (if full time) Higher National Certificate

The general availability of NVQs, GNVQs, and SVQs from 1992/3 is likely to affect this list. In its White Paper *Education and Training for the 21st Century*, the Government announced that it 'would regulate all full-time provision offered to students over the age of sixteen and to full-time students in further education colleges. This will be a means of requiring colleges and schools to offer only NVQs to students pursuing vocational options'.

The following courses are *non-designated*, which means the only sort of grant they can attract, if at all, is a discretionary one:

- City and Guilds and other craft courses*.

- BTEC Firsts*, National Diplomas*, National Certificates* and Higher National Certificates.

- SCOTVEC National Certificate*, and Higher National Certificate.

- HCIMA Professional Diploma.

- Postgraduate and part-time courses including distance learning, Open College and Open University postgraduate diplomas (with some exceptions in Scotland) and masters degrees.

There are no tuition fees for those courses asterisked for students under the age of eighteen (or in some cases, nineteen, twenty or twenty-one) providing they attend a college within their home local authority or region.

Conditions for a mandatory grant

To get a mandatory grant you have to meet certain conditions. The final decision on whether or not you are eligible rests with the grant-awarding authority, but you will probably qualify if you:

- live in the UK or another country within the European Community, and have done so for at leat three years before the course starts,

- are applying for a Scottish Education Department grant, you must also have been ordinarily resident in Scotland on a certain date a few months before the course begins: 30 June for courses starting in September/ October, 31 October for courses starting in January, 28 February for courses starting in March/April.

If you are from another EC country you should ask at the college where you intend to study, which grant awarding authority you should apply to – this grant will only cover the fee element, unless you or your parents can establish 'migrant worker' status in the UK.

You will probably *not* qualify if you have:

- primarily been in the UK to receive full-time education and would normally live in a country outside the EC,

- previously attended, with grant, just one course for longer than one term and seven weeks, and the course itself was of more than two years' duration (if the course itself was two years or shorter, you will be considered for a reduced grant),

- attended two or more courses with grant.

Conditions for a discretionary grant

Whether you get a discretionary grant will depend on what funds the grant awarding authority has available for this purpose. The authority will set its own rules of eligibility. For example, you might find that your examination results are taken into account, and restrictions are made on where you study.

Applying for a grant in England and Wales

Application forms are available from local education offices, and most schools are issued with forms. There will probably be three forms which need to be completed at different stages:

- *Application form* – to establish that you are entitled to a grant.

- *Grant assessment form* – to provide the local authority with the information it needs to decide how much you should receive. It is very important to get your parents' cooperation in completing this form. If they do not – for any reason – give information about their income and other details requested you will receive no grant towards maintenance.

- *College acceptance form* – you should send this straight away to the college when a place has been offered unconditionally. If acceptance depends on your examination results, you should send the form to the college as soon as your results are known. The college then completes the form, confirming that you have been accepted for the course, and returns it to the local authority. No money, fees or maintenance will be paid until this form has been received back by the local authority.

You should submit at least a general application to your grant awarding authority as soon as possible, although not before January for a course starting the following autumn. Don't wait until you get your exam results, or a firm offer of a place. Late applications may not be dealt with until after the course has started, and this will put you in a difficult position as fees generally have to be paid at the time of enrolment.

Applying for a grant in Scotland

You should apply as soon as you have received an unconditional offer of a place on your chosen course. The unconditional offer must be sent with your completed application form.

Mature students

If you are aged twenty-six or over, and have earned, or received in taxable unemployment or supplementary benefits or income support, at least £12,000 in total during the three years before the start of the course, you may be eligible for an additional amount to cover fifty-two weeks of the year. The amount depends on your age at the start of the course, £280 at twenty-six, £500 at twenty-seven, £750 at twenty-eight and £980 at twenty-nine or over. (All 1992–93 figures.)

In calculating the maintenance element of your grant, no contribution from your parent is expected if you have, before the start of the course:

- reached the age of twenty-five,
- been self-supporting (including any periods of unemployment or place-ment on Government training schemes) for any three years,
- been married at least two years.

Some of the other details

Changing course   When you receive a grant, it is for a specific course. If you decide to change courses, for example, from a HND programme to a degree, you need permission in order for the grant to be transferred.

Studying abroad   If the course requires you to study abroad for at least one term, the grant you receive will depend on the country in which you are studying.

Special personal circumstances   There are special provisions if you have dependants, and for the disabled. Additional help is also available to students aged nineteen or over, who are on full-time courses, and have particular difficulties in meeting their living costs – if you are in this situation, ask the student services or student support officer at your college about *access funds*. Your college is entirely responsible for deciding which students should re-ceive payments from the access funds at its disposal, how much, and so forth.

Working during vacations   If you earn money by working during vacations or weekends, this will not affect your grant.

Sponsorship/release with pay to attend course   If your employer is sponsor-ing you to attend the course – and this includes releasing you with pay for the time you spend at college – to the value of more than £3,550 (1992/3) during the academic year, your entitlement to a grant may be progressively reduced to the point where you get no grant at all.

Sandwich course students   You do not receive grant for any year in which there are no periods of full-time study.

Student loans

A government funded top-up loan is also available to help you meet your day-to-day living costs if you:

- Are under the age of fifty.
- Meet the residence requirements for a mandatory grant (see above).
- Are on a full-time course of at least one year's duration, and the course is one of those for which mandatory grants are available (see above), or qualifies on special grounds.
- Do not already have a loan for the course.
- Are not in default on repayments on a loan obtained on a previous course.

The loan is in addition to other forms of financial support you may be receiving, such as the maintenance grant. And the amount you can borrow is not affected by the level of your grant, your parent's income, or any similar condition.

You can borrow any amount up to the maximum in one year. The maximum depends on where you are living (in 1992–93 it was between £570 and £830). In the final year of your course the maximum loan is somewhat lower, because it is not required to cover the summer vacation following the end of the course (in 1992–93 the final year maximum was between £415 and £605).

Applying for a student loan

You cannot apply for a loan until you have started your course, and you must apply before the end of the academic year (not later than 31 July) in which you wish to receive a loan. Follow the procedure carefully:

1 Ask your college for the three forms which are required. Take with you your (a) birth or adoption certificate if you were born in the UK; (b) passport, if you were born outside the UK, and an official letter or other document which establishes the date, place and country of your birth, and your names at birth; (c) grant letter (if you have a grant or award); (d) cheque book or building society pass book, or other proof of your bank or building society account number and sort code.

2 A member of college staff will help you fill in the forms, which establish that you are eligible for a loan.

3 If you are eligible, the college will issue an eligibility certificate. It will send one copy of this to the Student Loan Company, keep one copy for itself, and give two copies to you. With both your copies will be attached an application form.

4 You then complete the application forms. One copy is for you, the main copy you send direct to the Student Loans Company. Remember to indicate on the forms:

   • How much money you wish to borrow (up to the maximum) – you can only make one application per year, so if you apply for less than the maximum you cannot apply for more later.

   • How you want the loan money paid into your account: in one, two or three instalments – if you apply late in the year, you may not be able to receive the loan in more than one instalment.

   • The names, addresses and telephone numbers of two contacts – you should ask them in advance to agree to undertake this role, explaining that they are not acting as referees or guarantors of your loan, but that they may be contacted to provide an address if the loan company loses touch with you.

- Whether you have ever been declared bankrupt – it is a legal requirement when applying for a loan to answer this question, but if you have been declared bankrupt, it will not affect your eligibility for a student loan.

5 As soon as you receive it, sign and return the formal loan agreement to the Student Loans Company. This will include an authorization for a direct debit to be made from your account after you leave your course in order to repay the loan.

Repaying the loan

The amount you have outstanding will be indexed to inflation. This means that the value of the sum you repay will be the same, in real terms, as the value of the sum you borrowed. There is no interest to pay.

Loan repayments are made by direct debit from your bank or building society account, in equal monthly amounts, adjusted annually to take account of changes in the rate of indexation. The repayments will start in the April after you complete or leave your course, and continue for the next five years or more. If you wish, you can repay the loan more quickly, and there are special arrangements for those who encounter difficulty in paying.

Postgraduate study

A very limited range of grants for postgraduate study is available. In the main, grants for vocationally related programmes are provided by the three national Government education departments (DE, SED and DENI) – see end of chapter – but from time to time some colleges and individuals have been successful in securing funding from the Employment Department, TECs and lecs, and from employers.

If you are considering doing postgraduate study, you should start making enquiries about suitable courses (see Chapter 10) and likely sources of funding as soon as possible – eighteen months to a year in advance.

Applying for a course

The general rule is to apply as soon as possible. If you are a school leaver, there is no need to wait for your exam results before applying. Colleges, used to dealing with such uncertainty, will offer a conditional place.

Admission procedures vary according to the level of course and type of institution. The prospectus will make clear what you should do:

- UCCA for all full-time and full-time (sandwich) first degree courses at, or validated by universities in the UK,

- PCAS for full-time and full-time (sandwich) first degree courses, DipHEs and BTEC and SCOTVEC HNDs at institutions that belong to the PCAS system.

And direct to the institution for most other courses, including:

- all part-time programmes,
- BTEC and SCOTVEC National Diplomas and Certificates, GN/SVQs levels 2 and 3, City and Guilds schemes,
- BTEC and SCOTVEC Higher National Certificates,
- HCIMA courses,
- postgraduate diplomas, taught masters and research degrees.

A combined application form has been in use for UCCA and PCAS since 1992. However, the copies of your form made for circulation to the institutions to which you have applied, are done selectively. So your choices in PCAS will not appear in the details sent to any universities, and vice versa. For entry from 1994 there will be a single admissions system.

Application via UCCA or PCAS

If you want to have the best choice for an HND or degree course, it is vital your application is put in as early as possible in the preceding academic year.

The official application period is from 1 September of the year before you will actually start the course, to 15 December. Applications received after that time will be considered if suitable vacancies remain. There are special arrangements for late applications, and for publishing details of remaining vacancies in national newspapers in August.

For other courses

Unless you are applying for an HND or degree course at a college which works through the PCAS and UCCA system, you should apply direct to the college. An application form will usually be sent with the prospectus or course details, otherwise you should phone student admissions at the college, and ask to be sent one.

Some tips

1　Read carefully the instructions for applying which the college send you. It's usually a good idea to read the entire form quickly before you start writing anything, otherwise you might find you have filled in a section which does not apply to you.

2   Think about each question first. What information are you being asked for? What order should you list your qualifications in? Do you need to get some more information before you can complete the form?

3   Write carefully and legibly, using black ink. Application forms are usually photocopied so they can be circulated to the appropriate people. To make this simpler, the photocopy may be smaller in size than your original. If your writing is very tiny, or rather untidy, it will not be easy to read.

4   If you are applying on the PCAS/UCCA form, there is space to list a maximum of five choices of university, and four choices of polytechnic/college. The advantage in naming more than one institution is that you reduce your risk of being turned down because of the number of applicants to a particular course. PCAS and UCCA will treat each application with equal status. And each institution will consider your application entirely on its merits, so you do not need to indicate an order or preference. In the UCCA box on the form, you will be asked to list your choices in university code number order.

5   Take a photocopy of the form before you hand it to your referee to complete his/her section. This will help you prepare for questions you might be asked later at the interview.

6   Do not attach or enclose diplomas, certificates or transcripts with your application form unless the instructions specifically ask for these.

7   Be particularly careful to follow instructions regarding acknowledgement of your application, and payment of the UCCA/PCAS fee.

If you are a mature student

Before making your application through UCCA or PCAS, you are advised to write direct to the admissions officer of the college you are interested in, with full personal details. Some colleges ask you to do this if you are applying to that college only – this is because the process can be quite time consuming.

The UCCA/PCAS application form is primarily designed for the needs of applicants who have recently left school or college, so you should use the form as flexibly as possible to provide information on your qualifications, study and work experience, and any other factors you feel are relevant to your application. The college will be looking for commitment to the subject, and evidence that you can study, so remember to list any professional or vocational qualifications you have taken.

If you have special needs

If you have a disability, or learning difficulties, the first step is to contact the college's special needs coordinator and explain your particular situation.

There are some parts of some colleges, where the design and age of the building make it very difficult for wheelchair access, but even in these circumstances the college will try hard to help you.

How your application will be considered

Once the UCCA/PCAS application form has been processed, the schemes remain separate. All decisions in either scheme are made without reference to those made in the other.

When the college receives your application, it will be considered carefully by the admissions staff and tutors. You may then be asked to go to college for an interview, when it is a good idea to take along any records of achievement you have and be prepared to discuss them.

Interview and open days

The interview presents you with a chance of finding out more about the college and its facilities, the course and the staff who will teach you. What options will you be able to take? What size are the tutorial and seminar groups? What accommodation is available? What sort of placements are arranged for industrial experience? Does the college have special relationships with employers? What sort of jobs have past students from the course got?

From the college's point of view, the interview is a means of selecting students who are enthusiastic, motivated and genuinely want to study the subject. Will you cope with the content and level of the course? What sort of contribution will you make to group learning activities, and to life in general at the college?

Offer of a place

An offer of a place takes two forms:

- *Unconditional* – you have satisfied all the immediate requirements for admission and have been accepted.

- *Conditional* – the offer is conditional on your obtaining certain qualifications or certain grades in examinations. A clear statement of the conditions will be contained in the letter of offer.

The letter of offer will also tell you how to accept or decline the offer. For courses within the UCCA and PCAS scheme, all decisions (except invitations for interview) will be conveyed to you, and you will be expected to respond, through UCCA or PCAS as appropriate, by a specified date.

For courses outside these systems, decisions will be communicated directly to you by the college, and you will be expected to reply direct to the college.

If you decide at an earlier stage to withdraw your application, you should let the admissions officer at the college know as soon as possible. That way you will be helping other students who have applied to that college.

You may, if you wish, hold offers through both UCCA and PCAS until the summer, when you know your examination results. You can hold two offers, but you must rank them in order: 'firm accept' and 'insurance accept'. Generally, you are then committed to the first accept, unless that college turns you down, when your hopes rest on the insurance accept.

You are expected, in fairness to other applicants, not to hold any offer longer than is necessary. Indeed, if you ignore reminders to reply, your offers will be withdrawn.

If you fail to get the required subject passes or grades, you should contact the admissions tutor at the college directly. The tutor may decide to accept you anyway. If not, then you may still get a place at another college through the clearing scheme. This operates in the autumn, and vacancies are advertised in the national press.

Joining instructions will be sent in good time before the course starts.

Enrolment

If your local education authority or another sponsoring body is paying your fees, when you enrol at the college you will need to have with you a letter from the authority or sponsor confirming that it will pay your fees.

If you are paying your own fees, you will usually be asked to pay in advance for the course, or the first full academic year of it. If you do not pay these fees by the last date of enrolment, you are likely to be excluded from the course.

Check carefully what other documents you need to take with you for the enrolment and registration process, such as your birth certificate, record of achievement, evidence of qualifications, and passport-size photographs (for your students' union card, identity card, college files, and so forth).

You will usually be expected to join the students' union or similar campus organization. This is a valuable way of getting information about developments which affect you as a student, both nationally and within the college. Most students' unions have a busy entertainment programme, and through their affiliation with the National Union of Students (NUS) you can enjoy travel concessions and low-cost personal insurance schemes.

Planning for college

Hopefully you will have seen something of the college, met some of your future colleagues and lecturers when you went for interview. Alternatively, you may have been able to attend an open day.

Before the course starts you will have a short induction programme to explain how to use the library, where the various lectures and seminars will take place, and where the students' union, banks, college restaurants, shops, bars, crèche facilities and so forth are located, as well as the arrangements for car parking, college rules and regulations.

Overseas students may be asked to attend a special induction programme. At Middlesex University, for example, this takes place over a week before the beginning of term. This gives university staff a chance to welcome overseas students to Middlesex and introduce them to life in London and British culture generally. Accommodation officers are available during the induction course to help students. The Middlesex induction course, which is free to all overseas students, includes a room in a hall of residence, meals and tuition.

If you have just left school, be prepared for some big differences. You will find you need to take much greater responsibility for your own learning. There will be little or no spoonfeeding, little or no learning by rote.

There will be emphasis on exercising initiative. There will be encouragement to develop personal transferable skills, such as communication and leadership. Employers will be more interested if you can *do things* as well as *know things*.

The teaching methods are likely to involve many different techniques, from *seminars* – group discussion involving one or more staff, of views, facts and conclusions put forward by members – and *tutorials* – meeting of a small number of students with a member of staff, to look in depth at an area of work – to practical laboratory classes, project work, games and simulations, role plays and a variety of small group exercises. Even the lectures are not simply a matter of unfolding information for you to absorb. The intention is often to challenge you, to make you think the subject through for yourself.

♦ The expression 'read for a degree' illustrates the point that reading is usually the key to understanding. Reading may be required as part of the preparation for a tutorial, seminar or essay. A tutor or lecturer may suggest specific reading as an aid to understanding some key area. It is the easiest part of the work to leave undone, yet reading is usually the source of the extra facts, ideas and inspirations which make the difference between a first-class tutorial or exam answer and a mediocre one. *University of Plymouth prospectus.*

You will be allocated a personal tutor, who will try and get to know you both as a person as well as a student. She/he will be an important source of academic counselling and advice.

If you encounter a problem relating to your course, college life, a personal matter, or simply need someone to talk things over with, the students' counsellor at the college will be able to help. He/she will seek to provide a setting within which you can talk freely and in confidence, as well as providing the day-to-day factual information which can be so important in new surroundings. Counsellors do not seek to impose their own values, or give advice. Instead they will try to help you to decide on more effective and satisfying ways of dealing with your situation, and to explore the implications of acting on those decisions.

Most colleges have full- or part-time chaplains from each of the main faiths. No matter what your denomination or faith, you will be welcome at the chaplaincy, where many students value the opportunity to meet together for coffee, or lunch, or to enjoy the peace and quiet.

Where to stay

A number of colleges have their own halls of residence, flats and other student accommodation. There may be restrictions on who can use this accommodation – for example, places may be reserved for students who live more than 50 miles away, or those in their first year.

Whether or not the college has its own student accommodation, there is usually an accommodation officer who will be able to help you find a suitable place. He/she can provide lists of rooms and flats within easy reach, where the landlords understand the needs and lifestyle of students!

What you will need

If you are going on a catering course you are likely to be required to provide some personal items of equipment and protective clothing. The college will give an estimate of the likely cost, and will usually have negotiated special terms with suppliers to keep that cost as low as practical. The typical cost for a set of knives and uniform for cookery courses is upwards of £250.

For most courses you will need to buy your own copies of the main text books. You might be lucky to beat everyone else to the library, but even then you won't be able to borrow the books for long! There is often a bookshop on the college campus where you can find these books, or a bookseller in the town that will supply them.

If the course involves field trips or other activities away from the college, you will be required to contribute to the cost of these.

You will also have to pay registration or examination entry fees to the appropriate awarding body. If you are on an HCIMA course, you will have to become a student member of the Association.

You should open a bank or building society account before arriving at college – indeed if you are getting a student loan, this is essential. Most banks are keen to have new student customers and usually offer attractive incentives.

Consider taking out an insurance policy to protect your personal possessions. The students' union might be able to put you in touch with a company offering low-cost policies for students.

What will be involved in work experience

If you have decided on a National Diploma, Higher National Diploma or degree course, it is very likely that a large part of the programme – up to a year – will be spent gaining work experience. Most other full-time college courses include an element of industrial experience, unless they have been designed for students who have already been working in the industry.

So what's involved? In most cases, the arrangements are made by the college, including what sort of experience you will receive and how much you will be paid. If you do make the initial contact with an employer yourself, then the college will have to approve the plans. This is to try and make sure that you don't become the subject of one of those horror stories of exploitation by unscrupulous or hard-pressed employers. Fortunately, there are very few indeed like that, but it's best not to take the risk!

Your college and your employer will agree a programme of experience and training for you, so that you get a chance to work in a variety of jobs, with a varying level of responsibility. You may not enjoy some of the work at all, but wherever you are, it will put you in an excellent position to learn more about the industry, its customers and the people who work in it.

The college will monitor your progress closely, and at some stage you will be visited by a member of the college staff. He/she will spend time with you, and with your employer. Sometimes students return to college for a midway conference to discuss their experiences as a group and receive guidance and help. A special college newsletter may provide another means for maintaining contact with your tutors and colleagues.

To encourage you to get the most from the experience, you will usually be expected to do some report writing or project work related to what you have done.

And, as you will see from the many examples in this book, there is quite a good chance that part or all of your work experience will be spent in Europe or even further afield.

Purpose of work experience

The *Code of Practice for Work Experience* produced by the Council on Hospitality Management Education and the Hotel Employers Group points out that employers, colleges and students have specific objectives in their involvement in work experience, but all share some common aims:

- To develop individual maturity, self-awareness and confidence.

- To provide some structured practical experience of the industry, its operations, its customers and its staff.

- To consolidate skills learnt during studies and appreciate industrial standards and levels of performance.

- To enable industry to demonstrate the available career potential.

The Master Innholders Association has also drawn up a code of practice aimed at industrial placement students and those in their first job after college – see Chapter 6.

Studying in Europe

The European Community Action Scheme for the Mobility of University Students (ERASMUS) is a system whereby students studying in UK universities and colleges have the choice to study elsewhere in the EC for at least three months, receive full recognition for this period as an integral part of the overall course, and enhance their employment prospects in the Single Market. The ERASMUS period can include industrial training. From 1992/3, the scheme is expected to be widened to include Austria, Finland, Iceland, Norway, Sweden, Switzerland and Liechtenstein.

ERASMUS grants may be available on a top-up basis towards travel costs, maintenance in the destination EC country, and language preparation.

Currently, the majority of students participating in ERASMUS exchanges do so because they are on a course which belongs to Inter-University Cooperation Programmes (IPCs). (See Chapters 8, 9 and 10 for examples.)

The other method is by taking independent initiatives, as so-called 'freemovers'. If you wish to do this you should enquire at your college, whose help you will need in setting up the arrangements with the EC in Brussels and the ERASMUS National Grant Awarding Authority, which for the UK is based at the University of Kent in Canterbury (details at end of chapter).

ERASMUS is run by the Commission of the European Communities in Brussels. One of its main objectives is to encourage student mobility, but financial support is also available for teacher exchange programmes to conduct special courses in other universities and colleges, and for universities and colleges of different member states to cooperate in the development of courses or curricula on a joint-venture basis.

COMETT – Community Action Programme for Education and Training in Technology – also EC-funded, is orientated towards new technology and with the social implications of new technology. Further information available from the COMETT Liaison Office, Department for Education – address at end of this chapter.

How you will be assessed

Success on college-based schemes at levels 1 to 3 is usually measured through a combination of practical assessment in a simulated work situation, for example the training restaurant, and multi-choice or short answer examination. Project work plays an important role.

For the work-based qualifications the assessment is carried out on the job by the candidate's own supervisor or manager, who must be qualified and competent to do so. (See Chapter 7.)

Success in BTEC and SCOTVEC programmes of study is measured through a combination of continuous assessment of practical work, essays, seminars and so forth, assignments or phase tests, project work and examinations or end of unit tests. Other learning activities which may be assessed include case studies, role play and similar group activities, oral and visual presentations.

For the HCIMA Professional Certificate, student performance is measured by a combination of college-devised assessment schemes moderated by the HCIMA, and a case study. The case study, set by HCIMA, marked by college tutors and moderated by HCIMA, is tested via two papers, one open book, one unseen. The open book paper is completed in the student's own time, the unseen paper is taken under examination conditions with three hours allowed for its completion.

The Professional Diploma is tested by three elements: college-devised assessment schemes, college-set and marked examinations (HCIMA moderated), and an integrative industry-based project demanding a written report and verbal presentation.

Progress on degree programmes of study is usually measured through a combination of examinations, project work and coursework assessment: practical and laboratory work, seminars and group exercises including case studies, essays and so forth.

Assessment of coursework and presentation of a project and/or thesis or dissertation, are normally the principal methods of determining the success or otherwise of students on programmes of study leading to a postgraduate diploma or masters degree.

If you are an overseas student

One of the first steps is to check how your qualifications match up with the course entry requirements. You may already know this from an adviser at your school or college – detailed lists of equivalences are given in reference books on the subject, and there are a number of useful publications (listed at end of this chapter).

The British Council in your country will be able to guide you through all the formalities, and in addition will hold a variety of videos and publications on education in the UK. If there is no British Council representative, you should get in touch with the British High Commission or Embassy in your own country.

The UK university or college to which you are applying will also help, and if you are already in the UK, you should consult the student adviser attached to your country's embassy or high commission.

It's important that you can communicate well in English. You will usually be expected to prove this, perhaps by a college-devised test, by passing a TOEFL test at an adequate grade, or by other accepted criteria such as the British Council ELTS scheme.

The lectures will be in English – and you can't rely on the lecturer speaking slowly, or repeating what has been said. To get the most from tutorials and discussion groups, you need to be able to participate fully. Supporting notes, text books and so forth will be in English, sometimes quite difficult English that your colleagues also have to work hard at understanding.

Allow yourself plenty of time. If you are applying through UCCA or PCAS, as you must for most degree and HND courses, aim at making your application in September of the year before you intend starting the course. Whatever the situation, you should apply at least four months before the course begins – this will allow enough time for your application to be considered and processed, and for you to make arrangements for somewhere to live when you start the course. Don't take the risk that answers to your enquiries, and the all-important application form will not reach you for many weeks, because they have been sent surface mail from the UK. Send an international reply coupon to guarantee airmail replies.

Check carefully where your application should be sent to. Some countries require their students to submit applications through their overseas students' office in London: Cyprus, Guyana, India, Luxembourg, Mauritius, Tanzania, and Thailand. There are special rules for private applicants from Ghana.

Overseas fees

Fees for overseas students studying in the UK are based on what it actually costs the college or university to provide the course. The reason overseas fees are substantially higher than they are for British students is because quite a large proportion of the taxes British people have to pay goes towards financing colleges and universities. In effect, fees for British students are subsidized by their Government.

Before accepting you, colleges will usually require evidence of your ability to pay the tuition fees, and to maintain yourself throughout the course. For example, confirmation from your government, agency or other sponsor that it will meet the relevant charges. Most colleges insist on payment in advance of all first year fees.

Students are regarded as being from overseas for fee purposes if they have not been resident in the UK, Channel Islands, Isle of Man or another country in the European Community for a period of three years immediately preceding the date of enrolment on the course.

Arrangements for industrial experience on sandwich courses

If you are taking a full-time sandwich course in the UK, you will require permission to undertake the work which is essential to that course. Normally the college will see to this, at the same time as making the arrangements with your employer.

The procedure involves the college writing to the Employment Department, Overseas Labour Section, giving full details of you and your course of study, and confirming that the work experience element is an essential part of the course.

Working in the UK at other times during your course

You need permission to take up free-time or vacation employment while you are in the UK as a student. Ask your employer to complete form OW1, and take this to the nearest Jobcentre with your passport, and a letter from your college confirming that the job will not interfere with your studies. The Jobcentre officers will grant permission if there is no suitable labour available locally to do the job you have applied for.

Coming to the UK for training or work experience

This is not particularly easy if you are from a non-EC country. To get a job in the UK you need a work permit, and work permits are only issued to overseas workers aged between twenty-three and fifty-four, for jobs where their skills are of particular value to the UK. The criteria include:

- Highly skilled and experienced workers for senior posts in hotel and catering work, who have successfully completed full-time training courses of at least two years at approved schools abroad (or, exceptionally, have other relevant specialized or uncommon skills and experience).

- Other key workers with a high or scarce qualification in an industry or occupation requiring expert knowledge or skills.

However an exception is made for those coming to the UK for a limited period of training or work experience. Under the Training and Work Experience Scheme, the employer makes the application confirming that the training or work experience you will be offered:

- Leads to an occupational skill or professional qualification that is not readily available in your home country, but will be of use there – a detailed programme for the training or work experience has to be provided.

- Is for a fixed length of time, agreed in advance – up to twelve months normally for work experience.

- Is for a minimum of thirty hours per week.

- *If it is a training scheme* – that you will be offered wages and other conditions which are not less favourable than those obtaining for similar on-the-job training in the area.

- *If it is work experience* – are surplus to the employer's normal staff needs, and will not be filling a vacancy which would otherwise be filled by a UK employee – unless the arrangement is part of a head-for-head exchange with an employer in your country providing work experience for someone from the UK.

- *If it is work experience* – you will only be paid pocket money or a maintenance allowance by your UK employer (but not less than the minimum statutory wage laid down by the Wages Council in the sectors of the industry where this applies) – unless as part of a head-for-head exchange arrangement, the UK person working in your country also gets full pay.

And that you:

- are suitable for, and able to benefit from the training – so your previous examination results may be taken into account,
- can meet the entry requirements to get the qualifications which are part of the training,
- are over eighteen,
- and *if it is a training scheme* – not older than fifty-four, or,
- *if it is work experience* – near the start of your career, and not over thirty-five.

If the UK hotel or restaurant where you want to work belongs to the British Hospitality Association, your potential employer will be able to get the BHA's help in completing the paper work and submitting the work permit application.

Studying overseas for UK qualifications

City and Guilds qualifications are available through approved colleges in various countries. BTEC courses usually require at least some attendance at the centre running the programme, so it is not generally possible for students to study by overseas correspondence for courses based in the UK.

In conjunction with Norwich City College, the HCIMA offers a correspondence course leading to its membership examinations.

Further information

Applying for a place on an HND, DipHE or degree programme at polytechnics and universities

Universities Central Council on Admissions (UCCA)

- Applications for degree programmes at universities.
  PO Box 28, Cheltenham, Gloucester GL50 3SA
  Tel: 0242 519091

Polytechnic Central Admissions System (PCAS)

- Applications for HND, DipHE and degree programmes at polytechnics and colleges in the PCAS system.
  Fulton House, Jessop Avenue, Cheltenham, Gloucester GL50 3SH
  Tel: 0242 227788

Skill: National Bureau for Students with Disabilities

- Advice and written guides concerning facilities in universities/colleges for students with disabilities and information on extra grants, personal support, etc.
  336 Brixton Road, London SW9 7AA
  Tel: 071 274 0565

Useful publications on applying for a place

The UCCA Handbook and *PCAS Guide for Applicants* – available free from schools and colleges, careers offices and UCCA/PCAS. Give details of how to apply and list all full-time and part-time (sandwich) university degrees (UCCA), and DipHE and HND courses at polytechnics and colleges in the PCAS scheme.

A Mature Student's Guide to Higher Education – PCAS and Committee of Directors of Polytechnics.

Mature Students: Universities Welcome You and *Going to University* – Committee of Vice-Chancellors and Principals, 29 Tavistock Square, London WC1H 9EZ.

Guide to the Colleges and Institutes of Higher Education – free annual guide, Standing Conference of Principals, Edge Hill College of Higher Education, Ormskirk, Lancs L39 4QP.

Sixth-Former's Guide to Visiting Universities, Polytechnics and Other Colleges – annual, CRAC/Hobsons Publishing (address at end of Chapter 6).

How to Live in Britain: A guide for students from overseas – British Council Printing and Publishing Department, 65 Davies Street, London W1Y 2AA.

The following are normally available for inspection in good public, school and college libraries, or ask at your careers office where you can find a copy:

- *The Directory of Further and Higher Education* – annual, CRAC/Hobsons (address at end of Chapter 6).

- *University Entrance: The Official Guide* – Sheed & Ward, London.

- *Scottish Universities: Entrance Guide* – Scottish Universities Council on Entrance.

- *Polytechnic Courses Handbook* – annual, Committee of Directors of Polytechnics.

- *The Potter Guide to Higher Education* – Dalebank Books, Huddersfield (concentrates on lifestyles and environmental factors).

- *Handbook for Students from Overseas and their Advisors* – the British Council and the Association of Commonwealth Universities.

- *Higher Education in the UK: A Handbook for Students and their Advisors* – Longman Group on behalf of the Association of Commonwealth Universities (written largely for overseas students).

Databases

ECCTIS 2000

- Database of all further and higher award-bearing courses of more than six weeks in the UK, with information on content, length, method of study, entry requirements, NVQ/SVQ levels, institution type.
  Fulton House, Jessop Avenue, Cheltenham, Glos GL50 3SH
  Tel: 0242 518724 Fax: 0242 225914

Centigrade Programme

- Available through schools, match an individual's interests, abilities and personal qualities with the requirements of higher education courses, and select a suitable range of these for careful research and consideration.

More information on grants and student loans

Department for Education

- Free booklet *Student Grants and Loans: a brief guide.*
  Sanctuary Buildings, Great Smith Street, London SW1P 3BT
  Tel: 071 925 5000 Fax: 071 925 6000

  Publications Despatch Centre
  PO Box 2193, London E15 2EU
  Tel: 081 533 2000 Fax: 081 533 7700

Scottish Office Education Department

- Free booklet *Student Grants in Scotland: A guide to undergraduate allowances.*

- Free booklet *Loans for Students: a brief guide.*
  Awards Branch, Gyleview House, 3 Redheughs Rigg, South Gyle, Edinburgh EH12 9HH
  Tel: 031 244 5869/5870 Switchboard: 031 556 8400 Fax 031 244 5887

Department of Education for Northern Ireland

- Free booklet *Awards and Loans to Students: a brief guide (for Northern Ireland).*
  Scholarships Branch, Rathgael House, Balloo Road, Bangor,
  Co Down BT19 2PR
  Tel: 0247 270077 Fax: 0247 456451

Student Loans Company

100 Bothwell Street, Glasgow G2 7JD
Tel: 0345 300 900

UCCA

- Free leaflet *Industrial Sponsorship and the Universities' Central Admissions Scheme*, address above

Other publications on grants and sponsorship

The following are normally available for inspection in good public, school and college libraries, or ask at your careers office where you can find a copy:

- *Sponsorships Offered to students by Employers and Professional Bodies for First Degrees, BTEC Higher Awards or Comparable Courses* – annual COIC/ISCO publication.

- *The Directory of Grant Making Trusts* – Charities Aid Foundation.

- *Charities Digest* – Family Welfare Association.

- *The Grant Register* – Macmillan Press.

- *Young people's guide to social security* – Department of Social Security, leaflet FB23.

Some other useful publications

- See also end Chapter 1.

- *Graduate Careers Information Booklets* – published by the Association of Graduate Careers Advisory Services; titles include: *Changing or Leaving Your Course, Postgraduate Study and Research, Postgraduate Management Education*, available through CSU (see end Chapter 2).

Overseas students

British Council

- For further information or advice on studying in the UK as an overseas student.
  10 Spring Gardens, London SW1A 2BN
  Tel: 071 930 8466 Fax: 071 839 6347

Employment Department Overseas Labour Section

- *Training and Work Experience Scheme: Guide for Employers* (leaflet OW21) and *Employment of Overseas Workers in the UK: Guide for Employers* (leaflet OW5).
  Caxton House, Tothill Street, London SW1H 9NF
  Tel: 071 273 3000 Fax: 071 273 5981

6
Finding a job

How you set about looking for a job depends on what you are looking for. If it is just a job you want, then the local Jobcentre, employment agencies, recruitment specialists, advertisements in the national and local newspapers, the trade press, on local radio and even the TV, are probably the best way of finding out what is available (main trade press titles listed at end of chapter).

For 'on spec' job applications to individual employers, the hotel, restaurant and pub guides published by the various motoring and consumer associations (available in most libraries and bookshops) provide a good source of information. The *Yellow Pages* and *Thomson Directory* will list hotels and catering businesses, leisure facilities and so forth in your locality. The *Travel Trade Directory* gives details of tour operators, travel agents and other facility providers. Your careers service will also help.

Personal contacts can be the very best source. It might help to take the initiative, by asking your friends to find out about job opportunities with their employers. Even consider part-time, or temporary jobs they tell you about, it is a way of getting your foot in the door.

Approaching employers 'on spec'

If it is your first job and you are also looking for training and possibly qualifications, you might of course learn about such opportunities from advertisements, but it will probably be more useful to approach the companies likely to offer such schemes individually. Indeed some employers rarely have to advertise vacancies – they don't need to, they get so many unsolicited applications.

The local careers service will be able to help. Good libraries have directories and books of companies offering training schemes, and the annual *Caterer & Hotelkeeper Careers Guide*, *The Handbook of Tourism and Leisure*, and *HCIMA Reference Book* are excellent starting points (details at end of chapter).

If you are writing to employers 'on spec', do try and tailor your approach to fit what each employer is most likely to respond favourably to. Do some research about the company first. Identify how you could contribute. Think in terms of what the employer needs, not what you want.

A blanket letter, especially if it has obviously been sent to many companies, will probably not get (and certainly doesn't deserve) an acknowledgement.

Timing such approaches to employers can be crucial. Avoid writing at the beginning of the low season, or to companies that have been making staff redundant – keep an eye on the press for news of such developments. Also keep a look out for companies that advertise regularly for staff. If none of the vacancies suit you, it might still be worthwhile writing to see what opportunities there are in your field.

♦ Be specific as to the type of job you want when writing 'on spec'. We're interested in self-motivated people, so mention any successes in life to date – academic awards, sports prizes, scouting or guiding awards. Show a little imagination when relating your talents to the job. *Chris Ripper, interviewed as personnel director of Thistle Hotels by Michael Helby of the* Caterer & Hotelkeeper.

Employers will value you for what you know. But remember that they are likely to be equally concerned about your ability to:

- communicate well,

- apply knowledge to solving problems or developing ideas,

- work with others,

- meet deadlines, and

- accept individual responsibility.

Making the most of your college resources

If you are a college student, the careers and appointments service will have information on employment opportunities. Often certain employers and colleges form strong links, with the result that you may have preference in being considered for an interview.

Career and job fairs, employer recruiting visits – the 'milk run' – talks by visiting speakers are some of the other ways in which you will get a chance to discuss your prospects with, and find out more about, potential employers.

Many students return from their industrial training period with an offer of employment when they finish the course.

Profile: Margaret Rose

Clubs/domestic and diplomatic service/training/further education

Margaret's catering career began in 1974, at Queen Margaret College, Edinburgh. With seven SCE O grades, she enrolled on the two-year Ordinary National Diploma in Hotel, Catering and Institutional Operations. That year she was one of six finalists in the 1974 'Young Cook of the Year Competition'.

After working for a short time as a cook with Lothian Regional Social Work Department, she became Head Cook at the Pitlochry Festival Theatre. There she was in charge of providing dinners and lunches before 'curtain up', and teas and snacks during the intervals. Her next career move quickly followed. After joining Edinburgh University Staff Club as Junior Assistant Club Manager at the end of 1977, she was promoted to Acting Club Manager.

Margaret became responsible for the staff of seventy, as well as the trading accounts and quality control of food sales. It was during this period that she won the Under-25 Cavendish Cup, organized by *The Catering Times* and Cavendish Hotel to find the most successful women in the industry, with her essay on the topic: 'Work problems and how I solved them'. She also gained the RIPHH Certificate in Food Hygiene and Handling of Food.

Blair Castle, the ancestral home of the Duke of Atholl, provided Margaret's next challenge. As Catering Manager/Housekeeper, with a staff of twenty and an assistant, her duties covered housekeeping for the castle, looking after the prestigious functions which took place and managing the Castle restaurant which catered for as many as a thousand customers on a busy day. Turnover in her first year increased by 20 per cent and Margaret successfully established the Castle's function trade. During her free time she gave demonstrations to Women's Rural Institute meetings in the Tayside Region, on various topics related to catering.

Then it was off to Berne in Switzerland as cook to the British Ambassador. At twenty-five, Margaret became one of the youngest chefs in the diplomatic service. VIP guests included several Swiss presidents – they changed on an annual basis – and Margaret Thatcher, for whom she created a special soufflé ornamented with cream, fruit and crystallized rose petals: 'Pavlova à la rose en été' (Pavlova like a summer rose).

Guests at the Women of Scotland luncheon in 1983, a year after Margaret took up the Berne post, heard of some of the difficulties which had to be overcome. Speaking on the theme 'A degree of tension', Margaret asked her audience to 'Imagine twenty-four of the Ambassador's guests waiting for their consommé. I pour the soup into the beauti-

Margaret Rose (*continued*)

ful porcelain serving bowl. It suddenly disintegrates! Stepping over the pool of soup forming on the kitchen floor, I rush to the cupboard, snatch two tins of consommé, and rapidly heat up the contents plus some stock cubes, a little water and a bottle of sherry. After the meal the Ambassador's wife came to the kitchen – now back to normal – to congratulate me on getting the consommé flavour 'just right'.

An excellent command of French-based Esperanto helped Margaret run things smoothly in the kitchen. In order to communicate even more effectively, she studied and passed the Italian Language Certificate of the Eurocentre of Florence. And on a visit to the UK in 1985 she went on a three-day Hotel and Catering Training Board course for her Trainer Skills One Certificate – now the Craft Trainer Award. This gave her an insight and interest in training, and in 1989, she became an instructor at British Telecom's Catering College in London. Here she developed her training skills, gained the HCTB Group Training Certificate and Training Practice and Assessment Certificate.

Switzerland beckoned again in 1990, when Margaret joined the staff of the Hotel Institute Montreux, as Head of Department (Food and Beverage). 'But I found working and living in an institution too restrictive. I missed the freedom of the commercial environment, and returned to the UK in October 1991 to become a freelance training consultant.'

With her various HCTB/HCTC trainer training qualifications (added to in 1991 with the Training Technique Development Certificate), and the IEHO Advanced Food Hygiene Certificate, she is able to offer clients a wide variety of tailor-made courses to suit their particular needs.

Margaret offers this advice to anyone wanting to enter the industry. 'One is always learning. When tensions increase in any situation, don't panic. Keep a sense of humour. Be ready to expect the unexpected. And in the event of a disaster, use your imagination'.

Applying for a job

Seen a company or job that attracts your interest? Now it's time to put your marketing skills into practice, so that you stand the best possible chance of getting an interview, and if that goes well and you like what you learn about the company, a job offer.

Take the trouble to spell correctly the name of the person and company you are writing to. Find out the person's job title, use it on the envelope and in the covering letter.

If you are responding to an advertisement, follow the instructions for applying carefully. Some employers will ask for a CV, others will give an address or telephone number to contact for an application form. A hand-written letter of application may be specified. Some leisure centres and seasonal businesses hold open days which anyone interested in working for the company is invited to attend.

If an age range is specified and you fall well outside it, don't waste your time or the employers by applying. Concealing your age in the hope that you will get an interview and convince the company to take you on is a high-risk strategy not recommended.

Application forms

Before starting to fill out the application form, make sure you understand what details are required and in what place. Not all application forms are as clear as they might be in this respect – it may not be your fault that you haven't given the best picture of yourself, but it won't help you get the job. So try and treat poor forms as a challenge to demonstrate your ingenuity.

If you are at all uncertain about getting the right information down on the form, the right way the first time, photocopy the form before you start to fill it in. Then use the photocopy as a dummy run.

1   Write neatly, using a black or blue pen so that photocopies of the form, which are likely to be made as your application is processed, are clear.
2   If the form is of a suitable size to fit into a typewriter, you may prefer to type. Take care if you have to fold the form to do this. If you are typing the last page of a four page form, for example, and have to fold it so that the two inside pages are facing each other, insert a thin sheet of paper between them first. Unless you do this, it is likely that the pressure of the typewriter keys will cause smudges on the inside pages.
3   Do not leave gaps on the form. If something does not apply to you, write 'N/A' (not applicable) to indicate that you have not overlooked the question.
4   Do remember to sign and date the form.
5   Check what you have written or typed carefully for spelling mistakes, and other errors. If you can, get a friend (preferably someone who has had experience of dealing with job applications from the employer's point of view), to check what you have written.
6   Take a photocopy of the completed form before you send it off. If you get to the interview stage, questions are likely to be based on what you wrote, so it's useful preparation to re-read the application form at that stage. Keeping a file of completed application forms, also helps when it comes to filling out future forms, especially if you have made a note after the interview of where, with hindsight, you could have given better information (without, of course, becoming dishonest). Aim to give a better presentation of yourself each time.
7   Return the application form promptly. Don't risk your application being ignored because it arrives after the closing date.

Profile: Nicholas Jones

Hotels/fast food/restaurateur

Nicholas is Managing Director of NBJ Leisure Ltd, his own company, formed to promote fast food outlets, aimed at the young, fast moving customer, with a taste for interesting, tasty and reasonably priced grills, pasta and salads.

With Economics at A level, and an ambition to have his own restaurant, Nicholas left school in 1981 and enrolled on the HCIMA Part A course at Westminster College. 'But I quickly decided to by-pass college and plunge myself into the real world as soon as possible.' His application for a place on Forte's five-year management course (then Trusthouse Forte/THF) was accepted.

The first year was spent working in kitchens, covering every task from the washing-up to vegetable preparation: six months in London, at the St George's Hotel, and six months in Paris, at La Plaza Atheni. 'Working with a very large kitchen brigade, I gained an enormous respect for French culinary skills.'

The restaurant, bar, banqueting and reception areas were next. Nicholas spent six months working through these departments at Brown's Hotel, London, before moving to the Westbury Hotel to gain experience in maintenance and housekeeping. Here he was given the opportunity to carry out shadow management duties – 'my first chance to carry a bleep!'

As Back of House Manager at the Hyde Park Hotel, the bleep was to become a more established part of Nicholas' life throughout 1984. This followed six months in the sales and marketing department at THF's London office, eighteen months as Assistant Product Manager, also at Head Office, followed by his first appointment as Marketing Manager at Grosvenor House, London.

In order to pursue plans for his own restaurant, Nicholas decided it was time to return to 'grass roots'. So he spent six months at Pastamania, London, covering all the kitchen duties, including washing up. 'That gave me a feel for the place and requirements of the fast food trade. And to get myself used to working unsocial hours, I then spent six months as Night Manager at Maxwells in Covent Garden, a busy fast food restaurant. Working nights meant I could spend some of the day trying to raise money to open my own restaurant.'

To complete this research into the fast food trade, Nicholas spent two weeks in the USA visiting outlets which would give him ideas, technical information and marketing methods.

NBJ Leisure Ltd was formed in 1988, with Nicholas as Managing Director and two shareholders. In October that year the company's first venture opened, the Over the Top Restaurant in Fulham Road, London – a busy trendy area, ideal for a fast food outlet with style! The name of the

Nicholas Jones (*continued*)

restaurant suggests extravagance, but the prices are reasonable, for a very innovative menu.

The experience Nicholas had gained since he left school in 1981 put him in good stead. Business prospered and in July 1989 NBJ Leisure opened a second Over the Top Restaurant. Situated in Whiteleys, Bayswater, a splendid and stylish shopping centre, it is well located for shoppers and cinema-goers.

Old Compton Street, Soho, was the location chosen for the third Over the Top Restaurant, which opened in January 1990. Despite the recession, trade was sufficiently good, first to justify opening the basement area as a Spanish Tapas bar, and then the re-development, in 1992, of the restaurant as the Café Boheme. A Parisienne concept restaurant, it will have French waiting staff.

Nicholas feels he has learnt more in the past two years than he could have achieved in any other job. 'You can never fully prepare yourself for running a business. Only experience, making mistakes and learning from them, gives you the impetus to look ahead to develop and reach higher targets.' Nicholas is very conscious of the part his team takes in running the business, 'Never get too big to know who works for you!'

The hard work and commitment involved in achieving his goal at such an early age, brought Nicholas an Acorn Award in 1990 (see Chapter 1).

The CV

A carefully laid out, typed CV, not longer than two pages, on good quality, plain white A4 size paper, without spelling, typing or grammatical errors, should be your aim. If you do not have access to a word processor, it can be time consuming preparing a fresh CV for each job application. High quality photocopies are certainly an acceptable alternative, and probably indistinguishable from an original. But if you are following this route, try not to settle for the all-purpose CV that looks as though it has been churned out to suit every need, including membership of a local sports and social club.

1   Begin the CV with your full name – it might be useful to underline the forename you prefer to be known by, and to put your surname in block capitals. You should also consider stating your gender, especially if it is not obvious from your forename whether you should be addressed as Miss, Ms, Mrs or Mr.

2   State your date of birth and age. It might seem silly to give both, but there may be regulations restricting employment of people under a certain age (as in the service of alcoholic drink, for example) and it may help the person looking at your CV to know exactly when you will reach the minimum age. Never be tempted to falsify your age. An experienced interviewer will soon spot the inconsistency.

3   Then give your home address and telephone contact numbers, if possible for day-time and the evenings. Give other contact addresses if you know you will be away for a length of time.

4   List all relevant qualifications, their grades where appropriate, what courses you have attended, when and where. Mention any you are studying for at present and when you hope to gain the award. If you have recently left school you should give similar details for your secondary school career. It is probably useful to begin with the qualifications that are most relevant to the job, and work backwards in time. Do mention training schemes and short courses you have attended.

5   Give details of your work experience, starting with your current or more recent job. Try to make this more than a list. Spend time thinking what you have done at each stage which will be of interest to the person considering your application. It might be certain areas of responsibility you had in a particular job rather than a long list of absolutely everything you have ever done. It might be the number of staff you were responsible for supervising, or the volume of trade. Whether you add a note of why you changed jobs and state your salary at each stage is a judgement that only you can make. If potential employers are concerned by the number of job changes, they are likely to raise the matter at interview, no matter what reasons you might give on the CV. Very often this sort of information is better explained in person than the printed word which can so easily be misinterpreted. Earning details can help reinforce your claim to have held responsibility, and if the job you are applying for is offering a lower salary – having been advertised without those details – you might save a lot of time.

◆   Your CV should be clear, concise and informative, giving details of objectives, achievements and responsibilities for the last two or three positions held, and thereafter a succinct list of jobs undertaken. Attach a good, smart head and shoulders photograph. *Roddy Watt of Berkeley Scott Personnel Consultants, writing in* HCIMA Reference Book.

6   Mention hobbies and special interests where you think these will help give a more complete picture of you – *anything that shows you've done something other than sit exams*, as one personnel director described it. Hobbies and special interests often provide a useful starting point at the interview, as the interviewer gets you to relax. If you have or are about to leave school and have no work experience, describing your interests and out of school activities will be a useful way of demonstrating particular talents and aptitudes.

7   Remember to mention other useful abilities such as a driving licence and computer skills.

8   Don't leave any unexplained gaps in your CV – they arouse suspicion. If you took a year off to travel or to do voluntary work, mention this and what you gained from the experience. If you have been unemployed for a period, mention how you used this time to develop other skills, for example word processing, learning a language.

9   The application instructions often state the procedure regarding refer-

ences. If not, it does no harm and could be quite useful to give the names, position or job title, addresses and telephone numbers of two referees at the end of your CV. The referees should be people in a position of responsibility who know your work well: former employers, college tutors, school teachers, and so forth – but not family or anyone who might be thought to be biased. As a matter of courtesy, and for practical reasons, you should ask their permission first. The employer will expect to be able to contact referees without alerting you first.

10   Use a suitable size envelope so that you don't have to fold your CV more than twice.

The covering letter

This is your main chance to distinguish your application from all the others that the employer is likely to receive. But don't resort to bright coloured paper to do so – that could ensure that your application is the first in the reject pile. And don't be tempted to take short cuts. A general letter that you get photocopied and send off to all and sundry, or so it would seem, is destined for the wastepaper basket.

1   Write neatly – or type, so that you won't end up with a letter that's covered with corrections. Pay attention to the layout: even, fairly wide margins on both sides, at the top and bottom of the letter. Follow a consistent style: don't indent one paragraph, and not another.

2   If you are writing to someone by name 'Dear Mrs Hughes', end the letter 'Yours sincerely'. If you have no option but to address the letter 'Dear Sir/Madam', end with 'Yours faithfully'. Print your name clearly at the foot of the letter so that people don't have to struggle reading your signature.

3   If appropriate, make clear what job you are applying for, and the source (advertisement in the *Morning Advertiser* of 16 June).

4   Try to present the information you want to get across in a logical order. Avoid jumping subjects within the same paragraph.

5   Try and concentrate in the letter on stating why you think you are suitable for the position being offered. Keep the letter down to one page. An A4 sheet of paper should give you plenty of space to state your case. The details should be in the CV, and the next stage, the interview, will give you a chance to expand. The sole object of your letter is to get that chance. Don't blow it by being too wordy.

6   Because you are writing an important letter there is no need to try and use posh language. A natural letter with the occasional mistake in grammar or rather unusual expression will be much more effective than a badly constructed formal letter.

7   Check the letter for spelling and punctuation mistakes. Show it to a friend who can comment on how successfully you have presented your case. Photocopy the letter before you send it off.

Profile: Maggie Tiltman

Public relations/training/local authority catering/school meals/store catering

'When I was a schoolgirl, my mother became seriously ill and died. So through force of circumstances, I became a good cook and housekeeper at an early age. This helped start my career. With good A levels in Domestic Science and Dressmaking, I was offered a place at the then Cardiff College of Domestic Art, now part of the University of Wales. The three-year Institutional Management Association Diploma was geared to the welfare services, and covered management-orientated subjects such as nutrition, science of food, food service, front of house and some craft.'

Restaurant Supervisor at the famous Kensington landmark Derry and Toms, was Maggie's first job. The Rainbow Room operated during the day as a public restaurant for shoppers in the store, while at night it became the second largest banqueting suite in London entertaining up to 1,500 people with cabaret appearances by famous stars such as Tom Jones and Engelbert Humperdinck.

On five or six nights a week she supervised functions as well as her daytime job, for which she took over responsibility for stores and purchasing for the whole catering department. 'The Store employed thirty to forty male chefs: women were not allowed to work in the kitchens. I well remember having to ask permission from the Head Chef to walk through his kitchens!'

'My wages were £10 a week, so I was very indignant to find that my male Stores Assistant was getting £12 a week. When I protested to my boss, he said "But he is a married man with responsibilities and you are single".' Maggie pointed out that she had all the responsibility for stores, which was parried by her employer, 'As a male, your assistant does all the heavy work.' Maggie won the day when she pointed out that her male assistant was a weedy man, 5'4" in height, compared to her 5'10" sturdy stature, thus striking a blow for women, at least six years before the Sex Discrimination Act!

After three years at Derry and Toms, she moved to the twelve bedroom Swan Hotel, Wooton-under-Edge, Gloucestershire as General Assistant. During her year at the Swan, Maggie attended the Hotel and Catering Training Board's new On the Job Training Course, 'I found great satisfaction in passing my skills on to others over the next few years as Craft Training Instructor for School Meals in the part of West Midlands which became Sandwell Metropolitan Borough Council.'

Maggie married John Tiltman in 1973 and two years later left work to start a family: Clifford was born in 1974 and Sarah in 1976. 'After devoting my time to raising a family for seven years, I decided to return to

Maggie Tiltman (*continued*)

full-time employment. Armed with the Further Education Teachers Certificate which I had studied for and passed in 1981, I decided my future lay in teaching adults.' In June 1981 she joined a team of seven qualified trainers in the County of Avon School Meals Service, with 450 kitchens to look after, serving 50,000 meals daily.

Promoted to County Catering Training Officer in 1985, Maggie was responsible for bringing into the Avon School Meals Service, the City and Guilds 706-1 examinations and the NEBSM Supervisory Management Certificate. All in-house training courses were linked to Avon's Quality Assurance Programme for kitchen managers.

The challenge of launching a *Healthy Eating for a Multi-cultural Society* campaign with no advertising budget, brought a new dimension to Maggie's work. 'To involve the local media I started "Think Fit" projects throughout Avon's schools. An early success story was Cabot School, in the infamous St Paul's area of Bristol. The press and TV gave good coverage to the luncheon guest of honour, David Lawrence, the popular black Gloucestershire County cricketer. The children were proud and delighted when the next day David was selected as "Young Cricketer of the Year" by the MCC.' The healthy eating campaign included craft competitions for cooks and kitchen managers. The winner was entered in the *School Meals Practical Healthy Eating Competition* at Hotelympia, where she performed before the Queen Mother, gaining a gold medal and thus giving national and local media coverage for Avon's School Meals Service.

Months of hard study on top of her job and family responsibilities were rewarded when Maggie gained a Diploma in Management Studies at Bristol Polytechnic, having been sponsored by the County. Following the local Government Act 1988 (Compulsive Competitive Tendering), Maggie was appointed Client Officer for School Meals for Avon and became responsible for putting the school meals service out to tender. She was also elected Public Relations Officer for the Local Authority Caterers Association (LACA), a professional body for managers in the sector (see Chapter 11). She regularly writes for the magazine *Education*, and will give advice to any head teacher who is contemplating taking over the catering in her or his school. 'The full extent of the legal responsibilities involved is not often recognized by teachers or the public.'

Maggie is taking a Master in Business Administration at the University of West England (previously Bristol Polytechnic) which she hopes to pass in 1993. She is an advocate for nutrition being part of the National Curriculum, to make children aware of their bodily needs at an early age, and thus avoid being a victim of diseases and heart problems later in life.

Telephoning for a job

1 Make sure you know who you are phoning, what about, and have the advertisement handy just in case the first people you get put through to haven't been told about it.
2 Have by you: a pen and paper to make notes, and your diary so that you can confirm your availability for interview.
3 Get to the point quickly of why you are calling – be business-like.
4 Be clear in your own mind why you want the job. To say the job sounds as though it will suit your experience and interests is much more positive than 'Well, I need a job because I was made redundant from my last one.'
5 Be ready to explain what you have to offer. Don't take the risk of your mind going blank because you are so nervous: have some notes with you.
6 If the advertisement is not very specific, have a list of the questions you might need to ask: hours of work, training, pay, and so forth. These will always come in useful at the interview stage.
7 Listen carefully to what is being said. Speak clearly and not too fast.
8 If phoning from a call box, make sure you have enough money – it's probably better to use a phonecard, with a spare one in your pocket in case it takes you some time to get through.
9 Remember it's your chance to make a good first impression.
10 Smile while you're speaking, and if you're nervous, stand up: smiling definitely makes you sound more friendly, and standing up rather than sitting down makes you more on top of the situation.

Attending the interview

You are probably quite bored at being told that first impressions count. The advice is given because they do. Just as the lasting impression you have of a pub, restaurant or hotel is usually determined by what you see or don't see when you first arrive, and how the staff greet you.

The fact that you are being interviewed should encourage you. You have come through the first selection procedure on the basis of your application form, CV, and letter. What you now have to prove is that you are the right person for the job. It also gives you a chance to find out whether the job is the right one for you.

1 Prepare for the interview. Find out as much as you can about the employer and the business. If you know people who work for the company, speak to them. Obtain any literature published by the company itself – annual reports and accounts, in-house magazines and so forth. Your college library may keep press cuttings files on the larger companies – the HCIMA does this, and providing help of this sort is one of the Association's service to members.

2   If it's a local business, try and go there first as a customer. If it is an expensive place, you might have to settle for a quick walk through, a cup of coffee, or a telephone call to ask for the brochure to be sent to you. If you do visit, try and find an opportunity to explain your interest and ask one or two members of staff what it is like to work there.

3   Collect together documents you need to take to the interview: any that the company has requested, your Record of Achievement, relevant work experience reports, and so on.

4   Think what questions you might be asked – why you want to do the work/to join the company, why you think you will be good at it, what ambitions you have, what prospects you see for yourself, and so forth. Plan your answers. Prepare also for questions designed to find out about your personality, temperament, values, interests, and so forth. What are your strong points which you want to get across? Ask a friend who has more experience at being interviewed to help. It might even be useful to have a trial run. Re-read your application form, CV and letter, to remind yourself of the selling points you used in those.

5   Plan the questions you want to ask. Your objective by the end of the interview is to have a good idea of the nature of the work you might be offered, the working environment, opportunities for training and further qualifications, earning and promotion prospects, and so forth. You want to be offered a salary that represents what you are worth. If you do not know what the salary band is in advance, this might involve some research into the going rates for the sort of job you are applying for. If you get an offer and accept it, will the move be a good one for your career? Will the skills and experience you acquire be in demand later? If it helps, take a short list of questions with you, and refer to it during the interview. With a very small employer it won't show much understanding if you ask about promotion prospects. Questions that build on what you have learnt about the business, its style of operation, customers, and other staff might be more appropriate. If the company is larger, a question about career prospects in the light of your experience and what the employer is offering, may give you a useful insight and show the interviewer that you are self-motivated. Avoid giving the impression that you're obsessed with pay, hours of work, holidays and so forth. The interviewer will respect your right to know this information, but questions that show an interest in the company may create a better impression, especially if the other information is available elsewhere.

6   Think carefully about your hairstyle, make-up and clothes. Will they give a true picture of what you would look like in the job? Your potential employer is not interested in what you might look like in off-duty times, when you are relaxing. Wearing a T shirt and jeans might be OK for a job interview to work in the discothèque or as a pool attendant at a modern, luxury hotel. But it won't get you far if you want to be a receptionist or trainee manager. Check that the clothes you are wearing are as they should be: it won't help your pre-interview nerves if you suddenly find a button missing, or a stain that you had forgotten about.

7   Establish clearly where you have got to be and when. Arrive in plenty of time, even the best excuse may not make up for being late. Nor will it help at the interview if you're breathless and flustered as a result of rushing. If it's a big building you are going to, or the security procedures are elaborate, allow extra time to get to the interview location.

8   If the worst does happen and you get delayed, break your journey to telephone and explain what has happened.

9   Bear in mind that the impression you give reception staff and anyone else who meets you on your way to and from the interview room, may be crucial. It could be the managing director that you bump into without apologizing.

10 If you need to go through a closed door into an office, knock first with confidence and when you get the signal, walk in. Be prepared to shake hands (with a firm handshake), or not to shake hands. Interviewers will vary in their approach, so wait for the first move and then respond quickly. If your hands are hot and clammy, it's an idea to wash them under cold water before you go into the interview room. Don't sit down until you are offered a chair. If you are not clear where to sit, ask rather than taking the nearest seat. The last thing you want to happen in the crucial first few moments is to be embarrassed – even when it is not your fault.

11 It's quite natural to feel nervous and anxious. The interviewer will make allowance for this. It will help to take a series of deep breaths before you enter the interview room. Avoid excesses of any kind the day before the interview, and try and get a good night's sleep. Try to avoid gestures or remarks which draw attention to how ill at ease you feel. So don't look at your watch, wriggle or fidget. Avoid ending comments by saying 'you know' or 'sort of'.

12 Be courteous and polite throughout the interview. Use the interviewer's name from time to time, and look the person in the face as you listen and speak. It is generally regarded as rude for interviewers or interviewees to smoke or chew during an interview.

13 Do show enthusiasm, enjoyment and smile! A smiling, positive approach goes a long way with an interviewer.

14 Listen carefully to the questions and if necessary pause a moment before answering. Avoid yes and no answers, unless it is a direct question like 'Can you drive?'

15 Don't say things for the sake of it. Some interviewers use the technique of long silences to unsettle candidates into saying a bit more – unless you keep in command of yourself, you will come away regretting what you said in these unguarded moments.

16 Avoid getting angry if the questioning become awkward or aggressive. This may be a way of testing to see how you react under pressure. Don't feel you have to agree with the interviewer – especially if it's a subject where you are sure of your grounds. There should be no harm in arguing politely, indeed the interviewer may be challenging you on purpose.

17   Never criticize a past employer, whatever the reason, or be over-familiar regarding the circumstances of your departure.

18   If the interview has gone well, you will have the chance to ask those questions you have prepared. If necessary, ask if you may ask questions.

19   You may be faced with an interview panel. This can be rather daunting, but try and keep calm and adjust as quickly as you can to the questioning techniques used by each of the interviewers. Don't be distracted if one of the interviewers seems to be making lots of notes.

20   Particularly for management jobs, some interviews can be quite drawn out processes with tests to complete, presentations to make, face-to-face interviews with a number of different people, a tour of the business, lunch with the interviewers, their senior colleagues in the company and with other interviewees. The temptation may be to relax completely during the 'social sessions', and enjoy the good food and wine. Watch out! You are being watched carefully throughout the time.

What are the qualities necessary to cope with the pressures of international hotel management?

The ITT Sheraton group looks for the following in an applicant, says Thomas Hegarty writing in *HCIMA Reference Book*:

- *Leadership* – people should be able to think on their feet and come up with a reasonable working solution.

- *Communication* – the ability to listen is vital. Think about what is being said and then reply effectively.

- *Clear thinking* – express complicated issues with logic, quality and style and with a respect for the evidence.

- *Motivation* – be enthusiastic and have a commitment to tasks. Set a high standard of performance.

- *Personal qualities* – persistence, profit-motivated attention to detail, ability to absorb new ideas and apply them.

- *Interpersonal skills* – work as a member of a team. Balance the good and the bad. Do not be afraid to go to superiors with an idea and stick to it if you believe in it. Do not be swayed at the first hurdle.

'As well as the abilities outlined above', Hegarty adds, 'hotel companies are very hot on four other main points when interviewing applicants for management positions: appearance, personality, intelligence and attitude.'

Employer-based training schemes

Most of the larger employers offer one, or a number of different training schemes, designed for entrants with a particular level qualification. The extracts below – from recruitment literature in most cases – give a flavour of what is available, and how the different schemes work. It is *not* a comprehensive list.

- All **brewers** run training courses, ranging from a couple of weeks to several months for new managers. Such training is likely to include working alongside established trainer managers, then on to a period of relief management, perhaps in a number of different pubs.

- **Gardner Merchant's** twelve-month development programme for hotel and catering or business studies graduates is designed to enable you to become a junior district manager as your first appointment. The programme covers every aspect of our business. You spend time with personnel, sales, food production, and finance, learning the individual functions of these service departments, and how they link up to form a structured network. You will be expected to manage one of our units. This involves you in everything from menu planning and budgeting, to the principles of inter-personal skills, and the formation of sound relationships with clients. Finally, you will be given training in the key functions of a district manager.

- At **McDonald's** we are looking for enthusiastic leaders and motivators – people with at least four GCSEs, an outgoing personality and the ability to assume a high level of responsibility at an early stage. Management training begins with a twelve-week placement period in one of our restaurants, so you can appreciate the teamwork behind the smooth running of McDonald's restaurants. This is followed by basic, intermediate and advanced operations courses covering every aspect of business management from training and motivation to advanced leadership skills.

- At **Porterhouse Restaurants**, our style is relaxed but standards are high. A six-month training programme is structured to provide you with the varied skills and knowledge you need to progress. Career development can be fast for those who make the grade – what we need to see is two years experience of licensed catering and a positive attitude to achieving our style of hospitality.

- Our management training scheme at the **Sheraton Park Tower** is designed to fit each person's individual needs and interests . . . but when they come out they probably know more about the hotel than anyone else, they'll have made beds, changed light bulbs and worked on the front desk.

- The **Savoy Hotel's** programme for management training is designed to develop post-A level school leavers into junior hotel managers over a five-year period. It is intensive, concentrating on giving candidates experience of most departments in reasonable depth. In addition the group training centre provides regular off-job training courses in technical and supervisory skills. All trainees are encouraged to sit the HCIMA Professional Certificate and Diploma. One year of the scheme can be spent abroad to train managers at an international level.

Code of practice

Drawn up by the Master Innholders Association, laying down the minimum standards of employment guaranteed to any student working or training in its establishments. The code is aimed specifically at students on industrial placement, or in their first job after college.

Selection
- Rigorous selection procedures to ensure compatibility between the student and the business.

- Following an interview, a formal offer of appointment should be made in writing. This will include normal conditions such as position, hours of work and pay.

Contracts
- Accommodation should be provided which is clean, tidy and ready for use.

- The student/employee will be assigned a mentor appropriate to his/her level of expectations of the job.

- Hours of work will be the same as those for regular employees.

- Study periods – where appropriate – will be within the normal work schedule and suitable facilities and supervision will be provided.

- Progress assessments and appraisals will be carried out at regular pre-set intervals, at least every six months.

- An exit interview will be conducted by both the head of department/manager and a Master Innholder.

Careers
- Master Innholders will act as career mentors and counsellors for all students who previously worked for them or are working in their establishments.

- Where referred by one Master Innholder to another, the student/employee will be guaranteed an interview.

The Hotel Employers Group and the Standing Conference on Hospitality Management Education have a *Code of Practice for Work Experience* (see Chapter 5).

♦ Two trainees are recruited annually (with degree, HND or equivalent) on to the thirty-five- to forty-week management training scheme administered by the Office of the General Manager Catering. The training is mainly undertaken within the branch catering departments throughout the country and includes experience in all aspects of department store catering. Opportunity to attend off-job training courses covering aspects of management skills, team building and development as well as courses giving trainees an insight into the history and operation of the **John Lewis Partnership.**

♦ In the first year of the **Pontin's** trainee management scheme the emphasis is on acquiring job skills and participating in the comprehensive in-house training scheme. The second year concentrates on supervisory skills including interview and selection techniques, and the training and supervision of seasonal members of staff.

♦ Your training will be dynamic, challenging and highly participative. During the one-year programme you will be employed by a **Health Authority**, who will provide the practical experience to support the six, two-week modules at the residential training centre. **Hotel Services Unit of the National Health Service.**

Coping with unemployment

The hotel, catering and tourism industry offers better job opportunities than most, but that's no consolation to someone having trouble finding a suitable job.

Unemployment is much easier to cope with if you can keep a positive attitude. Avoid drifting into a state of apathy and depression – it's too easy to do so, and once you start on the downward slope it's increasingly difficult to climb back up again.

Try and keep a structure to your life, and a purpose to your activities. Not all your time can be spent job hunting, and even that activity may start to seem pointless, so that you start spending longer in bed, longer in front of the television, longer doing nothing very useful.

Building up your own routine will help avoid these dangers. Plan to spend a certain period of the day doing leisure activities, another researching job opportunities, another writing job applications and so forth. It can help to base one or more of the job hunting activities outside your home: so that, for example, you visit the library each morning to check job advertisements in the daily newspapers, and on their specific publication days the trade magazines.

Become much more systematic in tracking the progress of your job applications, and more rigorous in trying to establish why applications are unsuccessful. Spend more time preparing your applications, first of all finding out as much as you can about the employer so that you can match your abilities more closely to what's likely to be needed.

Getting the most from the Employment Service

The Employment Service (and in Northern Ireland, the Training and Employment Agency) exists to help people into work, and to fill employers' vacancies through the national network of Jobcentres (Agency offices).

Jobcentres are open to everyone. They have details of current vacancies – and not just those in the local area – and will quickly put you in touch with potential employers. They provide information on local employment and training opportunities available through government and other organizations. They will tell you of the various schemes and advisory services that are available to help you find employment, such as *Jobclubs, Jobsearch Seminars, Job Interview Guarantee* and *Restart*.

Working abroad

Experience abroad can be very broadening, and providing you make the right choices, it will almost certainly help your career. Don't let yourself be distracted by high salaries and impressive job titles.

Making job arrangements at long distance can have its pitfalls, so you need to give careful thought to:

- what sort of work, and what sort of employer you are letting yourself in for,

- the terms for which you will be working – and how they compare with what you are earning in the UK, considering the difference in cost of living between the two countries,

- arrangements for health care and personal insurance,

- work permits and visa requirements,

- inoculations and medical precautions which are advised,
  annual leave arrangements.

If you have a family:

- whether the family can join you, and where you will be living,

- what you do with your property in the UK, and if you do sell, how you can make sure you can afford to buy another when you return,

- arrangements for schooling of your children.

- Living in a totally different religious, moral and climatic environment can undoubtedly be a most enriching experience, but if you are unable to accept and conform to local customs, the whole experience may all too easily turn sour. *Mario Bianchin of VIP International Employment Consultants, writing in* HCIMA Reference Book.

Working in Europe

Free movement of labour within EC countries does not mean that work is easy to find. To have some chance of getting a reasonable job, you should know the local language adequately. You must also have a full UK/EC passport.

The *Young Worker Exchange Programme* is an EC scheme to help young people to expand their work experience in Europe, and enable them to discover, understand and enjoy the thinking and way of life of their European partners. You should be aged eighteen to twenty-eight, in, or seeking, employment, and have practical work experience or vocational training. The EC will contribute to living and travelling expenses, and in some cases, language courses. Exchanges vary in length from three weeks to sixteen months. It is promoted in the UK through the Central Bureau for Educational Visits and Exchanges (see end Chapter 5).

Through the Système Européen de Diffusion des Demandes d'Emploi Enrégistrées en Compensation Internationale (SEDOC), most Jobcentres can help provide lists of job vacancies in Europe and the experience needed. SEDOC exists to exchange information on job vacancies and applications between the employment services of EC member states. The SEDOC unit in the UK is based in the Overseas Placing Unit (OPU) of the Employment Department, Moorfoot, Sheffield.

Unfortunately countries do not always notify their vacancies to SEDOC, and when they do it tends to be for skills which are in short supply. Furthermore, the process is often long and bureaucratic, since your form has to be sent to the country (and specific town or area if one has been stated) where employment may be available. You may need to complete a copy of the form in each of the languages of the countries to which application is being made. A photograph and photocopies of diplomas and certificates will also be required.

Some recruitment specialists carry information on vacancies in Europe. From time to time job advertisements appear in newspapers and trade journals.

For many people, the easiest way to get work experience in another EC country is by joining a large company which has operations there.

Short-term work experience abroad

The British Hospitality Association (formerly BHRCA) will be able to help if you are working for a hotel or restaurant which belongs to the Association:

- for those who have a basic qualification and a minimum of one year practical experience: three to twelve months work placements in the EC through HOTREC's Stagiaires scheme, and

- for those who have a catering degree: twelve months work experience in Switzerland, organized with the Swiss Hotels Association.

The Central Bureau for Educational Visits and Exchanges, in cooperation with the Association of International Practical Training (AIPT) in the USA, operates programmes to promote transnational training for qualified individuals. These include the 'hotel and culinary exchange'. Participants must:

- be aged between nineteen and thirty-five,

- have completed, or presently studying a hotel and catering course,

- have gained some work experience in the hotel and catering industry, and

- not change jobs without good reason and full consultation with AIPT.

The application procedure takes two or three months, after which the trainee can apply for a J-1 visa from the US Embassy. This is valid for a maximum of eighteen months. Most people are able to identify their own work placements in the USA, or AIPT will help place applicants for an additional fee, but the procedure may then take six to nine months.

Harmonization of qualifications

The task of enabling qualifications in use within member states to be more readily compared has already engaged for many years the European Centre for the Development of National Training (CEDEFOP – see Chapter 11). Hotel and catering is one of the five occupational areas for which information sheets have been published: *Official Journal of the European Communities* (C166 volume 32 – 3 July 1989 available through HMSO bookshops).

The idea is that jobseekers can use the information sheets to demonstrate to a prospective employer in another EC country that their qualifications are relevant to the job being applied for. The sheet does not certify that the qualifications in both countries are equivalent, nor does it guarantee that the holder of the qualification(s) is able to do the job applied for.

The information sheet includes a common job description – elements of the job which apply to all EC countries – set out in the different languages of the member states. It also lists in table form for each country: the title of the certificates, diplomas and other vocational training qualifications which indicate that the holder has been trained to carry out the duties listed in the appropriate job description; the institutions providing vocational training; and the organizations entitled to award the listed qualifications. This information is written in the language of the country of origin.

Eight hotel and catering occupations are covered: receptionist, porter, storeperson, floor supervisor, waiter/waitress, barman/maid, chef and wine waiter/waitress. UK qualifications listed in the tables include City and Guilds, SCOTVEC National Certificate and Caterbase. In due course, NVQs and SVQs will feature.

Further information

Some useful publications for finding a job

Annual reference publications provide larger employers with a useful means of maintaining a high profile among potential employees. Advertisements and editorial announcements describe the various entry routes available, training schemes and so forth. These books are available in good libraries, and from the publishers:

- *HCIMA Reference Book* – Hotel Catering and Institutional Management Association, includes articles and advertisements on training and employment opportunities, directories of hotel operators, catering companies, organizations, periodicals and so forth (HCIMA address in Chapter 11).

- *The Handbook of Tourism and Leisure* – in association with ETB, WTB and STB, includes employer profiles and information on the careers and training they offer; Hobsons Publishing, Bateman Street, Cambridge CB2 1LZ   Tel: 0223 354551.

- *Careers Guide* – supplement to the *Caterer & Hotelkeeper*, usually published in January, and available separately throughout the year from the *Caterer* at a small charge (£1 in 1992), includes A to Z of employers offering training schemes; Quadrant House, The Quadrant, Sutton, Surrey SM2 5AS   Tel: 081 652 8680/3500   Fax: 081 652 8973.

Magazines and journals

Newspapers (local, national, daily, weekly) and trade publications provide employers with a useful means of filling job vacancies quickly. They will also give you an insight into what is going on in the industry, who the major employers are, and how their business is doing.

Most of the following are available through good newsagents, or on subscription from the publishers:

Arts Management Appointments – fortnightly, Rhinegold Publishing, London.
Caterer & Hotelkeeper – weekly, Consumer Industries Press, Croydon.
Hospitality – monthly, HCIMA, London.
Leisure Opportunities – weekly, Dicestar Ltd, Hitchin.
Leisure Week – weekly, Centaur Group, London.
Local Authority Week – weekly, L A Week, Croydon.
Morning Advertiser – daily, Society of Licensed Victuallers, London.
The Publican – fortnightly, Quantum Publishing, Croydon.
Restaurant Business – weekly, Centaur Group, London.
Hotel and Restaurant Magazine – monthly, Quantum Publishing, Croydon.
Scottish Licensed Trade Guardian – monthly, Peebles Publishing, Glasgow.

Scottish Travel Agent News – weekly, S&G Publishing, Stirling.
Travel Trade Gazette – weekly, Morgan Grampian, London.
Travel Weekly (inc. Travel News) – weekly, Reed Travel Group, London.

Also consult *HCIMA Directory of Periodicals* (available from the information office, and published in the *HCIMA Reference Book*). Most libraries hold reference books which give details of national, regional and specialist newspapers, magazines, journals and so forth.

Working or studying abroad

UK ERASMUS Student Grants Council

- Distributes EC funds on behalf of ERASMUS to UK colleges offering approved arrangements for studying and/or working in other EC countries as integral part of course.
  The University, Canterbury CT2 7PD
  Tel: 0227 764000.

Central Bureau for Educational Visits and Exchanges

- For advice about opportunities for career development abroad, including the European Community Young Worker Exchange Programme, and the UK/USA hotel and culinary exchange programme.
  Vocational and Technical Education Department, Seymour Mews House, Seymour Mews, London W1H 9PE
  Tel: 071 486 5101.

British Hospitality Association

- Formerly the BHRCA – through HOTREC scheme helps place trainees from BHA-member establishments in work experience in other EC countries; with Swiss Hotels Association, provides placements for UK degree holders sponsored by a BHA member; helps BHA members arrange work experience in their establishments for overseas students (address in Chapter 11).

ERASMUS

- For approval of student exchange and work experience schemes.
  15 rue d'Arlon, B-1040 Brussels, Belgium.

Commission of the European Communities Information Office

8 Storey's Gate, London SW1P 3AT
Tel: 071 222 8122.

Department of Social Security

Overseas Branch, Benton Park Road, Newcastle upon Tyne NE98 1YX
Tel: 091 213 5000.

Careers Europe

- The UK Centre for European Careers Information
  3rd Floor, Equity Chambers, 40 Piccadilly, Bradford BD1 3NN
  Tel: 0274 757521 Fax: 0274 742332.

Useful publications on working abroad

- *Working Abroad*, available free from Jobcentres, outlines the Jobcentre procedures for applying for permanent work in the other EC member countries. It also contains information on documents needed, rights to benefits and hints on questions to ask employers before accepting job offers.

- Social security guides for each of the EC countries are available from the Department of Social Security, Overseas Branch, Newcastle upon Tyne NE98 1YX.

- Details of unemployment benefits available in EC countries are given in Booklet UBL22, available from Employment Department Unemployment Benefit offices.

- A booklet and information about all private employment agencies licensed in the UK is available from the Employment Department, Caxton House, Tothill Street, London SW1H 9NF.

- *EUROPPS A Guide to Opportunities for Work and Study in the European Community*, 1991, produced by Somerset Careers Service and published by the Institute of Careers Guidance (see Chapter 11).

Comparability of qualifications

- Comparability of vocational qualifications in the EC, copies of the table of qualifications for hotel and catering occupations available to individuals. The Comparability Coordinator, Employment Department, Qualifications and Standards Branch – QS1, Room E454, Moorfoot, Sheffield S1 4PQ
  Tel: 0742 594144 (answerphone).

7

More about NVQs, SVQs and GN/SVQs

Far-reaching changes are underway, designed to make it possible for more people to obtain vocational qualifications, and for these qualifications to be better understood by all those concerned.

The first phase of these changes, in early 1992, saw the introduction of National Vocational Qualifications (NVQs) and Scottish Vocational Qualifications (SVQs) in catering and hospitality and travel services. The second phase began in autumn 1992 with the piloting of General National Vocational Qualifications (GNVQs) in leisure and tourism and General SVQs in hospitality, and leisure and tourism.

By the end of 1992, NVQs and SVQs will be available to over 80 per cent of the working population from basic skills to management. By the end of 1994, Government expects this coverage to be complete. The 1990 CBI report *Towards a Skills Revolution* outlined very specific targets:

- Immediate moves to ensure that by 1995 all young people attain NVQ/SVQ level 2 or its academic equivalent (see below).

- All young people should be given an entitlement to structured training, work experience or education leading to NVQ level 3 or its academic equivalent.

- By the year 2000 half of the age group should attain NVQ level 3 or its academic equivalent.

- All education and training provision should be structured and designed to develop self-reliance, flexibility and broad competence as well as specific skills.

The structure of levels

NVQs and SVQs are structured into a series of levels. This makes it much easier to see how you can progress to the qualifications appropriate for each stage of your career.

The five levels range from the ability to carry out tasks which are, in the main, routine and predictable (level 1), through to skills in complex technical areas, planning, problem solving and management (level 5). The levels can be cross-related in three ways:

	Traditional skill categories	Traditional vocational qualifications	Academic qualifications
Level 1	semi-skilled	pre-vocational certificate	national curriculum
Level 2	basic craft	broad-based craft certificate	GCSE
Level 3	advanced craft, technician, supervisor	national diploma/ advanced craft certificate	A/AS level
Level 4	higher technician, junior management	higher national diploma/degree	degree/HND
Level 5	middle management, professional	postgraduate diploma	postgraduate diploma/masters degree

Formal definitions
Level 1   Competence in the performance of a range of varied work activities, most of which may be routine and predictable.
Level 2   Competence in a significant range of varied work activities performed in a variety of contexts. Some of the activities are complex and non-routine, and there is some individual responsibility and autonomy. Collaboration with others, perhaps through membership of a work group or team, may often be a requirement.
Level 3   Competence in a broad range of varied work activities performed in a wide variety of contexts, most of which are complex and non-routine. There is considerable responsibility and autonomy, and control or guidance of others is often required.
Level 4   Competence in a broad range of complex, technical or professional work activities performed in a wide variety of contexts and with a substantial degree of personal responsibility and autonomy. Responsibility for the work of others and the allocation of resources is often present.
Level 5   Competence which involves the application of a significant range of fundamental principles and complex techniques across a wide and often unpredictable variety of contexts. Very substantial personal autonomy and often significant responsibility for the work of others and for the allocation of substantial resources feature strongly, as do personal accountabilities for analysis and diagnosis, design, planning, execution and evaluation.

Some of the advantages and characteristics of NVQs and SVQs

- They recognize *your* ability in *your* job, providing a permanent record of your achievement.

- Whatever your job, whatever sector of the industry you are working in, they provide a route to relevant, nationally recognized qualifications appropriate to each stage of your career.

- They are not linked to any specific courses or type of learning activity. If you don't have the appropriate abilities at the moment, you can choose whatever method or combination of methods that suit you to acquire them, in a time-scale you are able to work to, and which can be extended or shortened just as you please: self-study, distance learning, guidance from your supervisors, work colleagues or friends, short training courses, college courses, and so forth.

- It doesn't matter how young or old you are. You don't need any entry qualifications. And they recognize the skill and knowledge you have acquired in the past.

- You are assessed in workplace conditions, using methods which are specifically designed not to cause 'examination nerves', or put you under pressures that you would not normally encounter in a job.

- They are designed to meet current and future employment needs, and will be kept up-to-date as technology improves and new industry practices are introduced.

Evolving framework of NVQs and SVQs

A feature of the NVQ/SVQ framework is that it is kept current and relevant to industry needs. Already (in early 1992) development work was well underway on:

- advanced craft units for culinary and service skills at level 3 and possibly level 4,

- a level 2 housekeeping qualification,

- industry-specific units at level 5, to complement those of the Management Charter Initiative and Training and Development Lead Body,

- levels 2, 3 and 4 NVQs/SVQs in retail travel, business travel and tour operating (including resort representatives, travel escorts and guides) available in 1993.

Profile: Vivian Higgins

Chef/hotels/clubs

'My parents came to the UK from Jamaica in the early 1960s. My mother was a really good cook and my favourite childhood memories are of the wonderful combinations of food and flavourings she used.' Vivian carried this inspiration into his school work. At high school he was the only boy to take Home Economics. 'It took courage and determination to work with a class of girls in a school where boys thought cooking was a woman's work.'

At Birmingham College of Food and Domestic Arts, Vivian gained the City and Guilds 706-1, 706-2, 707-1 and the Patisserie Certificate. He also started a band with £500 from the Prince of Wales Trust.

'My first job was as a 1st commis under a French chef at the Club Sixty Four in Birmingham. I stayed for six months, then moved to the Strathallan Thistle Hotel, as a Chef de Partie. I watched all my supervisors closely, intending to become a head chef myself one day.'

Thistle Hotels offered him the chance to move to London. After a year as Chef de Partie at the Royal Horseguards Thistle Hotel, Vivian moved to the Dickens Inn, St Catherine's Dock, then to the nearby Tower Hotel, which offered very busy and more varied work. By now he had gained a reputation for reliability and high standards, so it was not surprising that after the refurbishment of the Dicken's Inn, he was asked back as Sous Chef in March 1988. During the next fifteen months Vivian coped with the busy kitchen work at the Inn, while he studied two evenings a week at Lewisham College to gain his NEBSM Certificate in Supervisory Management. 'I knew I had to learn management skills before I could be in charge of a kitchen.'

As Premier Sous Chef at the Athenaeum Club in London's Pall Mall, a busy and very challenging period of his life began in June 1989, with many new ventures. Vivian became proficient at fat-carving, and Sutcliffe Catering, contracted to provide the food at the club at that time, sponsored him to take part in competition work. In 1990 he won a Gold Medal in the Hotelympia Salon Culinaire Buffet Centre Piece, Senior Class. With more free time at the weekends, when the Club closed, Vivian set up a private catering and hire company, Crystal Cuisine Catering. He has two teams, who work from London and Birmingham.

Vivian's hard work at the Athenaeum to achieve and maintain high standards, and to establish a good working relationship with the kitchen team, was rewarded in April 1991 when he was promoted to Head Chef, so achieving his boyhood ambition.

Six months later he moved to the Law Society, as deputy to the Head Sous Chef. The contract is held by Charters Hospitality Service, Sutcliffe's elite catering division. In 1992 Vivian was promoted to Head Chef at Welcome Trust in Gower Place, taking over a brand new kitchen.

Titles of NVQs and SVQs

At the time of writing (March 1992) 25 NVQs/SVQs had been approved in catering and hospitality, the licensed trade and travel services.

They include two qualifications aimed at the smaller establishment, where staff carry out a greater variety of jobs, and perhaps do not need the full complement of skills needs for a NVQ/SVQ in one functional area:

- Catering and Hospitality (Guest Service) *level 1* – made up of some food and drinks service and some housekeeping units.
- Catering and Hospitality (General) *level 2* – made up of some reception units and some table service units.

Level 1
Travel Services

Catering and Hospitality
- Food Preparation and Cooking – General
  – Quick Service
- Serving Food and Drink – Bar
  – Table/Tray
  – Counter
  – Take-Away
- Housekeeping
- Reception and Portering
- Guest Service

Level 2

Catering and Hospitality
- Food Preparation and Cooking
- Serving Food and Drink – Restaurant
  – Bar
- Reception
- General

Level 3

Catering and Hospitality Supervisory Management
- Food Preparation and Cooking
- Food and Drink Service
- Housekeeping
- Reception

On-Licensed Premises Supervisory Management

Level 4

Catering and Hospitality Management
- Food Preparation and Cooking
- Food and Drink Service
- Housekeeping
- Reception

On-Line Premises Management

How NVQs and SVQs are built up

Examples from the catering and hospitality structure generally have been used in the explanation that follows, but the basic principles will apply equally to levels 2 to 4 travel and tour operating NVQs/SVQs as they are developed.

The structure defined by key role

At each level the principal types of industry activity are classified by what is known as their *key role*. In this way the standards are shaped into a comprehensive structure, and can be easily related to a particular job you are doing.

Levels 1 and 2	Levels 3 and 4
Prepare food for consumption or service.	Plan operations (level 4 only).
	Manage operations.
Serve food and drink to the customer.	Manage resources.
Provide serviced accommodation and facilities.	Manage people.
	Manage the environment.
Provide a reservation, reception and portering service.	Manage information.

Activities classified as units

A *unit of competence* describes one or more activities which form a significant part of your work. For example:

- Assisting travel customers – *level 1, Travel Services.*

- Maintain kegs and drinks dispense lines – *level 2, Serving Food and Drink – Bar.*

- Supervise the running of a function/event – *level 3, Reception.*

- Manage the housekeeping service – *level 4, Housekeeping.*

Competence is a wide concept which embodies the ability to transfer skills and knowledge to new situations within the occupational area. It encompasses organization and planning of work, innovation and coping with non-routine activities. It includes those qualities of personal effectiveness that are required in the workplace to deal with co-workers, managers and customers.

Each unit has value

Each unit has a value in its own right. Once you are competent in that unit, your success will be recognized as a *credit unit*. The awarding body will, on request, issue a certificate showing the credit units you have achieved.

Combinations of units form a NVQ or SVQ

In certain combinations, units make up a *National Vocational Qualification* or, if you are in Scotland, a *Scottish Vocational Qualification*. Levels 1 and 2 qualifications are made up of a set number of units: between six and thirteen. For example:

Travel Services, Level 1

Maintaining health, safety and security.
Assisting travel customers.
Displaying travel information and publicity materials.
Providing travel office support services.
Communicating travel information.
Contributing to business effectiveness.

Serving Food and Drink – Restaurant, Level 2

Maintain a safe and secure working environment.
Maintain a professional and hygienic appearance.
Deal with customers.
Operate a payment point and process payments.
Handle and record non-cash payments and refunds.
Prepare and clear areas for table service.
Provide a table service.
Provide a table drink service.
Provide a carvery or buffet service.
Prepare and serve bottle wine.

Levels 3 and 4 are made of up core and specialist units. At level 3 there are six core units, and between three and six specialist units. At level 4 there are eleven core units and between four and eight specialist units (see opposite).

Units common across different industries and free-standing units

Where qualifications include *generic* units, these have equal value in whatever industries they occur in. Levels 3 and 4 catering and hospitality NVQs/SVQs include units from the Management Charter Initiative (MCI) and Training and Development Lead Body (TDLB).

Free standing or *independent units* have a value in their own right, although they are not required for a particular NVQ or SVQ – generally because they are important to certain sectors of the industry only, or particular styles of establishment. For example, at level 2:

- Prepare and serve cocktails.
- Provide a silver service.

Free standing level 3 and level 4 units include those to do with assessing and verification (all TDLB generic units), such as:

- Design systems for the collection of evidence.
- Assess candidate performance.

Core units

Level 3

Maintain customer satisfaction.

Control the receipt, storage and issue of resources.

Contribute to the planning, organization and evaluation of work.

Contribute to the training and development of teams, individuals and self to enhance performance.

Monitor and maintain the health, safety and security of workers, customers, and other members of the public.

Provide information and advice for action towards meeting organizational objectives.

Level 4

Develop customer satisfaction.

Maintain the supply of equipment and supplies.

Record, monitor and operate cost controls.

Control budgets.

Contribute to the recruitment and selection of personnel.

Create, maintain and enhance effective working relationships.

Plan, allocate and evaluate work carried out by teams, individuals and self.

Develop teams, individuals and self to enhance performance.

Control the health, safety and security of other workers and members of the public.

Seek, evaluate and organize information for action.

Contribute to the implementation of change in services, products and systems.

Specialist units (two examples)

Housekeeping

Maintain the housekeeping service.

Contribute to the identification of equipment and supply needs.

Create, maintain and enhance productive working relationships.

Maintain the cleaning programme, furnishings and decorative order.

Food Preparation and Cooking

Manage food production operations.

Identify equipment and supply requirements.

Control and evaluate the stocktake within area of responsibility.

Produce and maintain a cleaning programme for the kitchen area.

Plan food production operations.

Plan menu, introduce and develop recipes.

Units made up of elements

Each unit consists of one or more elements of competence. An *element* is a description of an activity which you should be able to do. It is a description of an action, behaviour or outcome which you should be able to demonstrate. For example:

- Handle and transport customer and establishment property – *level 1*.
- Supervise operations within licensing laws – *level 3*.

How competent performance is defined

In describing what competent performance looks like, the *performance criteria* provide a clear measure against which an assessor is able to judge whether you can perform the activity specified in the element. He or she will not be judging how well you carry out the activity. The judgement the assessor has to make is *now*, or *not yet*. The evidence meets the performance criteria, or it does not. It is consistent with competence, or it is not. For example:

- Items are lifted and transported safely in accordance with laid down procedures – *level 1*.
- When appropriate, information relating to the licensing laws is communicated to the customer in the appropriate manner – *level 3*.

Situations in which competent performance must be demonstrated

You will be expected to demonstrate competent performance in a *range* of situations. The range statement describes significant classes or categories which define the scope of the element and performance criteria. For example in the level 1 element *handle and transport customer and establishment property*, the range specifies:

Items

- furniture
- electrical equipment
- customer luggage or laundry

Transportation methods

- by hand
- by trolley

Locations

- customers' rooms
- public areas
- storage areas

Laid down procedures

- all relevant health and safety legislation
- all relevant establishment procedures

For the level 3 element *supervise operations within licensing laws* the range specifies different types of licensing laws, and different breaches of regulations (for example, measures infringements, product description).

For the level 4 element *implement disciplinary and grievance procedures*, the range specifies the framework in which disciplinary and grievance procedures take place, who may initiate these procedures, the other parties involved, and who recommendations for improvement are passed by.

Evidence of underpinning knowledge

In order to be successful in an element at levels 1 and 2, you will be expected to possess the *underpinning knowledge*. This knowledge is regarded as essential to do the activity. For example:

* Why the security of property must be maintained at all times – *level 1*.

At levels 3 and 4 you will be expected to possess *knowledge of context*, which describes any factors in the general context which it may be necessary to consider to perform effectively, for example:

* Type of organization and type of licenses and permissions required – *level 3*.
* Organization's disciplinary and grievance procedures/code of practice – *level 4*.

also *knowledge of principles and methods*, which describes any theories, models or techniques necessary to perform effectively, for example:

* Communication with staff, customers and licensing and legal authorities – *level 3*
* Applying disciplinary and grievance procedures in practice; for example investigating incidents, taking evidence – including interviews, reaching a decision, making a recommendation, keeping an accurate record – *level 4*.

and also *knowledge of data*, which describes facts you either need to know, or how and where to obtain them in order to perform effectively, for example:

* All relevant legislation – *level 3*.
* Previous disciplinary breaches – *level 4*.

Assessment in the workplace or realistic work environment

For each element up to three *assessment methods* are specified: observation in the workplace or the *realistic work environment* (RWE) of a college or training centre; simulations in the form of case studies, role playing, assignments and work-based projects; and questioning. Observation is the most important method, supported, to a greater or lesser extent by supplementary evidence, for example documents extracted from the workplace, and questioning. The exception is where situations cannot be readily observed. So, for example, carrying out procedures in the event of an accident is assessed by simulation, or questioning, or both.

RWEs offer conditions which are as close as possible to those under which the competencies would actually be practised, that is, in the workplace. Their key feature is that the evidence collected in a RWE will ensure that the competence assessed can be sustained in employment. The awarding body's approval is required for RWE status. The criteria (available from HCTC) refer, among other aspects, to the work activities carried out, the hours worked by people in the RWE, customer perception of the RWE, and how the RWE is promoted and managed.

Assessing performance in the workplace or realistic work environment

This involves on-going observation of how you can carry out your day to day duties. The observation will be unobtrusive, so that it does not interrupt your normal work flow. It will also be planned so that the assessor can focus on the relevant elements and criteria.

If your supervisor or manager is not a registered assessor, then an arrangement can be made for someone who is registered to come and observe you at work. This may be as assessor from another department within your establishment, or a person from head office, or a person from another organization with whom your employer has an arrangement, for instance a college lecturer, or a training consultant. In the college situation, this is likely to be centred around the times you are working in the restaurant or kitchen. If the college does not have RWE approval, then an arrangement will probably be made for you to be assessed during the work experience element of the course.

When the assessor is unable to observe you deal with all the situations specified in the range statement, as part of your on-going work tasks and responsibilities, observation can be limited to a selection – for example three from the four types of pastry specified, and four of the five preparation methods specified. Supplementary evidence will then also be required. This might take the form of questioning, simulation, or evidence extracted from the workplace, or any combination of these.

The arrangement just described is particularly appropriate for small businesses where not all the range situations may apply, and when observation is by arrangement.

For some level 3 and 4 elements, assessment of on-going performance is simply not appropriate – for example, *maintain equipment for the rooms, public and work areas*. Assessment then relies on evidence extracted from the workplace – for example, records of equipment fault details, maintenance records and fault identification, supplemented by oral or written questioning and possibly work-based projects.

Evidence from prior achievements

This refers to pieces of work you have done in the past. This might take the form of a complimentary letter from a customer, a photograph of a cake you have decorated, a menu or recipe you have devised. If you work in a hotel reception or travel agency, this could be copies of faxes and telexes you have sent, messages you have taken, and so forth. Other examples include written reports of practical projects, staff training plans, health and safety audits, budget variance reports, meal production records, promotional literature, audio or video recordings.

Simulations

These are set up to recreate, as far as possible, the conditions and sort of pressures found in the working situation. They might take the form of case studies, role playing, assignments, work-based projects and so forth. For college-based students, simulations will often be the most practical way of demonstrating their competence. For everyone it is the safest way of checking that they know what to do if a fire breaks out, or in the event of an accident.

Questioning

Questions are the principal method of assessing underpinning knowledge. They may take the form of the sort of questions a supervisor or manager would normally ask when training you, to check that you have a good understanding of what is required. For example:

- Why protective clothing should be worn at all times.

- Why cleaning equipment used in bathroom areas should not be used elsewhere.

- Why cleaning materials should not be mixed.

- Why faults should be reported and dealt with as soon as they are discovered.

Sometimes it might be necessary to ask questions in an interview situation – especially if someone from outside your work area has to carry out the assessment procedure by arrangement. Sometimes, written questions might be used. In an off-job training session this might be a natural part of the course anyway. Computer-generated questions might be appropriate and feasible. Where used, questioning will supplement other assessment methods, not replace them.

How NVQs and SVQs are certificated

If you live in England, Wales or Northern Ireland, the system for keeping your own personal record of your achievements is the *National Record of Vocational Achievement*. SCOTVEC's certification system is called the *Record of Education and Training* or *RET* (see Chapter 4).

The certificates will be issued by the awarding bodies concerned, and will often be joint certificates, for instance City and Guilds and ABTA. They will also carry the full corporate logo of the National Council for Vocational Qualifications, indicating that they are accredited as NVQs, or the Scottish Vocational Education Council in the case of SVQs.

Most awarding bodies (see end Chapter 4) use sophisticated computer systems for recording and issuing certificates, so that the time period between gaining an NVQ/SVQ unit or qualification and receiving the certificate is normally less than five weeks.

Quality assurance of NVQs and SVQs

The quality of NVQs and SVQs is protected in a number of ways. First, the authority to assess your competence is only given to those who are themselves competent in the work you are doing. In addition the assessor must have the appropriate assessment skills – the Training and Development Lead Body has laid down what these are.

Second, there must be an appropriate system for monitoring or verifying that assessment is consistent. This may involve trained and qualified verifiers from your workplace or specialists brought in from another company, college or organization. The verifier will monitor the assessor's standards, and countersign assessments.

Third, there is an external verification process by which the awarding body ensures that, on a national basis, centres are operating to the same standard. This work is undertaken by verifiers appointed by the awarding body.

NVQs/SVQs in management

MCI, the lead body for management and supervision across all sectors, has defined three levels:

- *MCI Supervisors* – supervisors who carry out part of the management function – NVQ/SVQ level 3.

- *MCI Management 1* – first line managers – NVQ/SVQ level 4.

- *MCI Management 2* – managing managers – NVQ/SVQ level 5.

NEBSM is offering an NVQ level 4 in Management, based on the four key roles of management identified by MCI: managing operations, managing finance, managing people and managing information. Although these four areas have slightly different names from the four modules in the NEBSM Certificate (see Chapter 8), they relate to the same management roles, at higher levels of competence. The NEBSM award is based on the following MCI level 4 units:

- Maintain and improve service and product operations.

- Contribute to the implementation of change in services, products and systems.

- Recommend, monitor and control the use of resources.

- Contribute to the recruitment and selection of personnel.

- Develop teams, individuals and self to enhance performance.

- Plan, allocate and evaluate work carried out by teams, individuals and self.

- Create, maintain and enhance effective working relationships.

- Seek, evaluate and organize information for action.

- Exchange information to solve problems and make decisions.

BTEC's Certificate in Management Studies has been accredited by NCVQ at level 4 in management.

General NVQs

These new qualifications are initially being developed at NVQ levels 2 and 3, to offer young people between sixteen and nineteen in England, Wales and Northern Ireland qualifications that, although of equivalent rigour and value to A/AS levels, are more vocationally orientated. These first qualifications, piloted in colleges from September 1992, will be in five broad subject areas: administration and finance; production, maintenance and technology; health and caring; leisure and tourism; and design.

GNVQs are structured in units, like NVQs. Where they differ from NVQs is that they are not based directly on occupational competence. Instead they focus on the skills, knowledge and understanding required to underpin a range of NVQs within a broad occupational area.

The piloted GNVQs in leisure and tourism include the following core units:

Level 2	*Level 3*
Investigating leisure and tourism businesses.	Investigating the tourism and leisure industry.
Reviewing health, safety and security measures.	Maintaining health, safety and security.
Contributing to an event/service.	Providing customer care.
Maintaining customer satisfaction.	Marketing.
Promoting products and services.	Planning for an event or function.
Providing information.	Maintaining information services.
	Working in teams.
	Evaluating the performance of facilities.

Evidence from the core units is required from each of the four occupational contexts at level 3, and from at least two at level 2. For example, if a candidate completed the unit 'Marketing' in the accommodation and catering field, he or she might work on 'Providing customer care' in sports and recreation, 'Working in teams' in the entertainment and education field, and 'Planning for an event or function' in travel and tourism (this unit refers to one-off activities with significant requirements for planning, resources and evaluation specific to the event or function, such as a local travel fair).

General SVQs

General SVQs were accredited by SCOTVEC in Spring 1992 in five broad occupational areas: hospitality, leisure and tourism, business administration, care and technology. In addition to these qualifications (e.g. National Certificate (level 2) Hospitality, National Certificate (level 3) Leisure and Tourism), one very broadly-based General SVQ was introduced at level 1 and two preliminary awards at a more basic level than level 1: National Certificate (Skillstart 1 and 2).

Like GNVQs, the new qualifications are intended for those who are not in work: 16 to 19-year-olds in school and further education, adult learners, returners to the workplace and those who wish to prepare for a major career change. Being based on credits and levels, they offer clear routes of progression to SVQs, as well as to HNCs, HNDs and degrees, and are ideal for those unsure about exactly what career they want, or whether to go on to higher education.

Twelve credits are required for a level 2 award, eighteen for level 3. Communications, numeracy and information technology are among the mandatory core skill modules.

Further information

The various awarding and accrediting bodies are listed at the end of Chapter 4.

General enquiries

Training, Enterprise and Education Directorate (TEED)

- For up-to-date developments on the standards programme and lead body work, including progress on setting up the Tourism and Leisure Consortium – this will involve all the lead bodies below, plus many others such as Amenity Parks and Gardens, Arts and Entertainment, Inland Waterways, Languages, Theatre, Self-Employment.
  Qualifications and Standards Branch, Room E454, Moorfoot, Sheffield S1 4PQ
  Tel: 0742 593174 Fax: 0742 758316.

The Vocational Qualifications Unit (Northern Ireland)

Clarendon House, 9–21 Adelaide Street, Belfast BT2 8DT
Tel: 0232 244300.

Lead Bodies

These are organizations designated by the Government to act as a focus for developing occupational standards in their industry, or in a generic area. Around 180 lead bodies are in existence, some long established, such as the ABTANTB, others quite recent in origin such as the MCI.

Association of British Travel Agents.National Training Board

- For retail, business travel and tour operating – see Chapter 11.

Bus and Coach Training Ltd

- For bus and coach operations (including couriers).
  Gable House, 40 High Street, Rickmansworth, Herts WD3 1ER
  Tel: 0923 896607 Fax: 0923 896881.

Caravan Industry Training Organization

- For operation of caravan and leisure parks.
  88 Victoria Road, Aldershot, Hants GU11 1SS
  Tel: 0252 344170 Fax: 0252 22596.

Hotel and Catering Training Company

- For the catering and hospitality industry, and licensed trade – see chapter 11.

Local Government Management Board

- For local government and sports and recreation – see Chapter 11.

Management Charter Initiative (MCI)

- For supervisory and management.
  Russell Square House, 10–12 Russell Square, London WC1B 5BZ
  Tel: 071 872 9000 Fax: 071 872 9099.

Museum Training Institute

- For museums, galleries and heritage work.
  Kershaw House, 55 Well Street, Bradford BD1 5PS
  Tel: 0274 391092.

National Retail Training Council

- For the retail sector including shops in hotels, holiday centres, motorway services areas and so forth.
  Bedford House, 69–79 Fulham High Street, London SW6 3JW
  Tel: 071 371 5021 Fax: 071 371 9160.

Training and Development Lead Body

- For training and development.
  c/o NCITO, 5 George Lane, Royston, Hertfordshire SG8 9AR
  Tel: 0763 247285 Fax: 0763 247302.

8

More about the alternative qualifications

It should be no surprise that in such a diverse industry there is a considerable range of qualifications. In time some, perhaps many, of those described in this chapter will be moved into the framework of NVQs, SVQs and GN/SVQs. That the awarding bodies involved – BTEC, C&G, ABTANTB, HCIMA, HCTC, NEBSM – are also accredited to offer National and Scottish Vocational Qualifications will ensure a healthy, competitive environment, with good value available to employers and candidates alike.

Business and Technology Education Council (BTEC)

BTEC qualifications include the Foundation Programme, designed to be taken with GCSEs as part of a school's core or option programme; the First Certificate and Diploma, an initial vocational qualification for those who have chosen their areas of work (available at schools as well as colleges); the National Certificate and Diploma, for supervisory and junior management positions, also an accepted entry qualification for most degrees; and the Higher National Certificate and Diploma, for supervisory and managerial posts, also an accepted entry qualification for degrees giving two or three years exemption, and for some postgraduate programmes. BTEC's Continuing Education Certificates and Diplomas offer adults a short, flexible, concentrated way to update skills, improve knowledge of new technology or management techniques, or gain new expertise to help with promotion or career changes.

In late 1991 BTEC was approved by NCVQ as an awarding body for NVQs at levels 1 to 4 in the catering and hospitality industry and licensed trade (see Chapter 7). The expectation (March 1992) was that colleges would give students on full-time BTEC First, National and Higher National programmes the opportunity to gain units towards NVQs – through assessment during periods of industrial experience and in realistic work environments. Course content would also be influenced by the occupational standards (see Chapter 7), so that students were given support in gaining the underpinning knowledge and understanding they would need to be competent in the workplace.

Take-up of part-time programmes has never been strong, and it seems likely that NVQs will provide a more accessible route to qualifications for industry-based students.

From September 1992, General NVQs in leisure and tourism at levels 2 and 3 were being piloted in a number of colleges (see Chapter 7). These are likely to replace the National Diplomas in Travel and Tourism, and Leisure. A HND in Travel and Tourism was also being piloted.

BTEC First

Designed for young people who have chosen the area of work they wish to enter and seek a foundation for further study, the First programme provides an overview of the industry. The First Diploma is generally a one-year full-time course (or two-years part-time), the First Certificate one-year part-time.

Hotel and Catering Studies

The three core subjects are *introduction to the hotel and catering industry* – also covers health, safety and hygiene, planning and controlling costs, dealing with customers and colleagues; *introduction to food preparation and service* – buying, storing, preparing, presenting and serving food and drink; and *the clean environment* – also covers the basic cleaning skills.

The options available vary: catering in restaurants, catering for vegetarians, cleaning operations, food and drink service, food preparation, front office operations, hotel and catering costing and control, human nutrition, languages. At some colleges it is possible to specialize in accommodation services or hotel reception, and this will be reflected on the award title.

Leisure Studies

Working in leisure operations, the compulsory study area, gives an introduction to the different sectors of the industry, and develops such skills as working with other staff and customers, communicating, identifying and solving problems, numeracy, using information technology.

Options provide the chance to look at different sectors of the industry in more detail: arts and entertainment, countryside, cultural recreation, hospitality, sport and physical recreation, tourism.

BTEC National

The National Diploma is generally a two-year full-time programme, the National Certificate a two-year part-time programme.

Languages and European studies have become an important feature of many catering courses. Students on the BTEC National Diploma at Wakefield District College in Yorkshire, for example, can undertake a European unit in conjunction with the Lycee Professionel in Mazamet, south-west France. The range of languages offered varies, depending on the resources of the college. The choice usually includes French and German, and, at some of the larger colleges, Italian and Spanish.

The BTEC National Diploma at Herefordshire Technical College has been developed jointly with the hotels division of Forte plc. In addition to the practical aspects of hotel catering in general, the course focuses on the operation of the company's hotels, with integrated periods of work experience.

Some National Certificate programmes are designed to reflect the needs of specific sectors of the industry. Huddersfield Technical College, for example, offers a block release course for those working in country house hotels. All areas of hotel work are covered, with a special emphasis on customer contact skills and the principles of cuisine.

Programme content

The range of options (and in some cases what the core subjects are called) will vary between colleges.

Hotel, Catering and Institutional Operations

Six core subjects: *the hotel and catering industry* – its structure, how organizations are managed and run in a cost-effective way, customer care; *hotel and catering in context* – of the tourism and leisure markets, also law, sales and marketing skills; *hotel and catering administration* – office, keyboarding and computing skills; *people at work* – develops the confidence and abilities needed to relate to customers and colleagues; *applied science* – including nutrition; *purchasing, costing and finance*.

The course also develops practical skills in accommodation operations, food and drink service, food preparation, front office operations. General options include financial control, marketing, modern languages, tourism, small business enterprise, licensed house operations, and nutrition. Specialist options, reflected in the award title, include: accommodation services, catering operations, food and drink service, food preparation, food industry, front office operations, housekeeping, housekeeping and catering, vegetarian catering.

Travel and Tourism

Five core subjects: *people in organizations* – develops the skills and knowledge needed to be successful in the business, how the industry is structured, the importance of good communication skills; *the organization and its environment* – use of resources, impact of technology, working patterns, how organizations adapt to change, government policy, economic trends and legal requirements; *finance* – analysing and tackling problems from a financial point of view, planning and controlling costs; *the travel and tourism environment* – structure of the industry; *selling and marketing tourism* – includes product promotion, advertising and customer research.

Several options relating to particular sectors of the travel and tourism industry are available. Some colleges offer streams in tourism, retail travel or tour operation. The range may include: heritage tourism, incoming and domestic tourism, passenger transport operation, tourism in the public sector, travel geography, visitor attractions, arts and entertainment, cultural recreation, hospitality, modern languages.

Leisure Studies

The five core subjects are similar to those described above, with the emphasis on leisure: people in organizations; the organization and its environment; finance; the leisure environment; marketing leisure services.

National Diploma students choose three or four leisure options and two or three business options. National Certificate students choose two leisure options. Available leisure options may include: arts and entertainment, countryside, cultural recreation, hospitality, parks and amenity horticulture, sport and physical recreation, tourism. Business studies options may include: advertising, display, industrial relations, information processing, law, modern languages, statistics.

Business and Finance

Under this award title, a number of programmes put an emphasis on hotel and tourism administration, or leisure and tourism. Subjects covered include financial aspects, communications within organizations, the interaction between work organizations and their environment, marketing, incoming and domestic tourism, food service operations, human resource management, hotel front of house and accommodation services.

BTEC Higher

The Higher National Diploma is a two-year full-time programme, or three-year part-time or sandwich. For those following the A level entry route a three-year full-time sandwich course has been the norm, but a number of colleges are switching to a two-year programme. The Higher National Certificate is generally a two-year part-time programme.

At many universities, polytechnics and colleges where a degree course is also offered, HND students can transfer, with credit towards their degree. This is particularly straightforward when the degree and HND work on a modular system, with subjects or units common to both. A number of UK degree courses are specifically designed for HND diplomates. (Chapter 9 gives more details.)

Alternatively, the degree stage can be studied abroad. For example at Leeds Metropolitan University and Birmingham College of Food, Tourism and Creative Studies, HND diplomates can progress to the final year of the BSc (Hons) Hospitality Management, or to a BSc in Hospitality Studies at the New Hampshire College in the USA with internship with the Marriott Hotel Corporation for fifteen months.

Students on the HND Travel and Tourism at Herefordshire Technical College spend a study period in France at the University of Lille in year 1, and in Spain, at the Escuela de Turismo in La Coruna, in year 2. Work experience in France and Spain is also a feature of the programme. Those who wish to upgrade their HND to a BA (Hons) in Tourism Management can do so at Lille, or at Wolverhampton University (see Chapter 9). Core subjects include: business policy and organization, marketing for tourism, economic development and planning, personnel management. Specialist units include: dimensions of tourism, language studies, hospitality studies, heritage tourism, visitor attraction management, rural tourism, UK tourism, tourism in the EC.

The two-year HND at Henley College, Coventry, is an example of a 'thin' sandwich programme. The first period of industrial experience, from mid-December to late March of year 1, is spent in Bavaria, Germany, working in the kitchen, food service and housekeeping departments. The second period, from early July (at the end of year 1) to November is spent in the UK or Canada.

Plymouth College of Further Education offers a similar HND programme. Year 2 is spent in Tilburg, Holland at the Hotel School De Rooi Pennen, and in Saarbrucken, Germany, at the Technisch-Gewerbliches Berufsbildungszentrum. Year 2 also includes a twenty-six-week industrial placement in France, Germany or Holland. Students learn French and German in Plymouth and Saarbrucken, and take a basic course in Dutch in Tilburg.

The focus of Higher National subjects will reflect the strengths of the college concerned, as well as the needs of local industry. Thus at the University of Huddersfield (which offers a BSc in Catering and Applied Nutrition), the subjects include quality assurance and product development, catering science, technology and nutrition.

The Heritage Management HND at Cumbria College provides another example of how content varies. Specialism core subjects include: heritage and interpretation, historical studies, conservation, and developing heritage themes. Options include: exhibition design, promotion and publicity, edit and design, photography, desk-top publishing, arts administration, and interpreting through performance.

Programme content

As indicated by the examples above (all drawn from 1991 and 1992 prospectuses), colleges have some freedom in designing programmes within BTEC's guidelines.

Hotel, Catering and Institutional Management

Five core subjects: *work organizations* – covers the structure of organizations in the industry and looks at how they are managed in a cost effective way; *external environment* – how hotel and catering organizations respond to the economic, social and legal policies of local, central and international governments; *operational techniques and procedures* – develops the skills needed to run a hotel and catering business efficiently, including the use of computers and the importance of customer care; *physical resource management* – materials, equipment and property, including selection, purchasing, care and maintenance; *human resource management* – recruitment and training, legal and financial matters relating to the employment of staff.

Options may include a range of specialist management subjects, such as food and drink, accommodation, catering, conference and banqueting, licensed trade, leisure resources, public sector hotel services, tourism and hospitality, purchasing and materials, financial. Other options include: manpower studies and personnel administration, sales and marketing, small business enterprise, modern languages, applied nutrition, catering technology, gastronomy.

Leisure Studies

Six core subjects: *work organizations* – structure of different leisure organizations, how decisions are made and how policy is decided and put into practice; *external environment* – government policy, concern for conservation, social and economic trends and the increasing demand for indoor and outdoor leisure facilities; *operational techniques and procedures* – including planning cycles, market analysis, collection and use of data; *the need for leisure provision* – society's changing needs and demands, and the industry's success at satisfying them; *planning in the leisure industry* – in both local authority and commercial leisure organizations; *management of resources* – how different leisure organizations achieve their objectives by careful allocation and management of staff and resources.

Options may include: farm-based tourism and hospitality, planning for countryside recreation, sport and recreation provision, tourism and site management, water-based recreation.

Business and Finance

Options offered by a number of colleges include travel, tourism and leisure. Salford College of Technology, for example, offers an Urban Tourism option. The HNC Business and Financial Studies with Leisure Studies at Teesside University provides an example of course content. Year 1 includes work organization, organization environment, information management, leisure organization and issues, leisure and society or indoor recreation design technology and building services. Year 2 includes financial planning and control, operational management and leisure law, sport and physical recreation.

BTEC Continuing Education programmes

BTEC's Continuing Education programmes are specially designed for those at junior and middle management levels who wish to increase their effectiveness by acquiring new skills, updating specialized expertise, or acquiring knowledge of new technologies – perhaps because they seek promotion, new employment, or wish to set up their own business.

A typical Certificate in Management Studies (CMS) programme consists of 300 hours college-based study spread over a year, plus a work-based project. Five modules are covered: *managing people*, which includes communication, industrial relations, human resource development; *business skills*, which includes controlling budgets, marketing for non-marketing managers and enterprise skills; *recruitment and training*; *management techniques*; and *industry skills*, which will depend on the emphasis of the programme but might include: food production and service, menu planning, managing quality, catering law.

Southampton Institute provides an example of a specialist programme, for the BTEC Certificate in Management Studies (Leisure and Recreation). It is offered on a one-year part-time basis.

Profile: Sandy Ross

*Store catering/hotels/roadside catering/
contract catering/fast food*

His mind made up at sixteen that he wanted to go into the catering industry, Sandy gained his National Diploma in 1968 at what is now Brighton University. College holidays and any available spare time were put to good use to gain experience of working in hotels. (A formal period of industrial release was not required on the three-year National Diploma, unlike the Higher National Diploma which replaced it in 1968/69.)

From college Sandy went to the Garden House Hotel in Cambridge, where he worked in all departments for a year. A period of intensive management training and experience with the then Trust Houses company followed. There was plenty of variety too. Over the next few years he worked in five hotels and in head office in various positions including Food and Beverage Manager, Front of House Manager and Head of Personnel.

Meanwhile the family roadside restaurant business established by Michael Pickard, previously Managing Director of Trust Houses, was expanding rapidly and in 1973 Sandy became Happy Eater's first Area Manager. Sandy was soon promoted to Operations Director and Commercial Director. This period gave him extensive experience in operational, purchasing, personnel, training and public relations skills. And not least because he had to adjust twice to the different requirements of new owners, first the Imperial Group, then Hanson Trust.

Happy Eater changed ownership for the third time when THF took it over, and in August 1986 Sandy left to join contract caterers Compass Services, then part of Grandmet. As Regional Managing Director for nearly two years including the management buy-out, Sandy's area covered the South East of England, South London and City of London. 'I had 360 units in my patch and what can only be described as a great team of 4,500 support staff and managers.'

As Operations Director, Pizzaland International, from July 1988, Sandy set about improving standards and customer services in the company's 155 outlets. Improved scheduling reduced labour costs, food quality was better with stricter compliance with recipes, while new management performance accountabilities and a meaningful appraisal scheme benefited morale at all levels. Then United Biscuits decided to sell Pizzaland.

As the Group Merchandising Manager of the Catering Division at Selfridges since April 1990, Sandy's latest job is different again. 'I am enjoying the feeling of holding the reins as we undergo a series of exciting changes and a major refurbishment programme designed to

Sandy Ross (*continued*)

keep Selfridges in its position as one of the world's top stores during the next decade and beyond. The store has nine public restaurants, three staff restaurants, and I have 300 staff under my control.'

Despite the problems and pressures of work – not to mention the stress of being caught up in a string of company take-overs – Sandy has always been careful to reserve some time and energy for his wife, two daughters and son. He has recently walked the South Downs Way, plays cricket and loves the theatre, music and gardening.

To anyone entering the industry, who wants to reach a position of seniority, Sandy's advice is:

- Remain flexible at all times.

- Be prepared to change and move with the times.

- Always listen to people.

- Recognize that the team is the most important factor in the workplace.

- Create a positive environment to get the best out of people.

- Always remember to say 'please' and 'thank you' – courtesy counts!

Scottish Vocational Education Council (SCOTVEC)

SCOTVEC's modular approach, first developed for the National Certificate in 1984, was extended to the HNC and HND in 1990, with the introduction of Higher National units. A third type, the Workplace Assessed unit, has also been introduced, specifically designed to test competence in the workplace.

Modules and units can be taken individually or in groups which lead, for example, to Higher National Certificates (HNCs), Higher National Diplomas (HNDs), and SVQs. Each module or unit normally lasts around 40, 80 or 120 hours, covers a particular topic, and incorporates a number of skills or outcomes which must be achieved. To achieve an individual unit, a student must demonstrate ability in each of the required outcomes – that is, the system is competence-based. Training and assessment can take place in any suitable location, including the workplace.

SCOTVEC modules and units are available at a range of approved centres including colleges, schools and private training organizations, where they can be taken full-time, part-time or on a distance learning basis. Prior relevant skills and experience will result in credits for appropriate units, through the APL process (see Chapter 4).

SCOTVEC's Record of Education and Training (RET) certificate is updated automatically each time success in a SCOTVEC unit or group award is achieved – SVQs and the HND are two examples of a group award. The RET also records recognition of a qualification by the appropriate professional body.

SCOTVEC National Certificate

With nearly 3,000 modules, the SCOTVEC National Certificate provides qualification routes to suit most circumstances.

Foundation level modules include such titles as: *Function Waiting, Cost and Control in Catering, Food Service, Stocks and Sauces* and *Travel Agency Practice.*

Introductory level modules include: *Introduction to Computers, Work Experience, Mathematics, Introduction to Food Preparation Techniques* and *Introduction to Tourism.*

National Certificate

A two-year, full-time college programme which involves between forty and forty-eight modules, each involving around forty hours, is broadly equivalent to a BTEC National Diploma and the Ordinary National Diploma previously offered by SCOTEC.

Such a course will cover the core areas of hotel and catering operations, with options designed to equip students with the knowledge, skills and competencies for specific occupations. Typical modules include: customer contact, health and safety in the work environment, financial record keeping, reception, business documents and methods of payment, cost and control in catering, food service, alcoholic beverages, surface and cleaning procedures, cleaning agents, linen and bedding services, cookery processes, fats and oils, meat, poultry, bacon and game, stocks and sauces, personnel services, meal and menu planning, supervision and management.

From 1992/93 these programmes are likely to lead to the new General Scottish Vocational Qualifications in Hospitality and Tourism at levels 2 and 3.

SCOTVEC Higher National Certificate and Diploma

Scotland has generally been a year ahead of the rest of the UK in making changes in further education course provision. In 1990 the SCOTVEC Higher National Diploma (HND) was shortened to two years, and the one year Higher National Certificate (HNC) introduced in hotel, catering, leisure and tourism. The programmes became unit-based, making it possible to go from National Certificate through HNC and HND, through BA and BA (Hons) in an integrated fashion. Alternatively students may proceed from the

National Certificate to the HCIMA Professional Diploma, providing they have the appropriate units. Study is also possible on a distance learning basis.

The unit-based structure has opened up many different options, of which the following are examples.

HNC Hospitality Operations

Core subjects include: provision and service of food and alcoholic beverages, food hygiene, food and production processes, provision of accommodation services, financial accounting for the hospitality industry, and communication skills. Options include: human resource management, sales and marketing within the hospitality industry, computing, tourism, administration and control procedures.

HND Hospitality Management

Core subjects similar to the HNC with the addition of the following: management concepts for the hospitality industry, sales and marketing, human resource management, administration and control procedures, management accounting for the hospitality industry, the role of the hospitality industry within the economy, the management of food and beverage operations, foundation sciences for food studies, accommodation management, advising on premises and plant, and interior furnishings and fittings.

Optional subjects include: advanced service procedures, accommodation planning and design, utilizing the computer resource and foreign language for the hospitality industry.

HNC Food and Beverage Service Management

Designed to equip students with the necessary skills and knowledge to manage food and beverage operations. Core subjects include sales and marketing in the hospitality industry, administration and control procedures in the hospitality industry, the provision and service of food and alcoholic beverages, the management of food and beverage operations, food hygiene, human resource management, advanced service procedures, design and evaluation of workplace training and assessment, and the hospitality industry.

HNC Professional Culinary Arts

Designed to enable students to be responsible for the day-to-day production management of a commercial kitchen. Core subjects include preparation and presentation of food from the hot and cold kitchen, preparation and presentation of sweets and desserts, food and food product purchase specifications, food hygiene, design and evaluation of workplace training and assessment, organization and supervision of personnel in food preparation and the hospitality industry.

HNC Professional Patisserie

Designed to enable students to be responsible for the day-to-day production management of a commercial pastry section. Core subjects include pulled and brown sugar, chocolate, chocolate products and petits fours, pastillage and marzipan, fermented products, preparation and presentation of sweets and desserts, food hygiene, organization and supervision of personnel in food preparation, design and evaluation of workplace training and assessment, food and food product specifications, the hospitality industry.

HNC Tourism

Designed to meet the need for management trainees in the operations and marketing activities of local tourist organizations, and similar concerns. Core subjects include communication skills, interpretation of financial data, utilizing the computer resource, tourism operations and tourism marketing. Options include a second language, retail travel practice, tour operations, and managing a small business.

HNC/D Business Administration and Travel and Tourism/Business Administration with Travel and Tourism

Covers the administrative and managerial skills required in any business context, as well as those specific to retail travel, tourism and tourism operations. Core subjects include communication skills, interpretation of financial data, and utilizing the computer resource, working with people and teams. Options include retail travel practice and operations, tourism and tour operations.

The HND Business Administration has a further nine core subjects, which include many of those mentioned above as options on the HNC programmes. HND options include business law, developing personal effectiveness, managing change, international marketing and exporting, introduction to database management systems and document processing.

HNC/D Leisure Management

Core subjects include management in the leisure industry, planning organization and control, legal aspects, leisure in society, and customer care, structure and organization of sport and physical recreation, tourism, parks and amenities; and for the HND, the marketing of leisure services, and finance.

HNC Food Production Management

Developed jointly by Glasgow College of Food Technology, Telford College, Edinburgh, and Dundee College of Further Education, this programme is designed for those holding a craft qualification and appropriate experience in food production.

Hotel Catering and Institutional Management Association (HCIMA)

The HCIMA has always been an awarding and examining body. On the one hand, its courses serve as a benchmark for assessing the level of exemption given to alternative qualifications offered for membership of the Association. On the other hand – and more importantly for potential students – the Association has a tradition for providing routes to management qualifications where no others exist. This provision has continued in the 1990s with the introduction of the HCIMA Professional Certificate designed specifically for practitioners aspiring to, or working at supervisory level, and Professional Diploma for those employed as a supervisor or first line manager, or with experience in the industry, who aspire to more senior levels of management.

And from 1991, for the first time, HCIMA introduced a distance learning route to its qualifications, based around eleven support packages. Initially eight colleges have been approved to act as learning support centres (see Chapter 12): Brighton College of Technology, Brunel College (Bristol), Glasgow College of Food Technology, Herefordshire College of Technology, Newcastle College, Norwich City College, Thames Valley University, and Telford College (Edinburgh). For overseas students, a correspondence course is available through Norwich City College.

Students on HCIMA courses are expected to be members of the Association, and can make use of a wide range of membership services including access to one of the best stocked libraries in its subject area, a comprehensive information service and advice on careers, salaries and conditions of employment (see Chapter 11).

Professional Certificate

Part-time (two years – while working in the industry), or individual subject basis, or distance learning. Students are required to have previous experience, including some at supervisory level, and four GCSE passes at grades A, B or C, or other appropriate mix of work experience in the industry and qualifications, such as: three years' experience and success on a two-year part-time, or one-year full-time course leading to BTEC First or SCOTVEC National Certificate modules; or one year's experience and successful completion of a two-year full-time hotel and catering craft or supervisory course.

Under five subject headings, the Certificate includes food provision and control, food service and control, food commodities, alcoholic and non-alcoholic beverages, housekeeping and maintenance provision and control, front office provision and control, human resource organization and management, employee behaviour, social and supervisory skills, employment law, bookkeeping and basic accounting, cost and revenue control, pricing, sales and marketing.

Professional Diploma

Full-time (one year), full-time (sandwich) (two years), part-time (three years), or individual subject basis or distance learning. Students must have the Professional Certificate, or a profile of equivalent prior attainment such as: BTEC National Diploma; SCOTVEC National Certificate (in a specified number of modules from the agreed HCIMA/SCOTVEC equivalence list); BTEC Continuing Education Certificate in Hospitality Management; HCIMA Part A (the predecessor of the Professional Certificate). No formal entry qualifications are necessary for those with five or more years' experience as managers in the industry, provided they can demonstrate their ability through the HCIMA's Accreditation of Prior Learning scheme.

Where applicants cannot meet the twelve-month industrial experience entry requirement for the one-year full-time course, an acceptable alternative is a planned and supervised programme of at least forty-eight weeks experience, recorded in a Learning Diary portfolio and confirmed by the signature of an employer and/or course tutor.

In six areas of management study, the Diploma includes purchasing, managing food and beverage operations, servicing, maintaining and controlling accommodation operations, manpower planning, financial accounting, accounting for decision making, operational planning and control, project appraisals, market research and planning, pricing, promotion, organizational objectives and the management process, purchasing and stock control, control and measurement of performance.

HCIMA exceptional entry course

Full-time, one year, this intensive conversion course for non-hotel and catering graduates covers the same subjects as the Professional Diploma. Around ten weeks' experience in the industry is required before attending the course, and a further period of ten to twelve weeks' experience is included on the course.

National Examining Board for Supervisory Management (NEBSM)

NEBSM, for the time being, is adopting a dual approach to NVQs: continuing to offer the existing Certificate and Diploma (based on MCI standards – see Chapter 7), and in addition offering a competency based route to levels 3, 4 and 5 NVQs in management.

Introductory Course in Supervisory Management

Any mode of study, distance learning through Pergamon and Open College (seventy hours) – thirty hours is the recommended duration of this course, and the normal minimum age of entry is eighteen. It is designed for those undertaking supervisory duties for the first time. Content includes the role of the supervisor, managing resources, communications, motivation and leadership, training, health and safety, cost awareness, method study and interviewing.

Back-to-Work Introductory Award in Supervisory Management (for Women)

This part-time programme is intended for women wishing to prepare for a return to work at supervisory level, to increase their confidence and develop their skills. In about forty-five hours, supported by self-study, it covers four main areas: women into employment, women in supervisory management, skills of the supervisor, and preparing yourself for supervisory management.

Certificate in Supervisory Management

Any mode of study: full-time, eight weeks, part-time one to two years, or distance learning through Pergamon and Open College. Courses normally involve 240 hours of tuition, including in most cases a two-day residential element. For the distance learning route there are twenty-five units to be completed. For intending and new supervisors, aged eighteen or over, the NEBSM Certificate is designed to provide the practical knowledge and skills necessary to plan, organize and control a department or section of the business. The four modules are: managing products and services, managing human resources, managing information, and managing finance. Topics include quality of products and services, techniques of planning, organizing and controlling work, health and safety, managing people as individuals and as members of groups and teams, recruitment and selection, assessing, training and developing individuals, finance and cost control within the organization, budgetary control and performance, collection, storage, retrieval and use of information, speaking, writing and other communication skills.

Assessment is through a work-based assignment in each of the four modules, an open-book case study examination, a project and an interview.

Diploma in Supervisory Management

Any mode of study, one year, at least 180 hours, including a two-day residential element. The minimum age of entry is twenty-one, and candidates should have a minimum of three years' industrial experience including two at supervisory level, as well as an appropriate qualification, such as a BTEC National Certificate/Diploma.

Subjects, include: problem identification and analysis, problem solving and decision-making techniques, handling change at the workplace, analysing barriers to communication, improving listening and communications skills. Delegates also extend their knowledge and skills in a specialist technique relative to their work.

City and Guilds (C&G)

The 'comprehensive, progressive, accessible, industry-based' City and Guilds awards lead from pre-vocational education and foundation programmes for 14- to 16-year-olds, to the highest levels of professional practice, with the senior awards of Licentiateship, Graduateship, Membership and Fellowship.

C&G pre-vocational and foundation programmes

In 1991 the Government gave C&G sole responsibility for developing and strengthening Certificate of Pre-Vocational Education (CPVE) and Foundation programmes. New schemes leading to the Diploma of Vocational Education (described below) were piloted that year.

Introduction to Tourism in Britain

Usually component of full-time course, also distance learning through Open College (thirty hours). Provides a background to the industry, as well as the personal skills needed in handling visitors.

Profile: Warrant Officer Lou Hole

Army Catering Corps

Spending two years teaching culinary skills in Richmond, Virginia, USA, must be a challenging and rewarding part of anyone's career. Warrant Officer Lou Hole was selected by the Army Catering Corps to give a series of demonstrations to US servicemen, as well as to school and college students, and to compete in the Chicago Culinary Salon 1991 and other culinary competitions, in the USA, in Germany at the Frankfurt Culinary Olympics, and at Hotelympia 92, where he came third in the National Chef of the Year Competition.

Lou's career in catering began at Bughclere Secondary Modern School, Newbury, Berkshire. The school curriculum gave the opportunity to both sexes to take subjects not normally considered appropriate. So girls could take wood or metalwork studies and boys domestic science.

'I found I enjoyed cooking, and decided the Army Catering Corps would give me the best opportunity to develop my ability. The military training and the chance to travel abroad were very appealing. At 16-years-old I joined the Army Apprentice School in Aldershot.' There, for just under two years, Lou was instructed in cookery, and catering-related subjects, as well as weapon training, drill, first aid and fieldcraft.

His apprenticeship completed, Lou was attached in 1972 as Army Cook to the Royal Artillery. After a spell in Germany, he served two four-month tours in Northern Ireland, before the Regiment was posted to Catterick.

Two one-mouth tours to Calgary, Alberta, gave Lou some good experience at coping with new cooking techniques, and at dealing with the vast contrast in catering methods and equipment used in Canada.

Promotion to Lance Corporal came in 1975, when he was posted to Buller Barracks RCT. For the next two years Lou was encouraged to further develop his cookery skills, and he gained his City and Guilds 706/2. In 1978, while posted to Government House, Garrison Officer's Mess, Farnborough, Lou entered his first cookery competition, and won a gold medal in the cold fish section at the local Army Inter-District Competition.

Back in Aldershot at the Army School of Catering, he successfully completed the six month Cooks to Senior Officers Residence Course, and gained the City and Guilds 706/3 in Pastry Work.

At the Royal Military Academy, Sandhurst, Lou found 'a world of its own, with plenty of opportunities to develop my cooking ability, and I enjoyed the next two years immensely'. Lou and his staff catered for the special lunches, dinners and functions of the Commandant, General Sir Richard, and his wife Lady Vickers.

As Sergeant, he was next posted to Oslo, Norway as cook to the Commander in Chief Allied Forces Northern Europe, General Sir Richard

Warrant Officer Lou Hole (*continued*)

and Lady Lawson. He was also in charge of the Danish Army's kitchen in Copenhagen (which came under the same command, as part of the Northern Flank). This catered for important functions involving the Danish forces and other NATO members. Working in two kitchens, made life hectic for Lou, but never dull! He was also able to fulfil his schoolboy ambition to travel by visiting many European cities and enjoying at first hand their different ways of life.

After passing both the Education Promotion Certificate and the Advanced Catering Administration and Advanced Management courses, back in the UK, Lou was posted to Fallingbostel, West Germany as a Non-Commissioned Officer. In charge of production, he was able to get experience at managing supplies and staff.

Returning to Aldershot in 1987, to the Army Catering Training Centre, Lou was promoted to Staff Sergeant and took his Instructor Course, which gained him the City and Guilds 730 Teaching Certificate. After a break for the two-year assignment in America, Lou worked in the Officers' Mess and in 1990 became Master Chef of the Mess.

'During this time, I spent a week working at the Indigo Jones Restaurant in Covent Garden, alongside Chef de Cuisine Paul Gayler. It certainly helped me develop my knowledge of the latest cookery and presentation techniques, and gave me some valuable first experience at producing "the plated meal" under the watchful eye of the great master. I was able to introduce similar standards and style to the Cuisine Moderne concept for special dinners at the Officers' Mess.'

At the Expogast 90 World Cup Competition in Luxembourg, the coveted Gold Medal in the Restaurant of Nations Hot Kitchen Competition, was won by the UK team and also the Bronze Medal in the International Buffet Class. Lou, with two other Army Catering Corps representatives, was part of the British team, sponsored by the Cookery and Food Association and Multivac UK Ltd. 'For the gold we were judged on the quality, presentation, method of preparation, team working and cooking of a three course meal for 150 people. The food was later made available for sale, and was the first menu of the day to sell out!'

Communications Skills

Usually component of full-time course. Designed to develop proficiency in a wide range of communications skills and confidence in applying them to different situations. It covers reading, writing, listening, speaking – how to describe and explain, how to interpret information and how to set about finding information.

Numeracy

Usually component of full-time course, aims to develop the knowledge and confidence of anyone who has limited or no qualifications in mathematics. It covers the essential groundwork and everyday application of numeracy skills including arithmetic, decimals, fractions, ratios, percentages, elementary algebra and geometry.

Diploma of Vocational Education

Replaced the CPVE from 1991/92, the Diploma is designed to offer wider opportunities for young people aged fourteen to nineteen. It can be the main focus for a student's learning programme, or it can be taken alongside other courses such as GCSEs, A or AS level.

There are three levels: Foundation, Intermediate, and National. The foundation level gives students the opportunity to develop personal and social skills, and to acquire skills and knowledge within a broad vocational context, such as providing goods and services, providing business services, manufacturing and technical services.

Post-sixteen students are able to take the Intermediate and National levels, which are expected to be linked to GNVQs at levels 2 and 3. The Intermediate requires a minimum of fifteen days' work experience, the completion of an introductory module, an exploratory module, and five preparatory modules drawn from one of the vocational clusters. Modules from the generic group may be substituted for up to two of these five modules. Examples of module titles are: providing accommodation and catering services, popular catering, food service, reception duties, customer service, languages for work.

Certificate in UK Tourism

Designed to lead to a better understanding of the UK holiday and leisure market, and to give retail travel agency staff the knowledge and skills to sell and market UK-based holidays. The three units are assessed in different ways: the holiday product and travel geography by an open-book written test; practical skills, including communication are work-related and continuously assessed; marketing and behavioural skills require a case study, carried out over a period.

The Technological Baccalaureate

Piloted in 1991/92, the baccalaureate departs from many traditional courses in that it is not exclusively directed towards a specific vocational qualification. Instead it concentrates on providing the core skills and foundation subjects required for the National Curriculum (Key Stage 4), NVQs, GNVQs and A level programmes. The aim is to keep open the individual's career options, while providing a route for progression through to NVQ level 3; when awarded with credit: level 4; and when awarded with distinction: level 5 or degree. It falls into four parts:

• the exploration and development of individual potential,

• a common curriculum within a technological and commercial context,

• an elective curriculum related to the aesthetic or performing arts, the humanities or recreation, and

• an extension curriculum suited to the individual student's post-qualification intentions.

C&G and Association of British Travel Agents National Training Board (ABTANTB)

The NVQ/SVQ Travel Studies level 1 was approved in early 1992 (see Chapter 7). Levels 2, 3 and 4 qualifications in retail travel, business travel and tour operating were expected to be available from 1993.

Certificate of Travel Agency Competence (COTAC) (495)/Certificate/Diploma in Travel Skills

Any mode of study, including distance learning, the aim of this group of qualifications is to demonstrate competence over a range of skills most necessary to a travel agent. The tests are at two levels to cover the abilities expected after about eighteen to thirty months in employment. They are job-related, so any form of study should be supplemented by industry experience.

There are three components for both level I and level II tests. Successful candidates in the two written paper components receive the Certificate of Travel Agency Competence Level I/II, as appropriate. Candidates who also achieve success in the third component, workplace assessment, receive:

• at level I, the Certificate in Travel Skills (designatory letters CertTS), and

• at level II, the Diploma in Travel Skills (designatory letters DipTS).

The subjects covered in the level I written papers include world geography, use of airline guides and manuals, fares and ticket issues, UK holidays, European inclusive holidays, hotels, foreign currency, car rental, insurance, passports, visas and health, car carrying services. Workplace assessment covers the use of computerized systems, processing client bookings, customer service and communication skills, personal effectiveness.

Level II takes these subjects to greater depth, in particular, fares and ticketing, and also looks at package holidays, independent arrangements, and cruising. Workplace assessment concentrates on supervisory skills and tasks, including training.

Certificate in Travel Studies (499)

Full-time, one year, intended to develop the skills and knowledge of young people who wish to embark on a career in the UK travel industry, with particular emphasis on the retail sector, and for more mature people who wish to change career direction. It is based on an intensive college-based course (covering a similar content to COTAC level I), followed by six weeks of structured work experience.

Success in the two examination components which are identical to COTAC level I: Air and General, leads to the award of Certificate in Travel Agency Competence Level I. The other two components in which success is required for the Certificate in Travel Studies are: travel studies (general), and coursework assessment.

Certificate of Tour Operating Practice (COTOP) (497)

Any mode of study, including distance learning. In two parts, level I provides the practical skills and knowledge appropriate to employment with a tour operator, level II the detailed skills and knowledge up to supervisory level.

Level I covers the role of the tour operator within the structure and organization of the UK travel industry, cost and price calculations, legal aspects of tour operations, marketing, computers and other office technology, travel geography, ticketing and documentation.

Level II also looks at the planning and operational stages involved in the production of a tour programme, costings of inclusive tours, brochure production, pricing strategies, advertising and promotion, customer relations, business administration and supervisory skills.

Certificate of Travel Agency Management (COTAM) (496)

Any mode of study including distance learning, aims to develop the skills and knowledge of managers of travel agencies and to prepare other suitable staff for positions in management. Candidates are generally expected to have completed both levels of the Certificate of Travel Agency Competence (COTAC), or have worked in a travel agency for three years or more.

The syllabus is divided into six modules which can be taken in any order: financial control; office equipment and layout; office organization and administration; staff management; marketing; and the law and the travel agent. Each is examined by means of a written paper and assignment. Success in both components of staff management and any two other modules leads to the award of the Certificate of Travel Agency Management.

Regional examining bodies

A range of introductory and craft schemes are offered by the East Midland Further Education Council (EMFEC) and North West Regional Association of Education Authorities (CENTRA). These include the Introductory Catering Course (704) and the following:

EMFEC
Nutrition and Hygiene (710)
Pastry Cooks (711)
Book-keeping, Purchasing and
   Control, and Food Costing (713)
Modern Cookery (341)
Vegetarian Wholefood Cookery (703)

CENTRA
Food Hygiene (710–4)
Nutrition (710–5)
Pastry Cooks' and Patissiers' (711)
Cake Decoration (139)
Book-keeping and Food Costing
   (713)
Kitchen and Dining Room French
   (715)

The Yorkshire and Humberside Council for Further Education (YHCFHE) provides regional administration for various City and Guilds schemes.

Institute of Leisure and Amenity Management (ILAM)

The ILAM Certificate emphasizes the technical and operational aspects of the leisure business and introduces the functional areas of management. The BTEC Continuing Education Certificate in Leisure Management, designed jointly with ILAM, leads to exemption from all but one of the ILAM Certificate examinations. Similar exemption is given to those who have the appropriate SCOTVEC Higher National units. Partial exemption is given by the BTEC Certificate in Management Studies with leisure specialism, BTEC HNC Leisure Studies and DMS with leisure specialism.

Emphasis in the Diploma is on the managerial aspects of the leisure business. The areas of planning and providing leisure facilities and services, and the functional areas of management are of major importance, supported by economics, research and quantitative methods. Exemption from most of the Diploma examination papers – but not the compulsory case study – is given by the DMS with leisure and recreation, equivalent postgraduate diplomas and degrees. More limited exemption by a general DMS.

Institute of Baths and Recreation Management (IBRM)

The IBRM Recreation Management Certificate relates to the management of sports halls, leisure centres, swimming pools and associated facilities. The examination consists of four modules, exemption from one or more of which can be gained by an appropriate leisure management qualification: *resource management and administration* – financial control, human resource management, marketing; *sport and physical recreation* – range of facilities, the organizations involved; *indoor recreation design, technology and building services* – multi-use facilities, detailed design aspects; *operational management* – includes legal aspects, contracts, customer care, sponsorship, catering.

The Leisure Technician Scheme is a broad-based vocational training and accreditation programme which focuses on health and safety, effective customer care and the efficient technical operation of sport and recreation facilities. Modules include administration and supervisory studies, leisure centre supervision, pool plant operation, lifeguarding, sports coaching, leisure centre catering.

Exemptions can be gained from specific modules with, for example, a BTEC National Certificate/Diploma in leisure studies.

British Institute of Innkeeping (BII)

Success in the Business Management Certificate (distance learning or part-time course supported by distance learning) qualifies the candidate for full membership of the BII. Based on the *Pub Business* packs, it covers five areas: marketing, product development, staff development, finance and accounting, business information and control.

Hotel and Catering Training Company (HCTC)

HCTC's Training Division offers a full range of short courses from craft through to supervisory and management level. Many of these are designed to lead to NVQs and SVQs, as well as to NEBSM and BTEC awards. With the addition in 1992 of an assessor and verifier programme based on TDLB standards, trainer training remains a key area.

Operational Management Programme

One-day courses, supported by self-study and assignment work, designed to lead to level 3 NVQs/SVQs in catering and hospitality supervisory management. Core modules such as developing performance, managing resources, and maintaining customer satisfaction, plus specialist modules such as food production, housekeeping and pub management. Certain modules lead to the NEBSM Certificate in Supervisory Management.

Business Management Programme

Series of five-day residential courses. The nine modules cover *general management* – includes developing techniques for self-management, decision making, planning and controlling organizational change, organizational politics; *managing the market* – marketing techniques for business and customer analysis, designing a service package; *managing finance* – corporate balance sheet and profit and loss account, financial accounting techniques, preparation of capital expenditure forecasts; *managing personnel* – planning for future personnel requirements, designing a reward package, evaluating organizational culture; *management action* – reviewing and developing managerial style, goals and future directions both for the job and the manager; *systems management* – analysing and evaluating operating systems, quality control; *managing strategy* – product/market scope, strategic options, managing change; *information technology* – computers in context, development and utilization of databases, wordprocessing and integrated software; *managing the environment* – management roles and the external environment.

Success in the first five modules leads to the award of a BTEC Continuing Education Diploma in Hospitality Management. Success in all nine modules leads to a Diploma in Management Studies (DMS), and, gives exemption from the first year of the MBA programme at Middlesex University (see Chapter 10).

Craft Trainer Award (CTA)

Three-day course (previously Trainer Skills One, TS1) in one-to-one training, coaching and workplace assessment.

Training Certificate

Two separate modules – Group Training Techniques (GTT), three days, and Organizing Training and Assessment (OTA), two days – cover the writing of training objectives, designing and undertaking training sessions away from work pressures, preparing training aids, organizing and defining training responsibilities in the workplace.

Training Diploma

For training specialists who have a wide ranging responsibility for the organization and delivery of training and who, if required, wish to run other HCTC trainer skills programmes under licence. The first module, Training Practice and Assessment (TPA), five days, covers the skills required to run a Craft Trainer Award. The other two modules, Training Technique Development (TTD), two days, and Managing the Training Function (MTF), three days, cover the skills required to run a Training Certificate: group training techniques, and organizing training and assessment.

Food hygiene and nutrition

Many employers, colleges and other training providers offer courses in hygiene and nutrition by one or more of the following organizations (all described in Chapter 11). Most are available on a short or part-time basis, or as a component of a full-time college course, and some by distance learning through Open College (see Chapter 12).

Institution of Environmental Health Officers (IEHO)

Basic Food Hygiene Certificate

The fundamentals of good food hygiene practice. Based on six hours of tuition, subjects include: characteristics of bacteria, symptoms of food poisoning, prevention of food poisoning and food contamination, personal hygiene, pest control, cleaning and disinfection, legislation.

Intermediate Food Hygiene Certificate

Intended to equip supervisors with adequate knowledge to ensure that their units operate in an efficient, hygienic manner. The eighteen-hour course covers the relationships between hygiene and food poisoning, the structure and characteristics of bacteria and their potential to cause illness and spoil food, non-bacterial food poisoning, food-borne diseases, prevention and control measures, personal hygiene, food storage and temperature control, food preservation, design and construction of food premises and equipment, cleaning and disinfection, pest control, hygiene law.

Advanced Food Hygiene Certificate

Designed with management responsibilities in mind, this thirty-six-hour course covers in greater depth the syllabus of the intermediate course, also the training and education of food handlers, and management control techniques.

Royal Environmental Health Institute of Scotland (REHIS)

Elementary Food Hygiene Certificate

Six-hour course: identifies areas of major concern in the handling of food, and offers basic guidance on good practice. Covers similar areas to the IEHO course described above.

Intermediate Food Hygiene Certificate

Twelve-hour course, intended to provide a sound training in food hygiene and, by outlining the consequences of lapses in proper practices, make food handlers aware of the need for improved hygiene. Covers food poisoning and contamination, food-borne diseases, structure and characteristics of bacteria, personal hygiene, food storage and temperature control, food preservation, design and construction of food premises and equipment, cleaning, pest control and the legislation.

Diploma in Advanced Food Hygiene

Five days, usually residential, designed to equip those in a supervisory or management position with adequate knowledge to ensure that their units operate in a hygienic and efficient manner. In addition to covering food poisoning and its prevention in depth, a considerable part of the programme is given to hygiene trainer training, and the techniques involved in monitoring and controlling food standards. Candidates should possess the Intermediate Food Hygiene Certificate, or equivalent.

Royal Institute of Public Health and Hygiene (RIPHH)

Primary Certificate in Hygiene for Food Handlers

Based on a seven-hour course, it provides a simple scientific foundation for the understanding of food poisoning, explains the role of vermin in spreading food poisoning, and aims to develop an understanding of sound working practices which will prevent the occurrence of food poisoning, including personal standards appropriate to food handlers and approaching cleaning tasks in a methodical manner.

Certificate in Food Hygiene and the Handling of Food

Intended for supervisors and potential managers in food handling and catering. The syllabus, based on a sixteen-hour course, covers microbiology, food poisoning and other foodborne diseases, preservation of food, cleaning and disinfection, food premises, hygienic principles, pest control, and food hygiene law.

Diploma in Food Hygiene

Designed for managers in catering and related food industries. Minimum age is seventeen, and students should hold the Certificate in Food Hygiene and the Handling of Food, or equivalent. The syllabus, based on twenty-four hours of instruction, covers microbiology and food poisoning, design and equipment of food premises, legal requirements, the various methods of food preservation, cleaning and disinfection, control of pests, hygiene risks associated with the various products and types of establishment, food legislation, dealing with complaints, education and health control of food handlers.

Royal Society of Health (RSH)

Certificate in Essential Food Hygiene

Directed at those working in kitchens or undertaking first line duties in preparing, serving or retailing food. Recommended course length is six hours. Topics include: causes of food poisoning, bacteria, hygienic working methods, pest control, the law.

Certificate in Hygiene of Food Retailing and Catering

Designed for those who wish to study food hygiene to a greater depth. No previous knowledge is assumed, but on completion of the course (twenty-two hours minimum), the student should understand the causes and nature of food poisoning and be able to recognize risk situations and the corrective action required. The emphasis is on preventive aspects of food hygiene at the workplace.

Certificate in Nutrition in Relation to Catering and Cooking

Based on sixty hours of teaching, gives an introduction to nutrition, energy and nutrients, nutritional value of foods, applied nutrition, menu planning, and food hygiene.

Diploma in Food Hygiene Management

Intended for existing and potential managers and supervisors in catering, and food retailing, aged eighteen or over. Typical course length: forty hours. Recommended entry requirements: RSH Certificate in Food Retailing and Catering, or BTEC National Diploma, or City and Guilds 706–2, or equivalent. Syllabus covers the reasons for food hygiene, hygiene law, micro-organisms, food preservation, storage and fitness, cleaning and disinfection, construction and design of food premises, stalls and vehicles, equipment in food premises, personal hygiene and health education, pest control, risks associated with particular products and types of premises.

Diploma in Nutrition in Relation to Catering Management

Sixty-hour course, syllabus includes applied nutrition, energy and nutrients, nutritional value of foods, menu planning, food-related legislation, and hygiene. Entry requirements similar to Diploma in Food Hygiene, or two years' management experience.

Wine and drink knowledge and service

Three organizations (for more details, see Chapter 11) offer courses and examinations in wine and drink service and knowledge.

Academy of Wine Service

Wine Service Skills

Short course/distance learning, supported by a video, study guide and wine service workbook, covers the essentials of wine knowledge and service. Identifying, recommending and appreciating wines, how wine is made, fortified wines, cigars, liqueurs and brandy, stock control, safe working practices, and the legal aspects of serving alcohol.

Court of Master Sommeliers

Basic Certificate

Two-day course on the production methods of wines and spirits, wine service, social skills, and the legislation. Practical sessions on wine tasting skills enable candidates to detect basic faults, recognize typical characteristics of wine, and appreciate the harmony of food and wine.

Advanced Diploma and Master Sommelier Diploma

Three-day course for those with an extensive knowledge of wine service in the industry. For the Advanced Diploma a minimum pass of 60 per cent is required in each of the three examinations: practical service and salesmanship, knowledge of the sommelier, tasting of six wines. For the Master Sommelier Diploma the minimum pass mark is 75 per cent.

United Kingdom Bartenders Guild

The Guild's one day seminar programme includes basic bar skills and mixed drinks and cocktails.

The UKBG Education Scheme is in two parts. The first consists of a four-month correspondence scheme covering the knowledge aspects of barwork including wines, spirits, beers, costing and stocktaking. The second is a five-day residential course on the practical side of bartending, usually held in January. Entry to this course depends on achieving satisfactory standards in the correspondence course question papers and assignments.

Wine and Spirit Education Trust

Certificate

Part-time, distance learning: the principal wine-making and spirit-producing areas of the world, how to interpret labels on bottles, and make informed judgements about products. Basic explanation of wines, spirits, liqueurs, beers, ciders, and low alcoholic beverages. A typical course is divided into seven sessions of two hours.

Higher Certificate

Part-time, distance learning: provides the depth of knowledge required for the purchase, storage, marketing, retailing and service of wines, spirits, liqueurs and other alcoholic beverages. The course is normally divided into fourteen sessions of two hours.

Diploma

Part-time (two years), distance learning: gives a detailed and wide-ranging knowledge of wines, liqueurs and spirits. The course is divided into two parts, taken in separate years, in any order, each normally involving attendance for a full day each fortnight from January to the beginning of May.

Private schools and colleges

It is wise to check that the college is accredited by the appropriate organization before reserving a place on a course: the *Directory of Accredited Independent Colleges in Britain* is published regularly by the three organizations who monitor standards in independent colleges, schools, and organizations in the UK (addresses at end of chapter).

It is also important to check the standing of the qualifications the college offers. If they are not recognized nationally such as BTEC and City and Guilds, or do not help towards NVQs and SVQs, you should think carefully before proceeding. (A number of private establishments offer degree and postgraduate programmes, details in Chapters 9 and 10.)

Belair Education Centre

Offers a range of intensive courses including hotel reception and administration (eight weeks), and diploma courses in tourism and computers (six to nine months).

City College of Higher Education

Minimum entry requirements for the two-year full-time course leading to the Diploma in Hotel and Tourism Management are four GCSEs and one A level, or the equivalent. Each subject completed successfully leads to a Certificate awarded by the Educational Institute of the American Hotel and Motel Association, and success in all twelve subjects to the EIAHMA's Diploma. City College also awards its own Certificate at the end of year 1, and Diploma at the end of year 2. Generally, there are two intakes to the course each year: October and February.

Subjects include: introduction to hospitality management, human resource management, training/supervisory development, marketing, front office procedures, convention management and service, food and beverage management, tourism, hotel/motel law, financial accounting.

Greenwich College

The courses are full-time, last one academic year (two semesters), and generally commence in January, April, June and September each year. For the Diploma, five GCSE passes at grade C or above, or equivalent, are required;

for the Higher Diploma, successful completion of the Diploma or a course of equivalent length and content. There are no formal entry requirements for the Certificate in Travel and Tourism, which is only offered twice a year: June and September.

Diploma in Hotel and Catering Management

Economics, business law, accounting, computing and office automation, organizational behaviour, management (hospitality, front office, food and beverage), executive housekeeping, catering operations.

Diploma in Catering Management

Cooking for the catering industry, food and beverage service, principles of accounting, principles of management, marketing, human resource management, computing, business communications.

Higher Diploma in Hotel and Catering Management

Management/staff interface (recruitment and selection, supervision and leadership, training and development), tourism, marketing, law, conventions and trade shows, catering operations.

University of Oxford Delegacy Certificate in Travel and Tourism

World tourism, tourism in the home country, tourism impacts and planning, marketing.

Hotel Career Centre

Operates throughout the year, offering a very wide range of courses from one week to one year's duration. The longer courses include:

- Hotel and Catering Diploma (forty-seven weeks) which leads to a BTEC First and C&G certificates.
- Travel and Tourism Diploma (forty-two weeks).
- Hotel and Catering Management Diploma (twenty-three weeks), based on the syllabus of the Institute of Commercial Management.
- Hotel Operations Certificate (twelve weeks plus four weeks work experience).
- Travel and Tourism Certificate (ten weeks).

- Cookery Certificate (ten weeks plus two weeks work experience).

Other courses include: Food and Beverage Service (nine weeks), Hotel Reception (from two to ten weeks), Bar and Wine Service (two weeks), Bar/Pub Catering (one week), Buying and Running Your Own Hotel (one week), English for the Hospitality Industry (four weeks).

Speedwing Training

Called *Academy of Travel Management* until 1991, Speedwing is a wholly owned subsidiary of British Airways, set up in 1986 to provide training courses, consultancy services and distance learning material independently to the travel trade. Courses range from one to five days and cover every aspect of airline travel and related services, including customer service, selling skills, and IATA accredited fares and ticketing courses.

International Correspondence Schools

Offers a non-examination correspondence course leading to the ICS Diploma in Hotel and Catering Management. Subjects covered include: an introduction to management, hotel organization, control office procedures, economic aspects, legal aspects, book-keeping, accommodation studies, planning and operating hotel kitchens, catering hygiene, nutrition and food science, food and beverage studies.

Lakefield Catering and Educational Centre

A non-profit making institution and registered charity, specializing in training young women aged sixteen to eighteen whose aptitudes and interests lie in the practical field. It offers a two-year residential course leading to City and Guilds and other qualifications. The standard entry requirement is three GCSE grades D/E. The principal subjects are cookery and accommodation services, with other modules in food hygiene, first aid, communications (including a foreign language), and numeracy. The practical experience is gained in the catering and housekeeping departments of the Centre's hall of residence, where the students live in term time.

London City College

LCC is a section of Schiller International University, specializing in UK courses. The courses described below lead to the Institute of Commercial Management's qualifications (see Chapter 11), the travel and tourism courses are also endorsed by Speedwing (see above). Entry requirements depend on age: for students aged seventeen to twenty, five GCSEs or their equivalent are required for the Certificate. For entry to the Diploma, the Certificate or equivalent is required, or for students aged twenty-three or over, a minimum of three years relevant experience.

Both the Certificate and Diploma are full-time: from January to June, or September to December. The combined Certificate and Diploma course takes one academic year, from January to December, or September to June.

Certificate in Hotel and Catering Supervision

Fundamentals of the hotel and catering industry, restaurant services, front office control, accommodation studies, food and beverage supervision, business communications.

Diploma in Hotel and Catering Management

Hotel and catering law, starting a small business, computer applications in hotels, management of hotel and catering operations, marketing hotel and catering services, decision making in the hotel.

Certificate in Travel and Tourism

Structure of travel and tourism, retail travel operations, characteristics of world resorts, communication skills.

Diploma in Travel and Tourism Management

Managing a travel and tourism operation, promoting travel and tourism, starting and managing a business, computer and software appreciation, case studies in travel and tourism.

Schiller International University

In addition to its degree and postgraduate programmes (Chapters 9 and 10), Schiller offers the following.

Hotelingua

Full-time, one year; integrates intensive English and French, German or Spanish – depending on the location of the study centre chosen – with courses in hotel front office procedures, typing, accounting, front desk travel and tourism services, and restaurant operations.

Hotel Operational Management Diploma Programme

Full-time, one year followed by six months industrial experience. Primarily intended as a stand-alone course, subjects include principles of food and beverage service, introduction to hotel operations, office practices and procedures, food production, elementary German or French, introduction to hotel and restaurant management, housekeeping management, front office and office organization.

Cookery schools

This section concentrates on the main cookery schools, most of which supplement their programmes with demonstrations, part-time evening courses and so forth. Addresses are given in Chapter 12. Details of other cookery schools are published from time to time in *BBC Good Food*.

Le Cordon Bleu

In 1990 this school came under the same ownership as Le Cordon Bleu Paris. Each of the Certificate courses takes place over one term of eleven weeks.

Introductory Certificate and *Introductory Patisserie*

These two courses are structured so that they can be taken together over a full week. The Introductory Certificate gives instruction on basic and classic methods with an emphasis on French cuisine. The Patisserie course gives a thorough grounding in the preparation of all the various types of pastry.

Intermediate Certificate

For students who have the Introductory Certificate or other recognized basic training. Content includes recipes for fish, poultry dishes, regional cuisine, the preparation of many varieties of meat, vegetables, fruits, pastries and desserts. Students also take the school's wine course.

Advanced Certificate

For those with previous training and experience. Covers classic and contemporary cuisine: fish and shellfish, the boning of fish, meat and poultry, chaudfroid and aspic work, sauces, desserts for the sweet trolley and some pastry work.

Eastbourne College of Food and Fashion

Residential college for young ladies. The three single term courses (eleven or twelve weeks) described below are offered in such a way that they can form a one-year full-time course.

Intensive Cordon Bleu Diploma

Practical cookery with the emphasis on planning, cooking and serving menus for entertaining, dinner parties and some larger scale cooking for buffets.

Advanced Cordon Bleu Diploma

An extension of practical skills concentrating on complete menus, techniques of filleting, boning and carving, advanced fish, poultry and game cookery, pastry work, specialities such as flambé cookery, sugar and chocolate work, and a study of the various styles of cooking and famous chefs.

Diploma in Restaurant Management

Involves aspects of planning, ordering, costing, cooking and serving food, as well as the service of wine and keeping the accounts. Students are responsible for running the school's restaurant.

L'Ecole de Cuisine Française – Sabine de Mirbeck

Diploma and Diploma Superieur

The one-year Diploma, which incorporates management and wine courses, leads to five months training in a premier restaurant for the Diploma Superieur.

Beginners, Intermediate and Advanced Certificates

The Beginners is for school leavers or enthusiastic cooks interested in learning the basic skills, techniques and theory of French cuisine. The Intermediate provides further experience and covers more elaborate classical dishes. The Advanced concentrates on contemporary cuisine and the preparation of buffets and receptions. Each course lasts one term of ten weeks.

Leith's School of Food and Wine

Diploma in Food and Wine

The diploma (full-time, one year) is awarded to those who successfully complete the Beginner's, Intermediate and Advanced Certificate courses.

Beginner's Certificate in Food and Wine

Full-time, ten weeks; basic cooking methods are practised repeatedly, and three-course meals cooked most days. Dishes are generally uncomplicated but interesting. Supporting studies include hygiene, nutrition and diet, food presentation, buying of produce, deep-freezing.

Intermediate Certificate in Food and Wine

Full-time, eleven weeks; on similar lines to the Beginner's, but at a faster pace, with more sophisticated dishes tackled. Emphasis is given, for example, to soufflés, bisques, seafood dishes, advanced yeast and pastry cookery, microwave cooking, preserving and deep frying. As well as wine lectures and tastings, supporting studies include unusual vegetables, butchery, catering and restaurant methods in the kitchen, Indonesian, Chinese, Indian and Italian cooking.

Advanced Certificate in Food and Wine

Full-time, eleven weeks; the work covered is sophisticated and includes, among other subjects, the making of boned poultry dishes, seafood and fish dishes, aspics, petits fours, pastry work, ice creams and sorbets, nouvelle cuisine and low fat cookery. There are also wine tastings and lectures, and supporting studies on restaurant and catering management, cooking in commercial quantities and recipe writing.

Credential Certificate in Food and Wine

Full-time, six months; designed for those who already have a sound basic knowledge of cookery and wish to take up cooking professionally, the work covered on this course is that of the Intermediate and Advanced Certificate.

Tante Marie School of Cookery

Diploma

Full-time, one year, or two terms of twelve weeks (intensive course); covers traditional British cookery and a wide spectrum of French cuisine. Includes the preparation and cooking of meat, poultry, game, fish, shellfish, eggs, vegetables, stocks, sauces, as well as aspic work, canapés, pastries, gâteaux, icing and chocolate work. Supporting classes include nutrition, vegetarian cooking, menu planning, practical business skills, and flower arranging. Also leads to the Wine and Spirit Education Trust Certificate. The intensive course is designed for those who have some previous cookery experience, whereas the one-year course assumes no prior cooking knowledge or skills.

Certificate

Full-time, twelve weeks; primarily intended for those who want to learn to cook well for family and friends. Menus are selected to provide a balanced repertoire for family cooking, entertaining and parties of all kinds.

Vegetarian Society

Weekend catering courses are offered for experienced cooks who wish to set up their own vegetarian catering business, and those who wish to teach vegetarian cookery. The Society (more details in Chapter 11) awards a Cordon Vert Diploma to students who satisfactorily complete its four foundation courses. The first of these is an introduction to the basic principles of vegetarian cookery; the other three introduce more unusual foods and cooking techniques.

Further information

Addresses of awarding bodies in Chapter 11, addresses of colleges in Chapter 12.

Accrediting bodies: private schools and colleges

British Accreditation Council for Independent Further and Higher Education (BAC)

All Saints, White Hart Lane, London N17 8HR
Tel: 081 368 1299.

British Council English Language Schools Recognition Scheme (BC)

27 Marylebone Road, London NW1 5JS
Tel: 071 935 5391.

Council for the Accreditation of Correspondence Colleges (CACC)

Accreditation Unit, English Language Management Department (Home), 10 Spring Gardens, London SW1A 2BN
Tel: 071 389 4025/3.

9

More about degree programmes

In the mid-1960s there were only two hotel and catering degree courses available in the UK. By the mid-1970s the number had increased to ten, of which six were validated by the Council of National Academic Awards (CNAA). By the mid-1980s the number of hotel and catering degrees had doubled to twenty. And in the pages that follow, over seventy are described, including many which have been developed in the past ten years in tourism and leisure.

The Government's White Paper *Education and Training for the 21st Century*, published in May 1991, announced that the distinction between universities and polytechnics would be abolished. Polytechnics and some colleges of higher education will have the power to award their own degrees. The Council for National Academic Awards (CNAA), until then the principal degree awarding body outside the university sector, would be closed. Those not granted degree-awarding status will be able to approach accredited institutions, as a number already do – for example Duncan of Jordanstown College of Arts. Polytechnics will be able to adopt the title of university. These new titles, which must be approved by the Privy Council, may be obvious and easy – Brighton Polytechnic, for example, has become the University of Brighton. In cities where there is already a university, for example Leeds, Manchester and Oxford, the choice of name has been more difficult.

It is becoming easier for mature students to gain entry to management programmes on the basis of their experience (see Chapter 5 for entry requirements). Exemption from certain parts of programmes is given more readily, including the industrial experience element.

Transfer from Higher National Diploma to degree is generally straightforward, indeed a number of HND and degree programmes have been specifically designed with this in mind. In some cases the switch can take place during the HND, at the end of year 1 or year 2. In other cases the degree programme is intended for HND diplomates (not A level entrants), usually from that particular college (a necessary proviso in view of the different emphasis of the various HND programmes).

The majority of degree programmes include the study of one or more modern languages. Some include study abroad, in Europe, North America and as far afield as Australia. At Oxford Polytechnic, for example, one-term exchanges are possible with various educational establishments in the USA and Australia. Hotel and catering students are also eligible for exchanges with Florida International University at Miami, University of Massachusetts at Amherst, and Virginia Polytechnic Institute.

The modular structure of many programmes means that individuals have a greater choice of subjects and award combinations, and it is easier to change to another degree, should the original choice prove unsuitable. At several colleges the Certificate of Higher Education (CertHE) and Diploma of Higher Education (DipHE) are available to those who want a shorter programme, or those who, some way through the degree course, decide they cannot continue at college for some reason. (These awards are made on successful completion of a programme of study equivalent in standard to that of the first year of a degree course for the CertHE, the first two years for the DipHE. The entry requirements are essentially the same as a degree course, and one of the attractions of the CertHe/DipHE is the facility they offer of transferring to a degree course without loss of time.)

Some degree programmes are organized in two semesters per year rather than three terms. Most hotel and catering degrees are four years, usually with a year's industrial experience, but shorter programmes are likely to be more readily available, with a two-year degree possible before the end of the 1990s.

The degree programme at South Bank University provides a good example of how education and industry can, and do work together. The Hotel Employers Group helped during the development stage, provide specialist teaching expertise, case study material, software programs, industry attachments for all students in the third year, and tutorial visits to hotels.

Directory of degree, certificate and diploma programmes

Some degree courses have been designed with specific career routes in mind, hotel management, for example, others are more general. In spite of these similar aims, the structure, content and approach of the various degree programmes varies considerably. The details that follow are given in alphabetic order, by the town or city in which the college, polytechnic or university is located.

Details have not been included on the wide range of food studies, food science, food marketing, food quality, food microbiology, nutrition, applied consumer sciences and related programmes. The UCCA and PCAS guides will help identify these, and the addresses of the establishments offering them.

The UCCA and PCAS guides will also help identify degree programmes which have been approved since the information for this chapter was updated (March 1992). These include the BA (Hons) Leisure Studies at Leeds Metropolitan University and the BA (Hons) Leisure Management at Manchester University.

Aberdeen: The Robert Gordon University

BA (Hons) Hospitality Management

Full-time (sandwich), BA three years, BA Hons four years. Technical innovation, international trading and dynamic operating environments provide the main themes. Core subjects include human resource management, food production processes, management, marketing, control and financial accounting, food commodities, food hygiene, computing and communications. Options include French, off-shore catering, facilities planning, nutrition, leisure management and tourism. The fourth (honours) year provides a study of operations and risk management, corporate and business policy and business planning. There is a twenty-eight week industrial placement between years 2 and 3.

Bedford College of Higher Education

BA/BSc (Hons) Leisure and Recreation

Full-time, three years. A modular programme offering considerable choice of subjects both within and outside the leisure and recreation pathway. The award of a BA or BSc depends on the subject selection in years 2 and 3.

In the first year, the focus is on the demand for leisure activities, the nature of participation and the psychological factors involved. This is seen in the context of historical developments, the effects of social class and personal wealth. The provision and experience of leisure activities is looked at in depth in the second year, leisure resources in Britain and the rest of Europe, and what they offer the consumer.

Planning and management are examined in the third year: how demand and provision can be matched and managed, the problems that arise and how they might be solved.

Birmingham College of Food, Tourism and Creative Studies and University of Central England at Birmingham/University of Birmingham

BA (Hons) Hotel and Catering Management

Full-time (sandwich), four years. Catering and accommodation studies are covered in years 1 and 2, as well as the support subjects of marketing, economics, quantitative methods and information technology, law, accounting and behavioural studies. Year 3 is spent on an industrial placement in the UK, Europe or USA. Operations management, organizational decision-making, human-resource management and financial management are studied in the final year.

BSocSc (Hons) Travel and Tourism Management

Full-time, three years. Validated by the University of Birmingham, specific emphasis is placed on business skills to enable the student to join a tourism organization, and within a short time make an effective contribution to its management. Subjects include: tourism and leisure, economics, cultural studies, psychology, information management, organizational behaviour, planning corporate strategy, resource management, and, as an option, either events tourism, a modern language, or third world tourism. The final year concentrates on change: the contemporary issues bringing about change and the role of management in formulating effective strategies to produce responsive and sustainable tourism.

Bolton Institute of Higher Education

BA/BSc (Hons) Tourism Studies/Leisure Studies (modular course)

Full-time, three years; part-time, five years. Tourism and leisure can separately: form the major subject, with the other (leisure/tourism) or a different subject altogether, as a minor subject; be combined with each other or any other subject for a joint honours degree; or, be combined with a total of three subjects in a 'minor-minor-minor' mode. Other subjects available include European languages, business studies, design, urban and cultural studies. The programme is organized in two semesters of fifteen weeks per year. It can also lead to a CertHE or DipHE.

Tourism subjects include principles of tourism, the tourist industry, passenger transport, tour operations and travel retailing, planning, development and administration of tourism. The leisure pathway investigates three distinct elements: leisure as a social phenomenon, leisure provision, and leisure management.

Bournemouth University

BA (Hons) Hospitality Management

BSc (Hons) Food and Catering Management

Full-time (sandwich), four years. Both courses share the core studies. A grounding in theoretical and practical aspects of the industry is provided in year 1. Practical skills are developed in food production and restaurant service as well as in classroom-based activities such as the use of computers and accounting techniques. Specialist studies for the BA focus on hotel and leisure facility operations and design, and for the BSc on food science investigations.

In year 2, students gain experience by managing the department's commercially oriented restaurant and food production operations. Other core studies include people, organization and management, marketing. Specialist studies on the BA include accommodation management, catering design and tourism. The BSc includes catering technology, food hygiene and microbiology, nutrition.

Extensive project work in year 4 consolidates these studies with the practical experience of the preceding industrial training year, and helps students develop their creative, analytical and organizational abilities, to appraise current corporate business situations, and to make decisions. Core subjects include consumer behaviour, human-resource management and financial management. BA specialist subjects include small-business management, and either leisure and facilities management, or food and culture.

BA (Hons) Tourism Studies

Full-time (sandwich), four years. The nature and effects of tourism are covered in year 1, the place of tourism in the economy, as well as supporting business, finance and information skills. Specific aspects of tourism, tourists and their destinations, and public and private sector tourism operations are examined in year 2.

Tourists and destinations, and business in tourism form the core subjects of the final year. In addition, students undertake an extended project and study three options from a list which includes transportation management, planning and policy, hospitality management, the management of the arts and sports, marketing communications, information technology and computing in tourism.

University-based studies are supported by fieldwork, with a five-day visit to a tourist area in the UK in the first year, and a seven-day visit outside the UK in the second year. All year 3 is spent in a tourism-related organization.

BA (Hons) Leisure Marketing

Full time, three years. The programme is divided into three inter-related strands: core, applications and personal skills. The core subjects address the process of marketing in the leisure context. The second year unit involves local case studies, and there is a project in year 3.

The applications units develop knowledge of specific subject areas, beginning in the first year with those required to underpin marketing (such as economics, accounting, and consumer behaviour), studying in depth specific elements of marketing such as advertising in the second year, and progressing by the final year to examine sectors of the leisure industry such as arts, sport, hospitality or tour operations.

The personal skills strand develops the essential practical skills which enhance managerial ability and marketing competence, including computing, language, marketing research and financial performance, and in the final year computers and design, media production and law.

Brighton: University of Brighton

BA (Hons) International Hospitality Management

Full-time (sandwich), four years. During the first two years hotel/catering operations, two business subjects and a language (Spanish or French, or English for students whose first language is not English) are studied on a semester basis in each half year. The business subjects include management information and control, marketing, management accounting, business environment, behavioural studies, service delivery systems and human-resource management. In year 3 students spend six months working in a country other than their home country (locations include North America, Australia, France, Spain and Belgium), and six months working in the UK. Final year subjects include hospitality management, business policy and international management.

BA (Hons) International Tourism Management

Full-time (sandwich), four years. The arrangement and subjects studied are similar to the International Hospitality Management programme, with the addition in year 4 of international tourism planning, or international tourism marketing.

Buckingham: University of Buckingham

Buckingham, Britain's only chartered independent university, accepts no support from Government funds. (The BSc does attract a mandatory grant, but this comes to less than a quarter of the tuition fees.) Its forty-week, four-term academic year begins in January.

BSc (Hons) Business Studies (International Hotel Management)

Full-time (sandwich), three years. Year 1 is spent at Buckingham. Courses include language studies, international hotel management, introduction to accounting, business, and computing, principles of economics, mathematics, statistical methods and sources, marketing, production and operations management, accounting and financial management, human-resource management.

The first half of year 2 in spent at the César Ritz Institute of Hotel Management in Switzerland, where courses relate to the main operational departments within the hotel. They include: food production, food service operations, beverage management, front office operations and systems, human relations. Placement in a selected major European hotel for seven months follows.

Year 3 is located back at Buckingham. Students develop hotel management skills and specialize in selected areas relevant to their own interests.

Canterbury Christ Church College of Higher Education

BA/BSc (Hons) Tourism Studies and Business Studies

Full-time, three years. Tourism is taken with Business Studies for a joint honours degree, or another subject such as Sport Science, Information Technology and History. A foreign language (French, German or Spanish) is studied in each year of the course, and students have the opportunity to study for up to three months at a European institution. Year 1 consists of foundation studies: introduction to tourism, leisure and recreation. Year 2 covers the geography of tourism, leisure and recreation management. In years 1 and 2, those following the business studies route would also do: the business environment, and business information. Service sector marketing and management, and management styles and practices in an international context in year 3 are supported by two options. These include heritage studies, tourism destination studies, outdoor recreation management and tourism in the EC. The business options include financial management, personnel management and marketing.

Cardiff Institute of Higher Education

BA Hotel Management

Full-time (sandwich), four years. This programme – validated by the University of Wales – is designed to give an understanding of the business environment in the context of hotel operations together with skills relating to food, beverage, accommodation and front office operations. As the course progresses, the emphasis changes towards strategic management considerations such as marketing and quality control. Year 4 options include tourism, information technology, and quality assurance. The third year is spent in industry and throughout the course students have contact with industry through hotel-based group enterprise projects.

BA (Hons) Tourism

Full-time (sandwich), four years. In addition to tourism studies, subjects include law, economics, business finance, organizational analysis and behaviour, information technology and environmental analysis. Year 3 is spent in industry. Final year subjects include tourism marketing, policy formulation and resource management; and two options from international law, international finance, local authority tourism promotion, and tourism in Wales. The degree is validated by the University of Wales.

Cardiff: University of Wales College of Cardiff

BSc (Hons) Hotel and Institutional Management

Full-time, three years. An understanding of the management of personnel and resources in a socio-economic setting is provided on this programme. Emphasis is placed on human behaviour, social factors, business acumen, and technological awareness. Industrial practice takes place mainly in the summer vacations, for around twenty-eight weeks.

The first year (Part I) consists of three foundation courses: *management* – including economics, law, accountancy, use of computers; *operational management* – food preparation, theory and practice of catering and accommodation services, front office services, beverage management, safety and hygiene standards, consumer requirements, maintenance of buildings, plant and equipment, purchasing/stock control, food costing; *applied science* – including scientific method and measurement, applied microbiology, hygiene and food handling, properties of materials.

Years 2 and 3 (Part II) also consist of three subjects: *applied management* – including financial management, management training, organizational behaviour, personnel management, marketing and tourism; *operational management* – including food and beverage, accommodation and control systems, planning and design; *applied science and technology* – including food technology, food legislation, nutrition, ergonomics and environmental physics.

Cheltenham and Gloucester College of Higher Education

BA (Hons) Hotel Management/Catering Management/Tourism Management/Leisure Management modular scheme

Full-time (sandwich), four years; part-time variable. There is considerable choice of subjects on these modular courses, from within the field and from related fields. The awards of CertHE and DipHE are also available. The programme is organized in three levels, as illustrated by the following subjects common to the four fields: issues in leisure, tourism and hospitality (level I); marketing and finance in leisure, tourism and hospitality (level II); small business enterprise (level III).

The *hotel management* field also includes, for example: hotel operations; management information systems in hotel management; international aspects of hotel management; customer care and quality management; project planning; hotel design and development.

Catering management includes: food and beverage operations management; international gastronomy; the geography of wine; catering systems; food, nutrition and society.

Tourism management includes: tourism decision-makers; structure of tourism; communications in tourism; tourism development process; transportation issues; heritage tourism; strategic planning; environmental quality and tourism.

Bushey, Herts: United States International University-Europe

The campus works on a 'quarter' system, with ten working weeks constituting a quarter. Students may start their course at the beginning of any quarter: January, April, June or September, and progress is largely determined by their drive and ability. Thus the BS (Bachelor of Science) programme can be taken over three years – four quarters × three classes, or four years – three quarters × three classes. Most BS students graduate in three years or less.

The courses are accredited by the Western Association of Schools and Colleges (WASC) of USA. This means that courses taken are accepted by US universities, and vice versa, should a student wish to move. Movement between any of the four campuses of the university is also straightforward: Nairobi, Mexico City, London and San Diego, the main campus.

BS Hotel, Restaurant and Tourism Management

Full-time, three or four years. The programme comprises thirty-six classes: a core of sixteen hotel, restaurant and tourism classes which include hospitality management, food production, marketing, information technology, management accounting, food and beverage cost control, hospitality maintenance and engineering, restaurant development and operations, international travel and tourism, travel and tourism management; eight compulsory classes in the humanities and social sciences; four compulsory classes in business studies; and eight electives.

Associate of Arts (AA) Hotel, Restaurant and Tourism Management

Full-time, two years. Eighteen classes are required for this award, of which thirteen are from the range included in the BS programme, and five cover English, public speaking, composition, critical thinking, technical writing and computer software applications.

Coventry University

BA/BSc (Hons) Leisure Management

Full-time (sandwich), four years. Developed with Henley College, Coventry, this programme embraces the issues of why people take leisure and how leisure is provided for in Britain. Subjects include business information systems, business organizations and policy, marketing, finance and human resource management in the leisure industry, planning and legal issues. The options include sports and physical recreation, fitness management, tourism, arts and entertainment, countryside recreation and hotel management.

The industrial experience element is either in two six-month blocks (at the beginning of year 2, and at the end of year 3), or one twelve month block at the end of year 2.

Derby: University of Derby

BA/BSc Tourism (modular degree)

Full-time, three years; full-time (sandwich), four years; part-time, variable. Tourism is one of the many subjects available in the university's modular scheme, as a major subject, or as a joint degree with one or two other subjects such as marketing, European studies, accounting, and business. The tourism course includes an analysis of the structure of the UK travel and tourism industry, destination studies and the impact of tourism on those destinations, marketing and planning for travel and tourism, and international tourism. The awards of CertHE and DipHE are also available.

Dundee: Duncan of Jordanstown College of Art

MA Hotel and Catering Management

Full-time, three years. Validated by the University of Dundee. Studies in three disciplines are covered progressively throughout the course: *catering operations* – food science, food production and service, accommodation services; *management studies* – management methods, communications, business law, management of organizations, personnel and marketing management; *finance* – accounting and costing, management accounting and finance. They culminate in year 3 in an integrated study of the management of catering operations, with two elective studies: industrial relations, tourism and leisure, auditing, special diets. Students who study practical French in year 2 are expected to continue with this subject as their elective in year 3. There is a twelve-week period of industrial experience between years 1 and 2, and years 2 and 3.

Edinburgh: Napier University

BA (Hons) Hospitality Management

Full-time (sandwich), BA three years, BA (Hons), four years. In years 1 to 3 a study of fundamental principles of hospitality operations, financial studies and human resources is undertaken. Economics, marketing and information studies examine the external factors affecting hospitality operations. Additionally, students study a European language during years 1 and 2. A twenty-four week industrial placement period is included between Easter and September of year 2. The advanced stage, year 4, addresses strategic and organization issues with hospitality strategy and implementation, policy analysis, and hospitality and tourism environments.

Edinburgh: Queen Margaret College

BA Hospitality Enterprise with Tourism

Full-time, three years. Compulsory modules – designed to develop a knowledge of the industry and its operation, and to foster competence in management – include hospitality studies, management and innovation, finance, communication and information studies, sales and marketing, and human-resources management. The entrepreneurial studies module is designed to help graduates start up their own businesses, and the study of Japanese and French in the language and culture modules anticipates the major growth in the Far Eastern and European tourist markets. Optional modules include: leisure and recreation; facilities operations and planning; food, culture, and health retailing; European tourism studies.

Each year there are two fourteen-week semesters in college with a further fourteen weeks in industry, either in the UK or abroad.

Glasgow: The Queen's College

BA (Hons) Hospitality Management

Full-time (sandwich), four years. Years 1 and 2 are shared with the SCOTVEC HND programme, also modular (see Chapter 8 for content). Year 3 begins with a six-month industrial placement, from June to November. Core subjects include: marketing, human resource management, communications, sociology of work and organization, organizational psychology, management action skills, strategic management, financial management strategy. Electives (one per year) include entrepreneurial studies, travel and tourism, gastronomy, language and culture. Project work forms a major part of year 4.

Glasgow: University of Strathclyde, Scottish Hotel School

BA (Hons) Hotel and Catering Management

Full-time, BA three years, BA (Hons) four years. This programme offers considerable choice. Hotel School subjects include: hotel management cuisine), accounting, hotel and catering operational management, people and the hotel industry. Specialist class options include: project planning and development, facilities management, contemporary cuisine, aesthetic cuisine, oenology, cuisine and culture, convention management, issues and controversies in hotel and tourism management. Subjects from other departments of the Strathclyde Business School include: administration, marketing, economics, and accounting. Practical experience is undertaken during the summer vacations.

Those who reach the required standard in the pass degree can proceed to the fourth year for the degree with honours, pursuing their studies within the Hotel School, or jointly with another subject area in the Business School. A joint programme can link hotel and catering management with tourism, administration, business law, economics, industrial relations and marketing.

BA (Hons) Tourism

Full-time, four years. Tourism can be studied to joint honours level with other subjects offered by Strathclyde Business School, such as accounting, economics, geography, marketing, or finance. Alternatively, tourism can be taken as a first or second principal subject in the BA Business School. The first year comprises two modules: international tourism, which examines world travel movements and their associated impacts on receiving countries; and the structure of the UK tourism industry. Year 2 also has two modules: UK resort development, which appraises different categories of local tourist industry, and comparative resort development, which examines the dynamics of resort development by reference to case studies in selected overseas countries. Year 3 provides an understanding of the marketing management of travel and tourism operations within both the public and private sectors. In year 4, international tourism development provides an understanding of the significance of the international tourism sector and studies tourism issues in developing and developed countries. Leisure management and planning considers techniques for appraising leisure and tourism markets.

Guildford: University of Surrey

BSc (Hons) Hotel and Catering Management

Full-time, four years. Years 1 and 2 cover four main areas: *management studies*; *quantitative studies* – includes accounting, management science and computing; *food and beverage management* – includes food production science and gastronomy; *business studies* – economics, law, marketing, languages (optional). During the first long vacation, students are expected to undertake eight weeks practical experience in the industry. Year 3 is spent in industry. Final year subjects are: hotel and catering management, human resource management, financial management, marketing management and tourism. The final term is used for completion of a project.

BSc Hotel Management

Full-time, three years, overseas students only. For most lectures, students join their colleagues on the Hotel and Catering Management degree programme. Tutorials are conducted separately, as are classes in economics, law, communication studies, office management, business management, and English as a foreign language.

Hatfield: University of Hertfordshire with De Havilland College

BA (Hons) Travel and Tourism

Full-time (sandwich), four years. Business subjects studied in the first year emphasize the travel and tourism industries: business operations, law, accounting, quantitative methods, and spatial patterns, which introduces geographical aspects of travel and tourism. Year 2 subjects include financial management, quantitative methods, marketing, travel and tourism operations and their human aspects. Students also study French, Spanish or German, and there are workshop sessions in computer literacy and a case-study based course on the strategic aspects of travel and tourism. Year 3 is spent working on a supervised industrial placement in the UK or abroad. Specialized travel and tourism studies continue in year 4, with project work, and an optional course from a range which includes international trade and finance, British heritage, comparative employment systems, European law and international accounting.

Herefordshire Technical College and Wolverhampton University/University of Lille

BA (Hons) Hotel Management/Tourism Management/Licensed Retail Management/Leisure Management

Full-time (sandwich), two years (for HND diplomates). Students completing the BTEC HND in Travel and Tourism or Leisure Management at the college can take a further one-year industrial placement mutually agreed and organized, before joining year 4 of the degree programme at Wolverhampton (see below). Alternatively, HND Travel and Tourism diplomates can continue their studies in France, at the University of Lille where part of the HND is based.

High Wycombe: The Buckinghamshire College

BA Leisure and Tourism

Full-time, one year. This modular degree is specifically aimed at diplomates with an appropriate HND such as Leisure Studies, or Business and Finance

(Travel and Tourism). It enables students to develop specific leisure interests such as tourism, or sport and physical recreation.

Huddersfield: The University of Huddersfield

BA (Hons) Hotel and Catering Business

Full-time (sandwich), four years. Centred around three main themes – technology, human behaviour and business – this course has an international focus. The modular format gives considerable choice of subjects. These include: hotel and catering operations, analysis and planning; social sciences, customer and worker behaviour, organization and management, corporate and worker behaviour; marketing, accounting, business economics, quantitative business techniques, strategic analysis and planning. Year 3 is spent in industry.

BSc (Hons) Catering and Applied Nutrition

Full-time, four years. With its emphasis on the inter-relationship between the catering and food industries, this course prepares students for employment in either field. The focus is on food quality – microbial, sensory and nutritional – and the link between quality assurance and product-development techniques. The course raises the awareness of nutrition and its importance in society and, in particular, the role played by the catering and food industries in promoting healthy diets for consumers. Options enable students to take these topics to greater depth. Year 3 is spent in supervised work experience within the catering and food manufacturing industries.

Hull: University of Humberside

BA (Hons) European Tourism

Full-time, three years. The focus is on tourism and leisure as an area of consumer spending and employment, and their impact on hotels and catering, retailing, tourism and leisure facilities, agriculture, transport, business, local and central government, communications and media. Year 1 provides a grounding in the main areas of study. Year 2 concentrates on special analysis of tourism development, European marketing, modern European business and languages. From Easter, students undertake a European placement and study period. The final year focuses on tourism management and tourism in Europe, underpinned by social science and geography.

Jordanstown and Londonderry: University of Ulster

BA (Hons) Hospitality Management

Full-time, four years. Subjects specific to hospitality management are supported in years 1 and 2 by: organization studies, information technology, economics, quantitative analysis, accounting, marketing, personnel studies, and either a European language or public sector studies. During year 3 – supervised work experience – students may opt to undertake placement related studies leading to the award of a Diploma in Industrial Studies. In the final year, students apply higher level business, analytical and technological techniques to the total management of most styles of operations within the hospitality industry. The three year DipHE programme (year 2 is industrial experience) covers similar subjects to years 1 and 2 of the degree.

BA (Hons) Hotel and Tourism Management

Full-time, four years. An overall understanding of hotels and restaurants, and of tourism in general is given in years 1 and 2. This stage examines the economic, social and legislative environment; the needs of customers, and the products and processes involved in satisfying customers and achieving commercial success. In year 3, supervised work experience, the award of Diploma in Industrial Studies is available. In year 4, four subjects are selected from: hotel/financial/marketing/personnel/tourism management, leisure studies, information technology. One option is studied from: information systems, European business studies, tourism, food studies, language.

Leeds Metropolitan University

BA (Hons) Hospitality Business Management

Full-time, three years; full-time (sandwich), four years. Designed to provide the organizational abilities necessary for directing and coordinating business units of varying sizes and complexities in both the public and private sectors, this programme is modular, with a virtually common first year with the BTEC HND. A year in industry before the final year is optional.

Subjects studied include food and beverage management, accommodation operations, property management, human resources, management principles, information technology, rooms division management, marketing, law, accounts, economics, qualitative studies and a wide variety of electives. These include languages (in years 1 and 2), tourism, leisure studies, and European business.

BSc (Hons) Hospitality Management and Related Services

Full-time, three years; part-time, variable. Designed principally for those with a good BTEC National Diploma, and those over twenty-one who have substantial industrial experience, but not necessarily formal academic qualifications, the emphasis of the course is on acquiring and developing operational management, interpersonal and entrepreneurial skills.

Modules include organization management, work systems, information technology, marketing, the consumer, human resources, the food, beverage, liquor and accommodation product, business enterprise development, and tourism. In addition, two sectors of industry are studied from the following: licensed trade, restaurants, hotels, education and health care, contracts.

BA (Hons) Tourism Management

Full-time (sandwich), four years. The three themes of this programme are the study of tourism, in particular the management of people and places, languages (possibly two), and marketing. Year 3 is spent in industry. The strong vocational orientation provided in year 4 can be reflected in the award title, for example Tourism and Recreation Management.

London: Middlesex University

BSc (Hons) Hotel and Restaurant Management

Full-time (sandwich), four years. Either French or information systems is followed as an option throughout the programme. Core subjects include marketing, finance, personnel and operations management, and their application in hotels, restaurants and tourism businesses. In year 4, general management issues are examined through a series of case studies.

Students are also taught food production and service skills, and reception and housekeeping procedures. These skills are put into practice during the industrial placement – generally two, six-month periods. Students on the French option must spend at least six months in France.

London: Schiller International University

Schiller offers the opportunity of following a US education programme combined with instruction in the practical Swiss methods of hotel management. With English the language of instruction at each of the school's five centres – Engelberg in Switzerland, Waterloo and Wickham Court in London, Paris and Strasbourg in France – movement between them is straightforward, and indeed necessary for some programmes. Transfer to and from other US universities is also possible, as Schiller is accredited by ACIS of

Washington, the Accrediting Commission of the Association of Independent Colleges and Schools.

The academic year at Schiller consists of two semesters, one in the autumn and one in the spring, each fifteen weeks long, and a summer session of seven weeks. During a full semester, students enrol on four to six courses, each worth three credits. In-service training is a compulsory element of the programmes.

ABA Diploma in Hotel Management

Full-time, two years. Sixty-two credits are required for the Associate of Business Administration degree. Course titles include: introduction to hotel/restaurant management and tourism, principles of food and beverage service, hotel and motel law, accounting, restaurant operations, housekeeping management, introduction to wine science (oenology), front office procedures, food and beverage purchasing. English composition, applied mathematics, a foreign language.

BBA Hotel Management

Full-time, four years. 142 credits are required for the Bachelor of Business Administration degree. This programme is available as a follow-on from the ABA degree. Extra subjects include hotel administration and accounting, convention management services, international travel, marketing for European/US tourism, training and supervision, statistics, introduction to economics, a foreign language.

Alternatively the BBA is available as a one-year course for students who have completed thirty to thirty-six months of formal education in hotel/restaurant management.

London: South Bank University

BA (Hons) Hotel Management

Full-time (sandwich), four years. Operations management, business management and human resources management form the three broad areas of this unit-based programme. Level 1 units (terms 1 and 2) include introduction to hotel operation, finance and accounting, and the business environment, information systems and a modern language (French, German or Spanish).

Level 2 units – in terms three, four and five – include accommodation operations, food and beverage production and service, hotel accounting and financial management, marketing and the environment, human resources management, analysis and communication skills, and a modern language.

A year in industrial experience leads to the level 3 units in the final four terms. These include a project, financial and marketing management, business environment and enterprise, and options: further study of a modern language (French, German or Spanish), information systems, destination marketing, corporate finance, quality management, managing change and organization development, gastronomy.

London: Thames Valley University

BA (Hons) Hospitality Management

Full-time (sandwich), four years; full-time, one year for HND diplomates. With its emphasis on developing managers for the sectors of the hospitality industry which serve the tourist market, this course involves the study of a foreign language in years 2 and 4. Year 3 consists of a planned programme of work experience, either in the UK or abroad. HND diplomates join year 4.

The course has three main themes: business environment, which includes such subjects as organizational behaviour, applied economics, financial management, and effective communication; operations, which includes food and beverage and rooms division management; hotel and catering administration, which includes information technology, quantitative business analysis, accounting, marketing and human resource management.

BA (Hons) Leisure Management (Tourism and Recreation)

Full-time (sandwich), four years. For students with language skills there is the possibility of studying and or working overseas. Subjects include the political and social context of leisure, working in leisure organizations, the legal and economic environment of business, management and administration, European leisure policy and practice, operational studies, decision making in the leisure industry.

London: University of North London

BA (Hons) International Hotel and Catering Management

Full-time (sandwich), four years. The emphasis is on problem solving, innovation and critical analysis across the whole curriculum, with the objective of developing thinking managers. University-based studies are divided into three subject streams: *business management* – including accounting and finance, economics, sales and marketing, human resources management and organizational behaviour; *operations management* – including food and beverage studies, facility management, leisure and tourism studies, gastronomy, catering systems, marketing and business development; *cross cultural management* – including one language (French, German or Spanish), politics, history and international business policy.

There are two, six-month industrial placements, one or both of which are spent within the country of the foreign language studied.

Direct entry to year 3 may be available to those with HND Hotel, Catering and Institutional Management and other equivalent qualifications.

BA (Hons) Leisure and Tourism Management

Full-time (sandwich), four years. Basic business disciplines and key concepts in leisure and tourism are covered in the first year, behavioural studies, accounting, computing and quantitative methods, plus French, German or Spanish. Before the first six-month period in industry, decision-making skills are developed in units in public policy for leisure and tourism, management accounting and marketing.

Polytechnic-based studies continue with organization and human-resource management, and students develop their research skills through involvement in real problems from the public and commercial sectors.

The second period of industrial experience, which like the first, can be spent abroad, is usually spent in a contrasting area of the industry.

In year 4, students have a choice of two option pathways from arts and entertainment management, leisure facility management, tourism destination and attraction management, and travel and transport management. Students may also spend part of this year studying at universities specializing in leisure and tourism in Spain, the Netherlands, Belgium or West Germany.

London: West London Institute of Higher Education

BA/BSc (Hons) Leisure Management (modular degree)

Full-time, three years. Students registering for the BA or BSc specify two subjects which will form the main part of their course, so leisure can be combined with Sports Studies, Geography, Computer Studies, American Studies and so forth – but not Business Studies because of the extensive overlap. In addition to various business studies modules, others examine the place of leisure in society, the management of leisure facilities and leisure marketing. The leisure industry sectors are offered as specialist modules: arts and entertainment, countryside planning and rural recreation, and physical recreation and play facilities.

Luton College of Higher Education

BA (Hons) Business Studies (Travel and Tourism)

Full-time (sandwich), four years. A broad base of business theory and practice leads to the travel and tourism specialism (or accountancy, or marketing). There is an opportunity to study French, German, Spanish or Japanese. Core modules in years 1 and 2 include business economics, accounting, business analysis, behavioural and organizational studies, business systems and computer applications, the legal context of business, business information and decision-making, marketing, international environment of business and corporate strategy. Year 3 is work experience. Year 4 studies concentrate on the chosen specialism. The three tourism subjects are: structure of UK travel and tourism industry, tourism planning and development, and international tourism.

Manchester Metropolitan University

BSc (Hons) Hotel and Catering Management

Full-time (sandwich), four years. Operations management, administration, and the hotel and catering environment form the three main themes. Subjects include food studies, accommodation and catering technology, accounting, personnel, marketing, information technology, economics, law and behavioural studies. The third year is spent in industry.

BA (Hons) International Hotel Management

Full-time (sandwich), four years. The language strand aims to develop competence in two European languages other than English. The practical and procedural skills necessary for the successful management of accommodation and food and beverage departments form the operational strand. The management strand aims to develop appropriate business studies skills and problem-solving abilities.

Both periods of industrial experience are normally located in the country of the student's main foreign language, and are supplemented by an intensive short course in the other language.

Newcastle: University of Northumbria at Newcastle

BA (Hons) Travel and Tourism

Full-time (sandwich), four years. Supported by ABTA and the first degree in travel and tourism to be offered in the UK, this programme provides a broad foundation in business studies in the context of travel and tourism. Compulsory subjects in years 1 and 2 include quantitative methods, information technology, management skills, law, finance, marketing, organization behaviour and personnel, spatial patterns in tourism, impacts of tourism, and operations of the travel and tourism industry. In year 1, students already proficient in a foreign language, can study a language as an optional subject.

In year 4 the compulsory core includes business decisions, strategic and marketing management, and management practice. Four electives build on subjects taught previously.

Year 1 is based at New College Durham, years 2 and 4 at Newcastle. Year 3 is spent in industry.

Newton Abbot/Plymouth: University of Plymouth in association with South Devon College and Plymouth College of Further Education

BSc (Hons) Hospitality Management

Full-time (sandwich), four years. The course is organized in three equal pathways on a modular basis: *catering management* – includes food and the consumer, food and beverage production and service, gastronomy, costing of food provision, market problems for the catering industry; *accommodation management* – includes tourism, accommodation and the consumer, buildings, services and staffing, front desk operations, information analysis; *business and management studies* – includes financial management, business planning, legislation and taxation, human-resource management, economics and marketing.

English speaking students will normally be required to study French, and if desired a second European language.

Year 3 is spent gaining experience in one or more European countries, however, students with appropriate industrial experience can gain exemption from this requirement. HND holders can apply for direct entry to year 2 of the course.

Norwich City College of Further and Higher Education

BA (Hons) Hospitality Management

Full-time (sandwich), four years. This course, of which year 3 is spent in industry, is designed to give students practical management skills and knowledge related to food, beverage, accommodation and tourism/travel operations. Inter-related technology and management skills include planning, implementing and evaluating the subject areas of finance, marketing, information systems, hotels, tourism and economics, and human aspects of management.

Nottingham: The Nottingham Trent University

BA (Hons) International Hospitality Management

Full-time (sandwich), four years. Core studies are common with the Business Studies, European Business and Business and Quality Management degree programmes. This means a wide range of options, including human resource management, marketing research, operations management and information technology – and greater flexibility to transfer programmes.

Specialist subjects include hospitality management, decision making, the business context of a selected country, international business strategy, international marketing and international hospitality environment. Year 3 is spent on an industrial placement in the UK or abroad. All students are expected to develop their language skills in French, German, Spanish or Italian.

BA (Hons) Hotel and Catering Management

Full-time, one year. A 'top up' programme for HND in hotel and catering management. There are three core subjects (hospitality enterprise, business policy and operations, organizations and management) a hospitality project and two options.

Oxford Brookes University

BSc/BA (Hons) Catering Management/Tourism (modular degree)

Full-time, three years; part-time, variable. With the very large possible combinations of subjects students can tailor their studies to suit their interest and career aspirations. Thus Catering Management and Tourism can be combined with each other, or with such subjects as: Food Science and Nutrition, History of Art, French Language and Contemporary Studies, German Language and Contemporary Studies, Retail Management, Accounting and Finance.

Over 900 modules – or course units – are available, and for each particular degree certain modules are classed as compulsory, recommended and acceptable. Each module represents between a third and a quarter of a term's work for most full-time students. A student progresses through the course by accumulating credits for each module passed. A CertHE can be achieved by studying ten modules, a DipHE by studying eighteen modules, a degree by studying twenty-six modules, and an honours degree by studying twenty-eight modules.

There are two compulsory modules for Catering Management: the hospitality industry, and food and beverage operations (double module). Accommodation operations, social aspects of hospitality, introduction to law, and microcomputer applications are on the recommended list. Acceptable modules include social and applied nutrition, catering technology, gastronomy, decision-making in the hospitality firm, hotel systems management, corporate management in the hospitality industry, financial analysis and control, marketing planning, management accounting, and industrial relations.

In the Tourism programme, stage I presents the general body of knowledge, reviews tourism behaviour and identifies tourism decision makers. Stage II builds on this knowledge, developing an analytical and evaluative approach to the tourism development and management process. The variety of options is probably unique with such subjects as leisure in industrial society, cartographic design and communication, introduction to contemporary publishing, wildlife management, and social psychology.

BSc (Hons) Hotel and Catering Management

Full-time (sandwich), four years; part-time, variable. There are four compulsory modules in year 1: accommodation operations, the hospitality industry, social aspects of hospitality, and food and beverage operations. Introduction to accounting, economics and law, and microcomputing applications are also recommended. Stage I concludes with a year's industrial placement (in year 2).

The wide range of subjects offered in stage II includes those listed under the Catering Management degree above, plus, in a business context, French, German, Italian and Spanish.

Portsmouth University and Highbury College of Technology

BA (Hons) Hotel and Catering Management

Full-time (sandwich), four years. Provides a general appreciation of the technical aspects of accommodation provision, an appreciation of the major characteristics of food and drink, and an understanding of the individual, social, economic, organizational and financial factors that shape the management of hotel and catering businesses. Year 3 is spent in industry. Year 4 subjects include financial management, management of human resources, business policy, management workshop and two options from the following: personnel and employee relations, promotion of travel and tourism, economics of travel and tourism, information systems, gastronomy, quantitative management, hospitality marketing management.

Preston and Blackpool: University of Central Lancashire and Blackpool and the Fylde College

BA (Hons) Hospitality Management

Full-time (sandwich), four years. Year 1 (largely based at Blackpool) covers three main areas of study: hospitality studies, analysis of business activity, people and hospitality operations. There is also a four-week period of industrial experience. Year 2 (with time at both sites) includes hospitality management, business operations, human-resources management, consultancy projects and one option from the following: French, German, Spanish, gastronomy, tourism and leisure. After a year of supervised industrial experience in the UK or overseas, students return to Preston to undertake a project, strategic hospitality management, hospitality industry consultancy management and two options from the following: licensed trade management, marketing and the media, international tourism, and volume production systems.

Sheffield Hallam University

BSc (Hons) Hotel and Catering Management

Full-time (sandwich), four years. In addition to the core foundation studies in year one – behavioural studies, business studies, management information and food studies – industry-specific units cover food and accommodation studies. Years 2 and 4 have six main areas of study (year 3 is spent in industry): *food studies* – bringing together food preparation, food science, nutrition and food microbiology; *food production and service* – organization and equipment for preparing, cooking, storing and serving food, together with the skills of planning for efficient layouts and work routines; *accommodation studies* – design, servicing and maintenance, presentation and marketing of hotel rooms and conference/banqueting facilities; *the human aspects of catering* – motivation of staff, creation of atmosphere, communication, advertising, decor and personality, as well as the legal constraints; *applied financial studies* – including taxation, raising capital to finance operations, monitoring income and expenditure; *hotel and catering systems* – which helps draw the course together, includes the study of systems theory, and the analysis of the operational methods of specific hotel and catering organizations.

BSc (Hons) Hotel and Tourism Management

Full-time (sandwich), four years. Year 1 is identical to the Hotel and Catering Management programme. Years 2 and 4 comprise six areas of study: *hotel and tourism facilities management; financial and quantitative analysis;*

human aspects; *marketing*; *tourism* – tourism frameworks, international tourism, tourism planning and development; *interdisciplinary studies* – to develop an integrated understanding of hotel and tourism management.

BA (Hons) Recreation and Tourism Management

Full-time, three years. Years 1 and 2 lead up to a twelve-week period of work experience in the tourism industry. Subjects studied relate to four complementary strands: the environmental context of recreation and tourism activities, the recreation client, recreation activity analysis, and business studies. In year 3, in addition to common courses in policy and planning of recreation management and project management in the recreation industry, students study tourism marketing, international tourism, tourism planning and management, and one other subject from a wide range of options. (A parallel route is available leading to a BA (Hons) Recreation Management.)

Southampton Institute of Higher Education

BA (Hons) Leisure Management

Full-time, three years. This programme specializes in water-based leisure and environmental issues. First year subjects include: water-based leisure and tourism, maritime science and technology, organization and management studies, law, recreation and leisure environment management. For years 2 and 3, students follow three from a choice of five pathways. These are: resource management, leisure and environment, water leisure operations, management operations and yacht operations. The optional sports development programme includes instructor awards in most water sports plus land-based sporting skills.

Staffordshire University

BA (Hons) Business Studies (Tourism)

Full-time (sandwich), four years. The structure of this programme gives a broad grounding in business skills such as planning, coordination and administration, accounting and finance, marketing, quantitative, computing and interpersonal skills, while allowing the development of talents in a range of specialist areas of which tourism is one. Year 3 is spent gaining appropriate experience.

Warrington: North Cheshire College

BA (Hons) Leisure and Recreation with Business Management

Full-time, three years. Validated by the University of Manchester: fifteen modules must be completed for an honours degree. The DipHE is available at the end of year 2 with a total of eleven modules.

The joint honours structure enables the student to develop and integrate business and leisure skills. It provides a wide perspective of the whole field and allows the development of specialist knowledge within the four major areas of arts and entertainment, sports and physical recreation, countryside and open space recreation, and tourism.

Wolverhampton University and Stafford College

BA (Hons) Hotel Management/Tourism Management/Licensed Retail Management/International Hospitality Management

Full-time (sandwich), four years; full-time, one year (for HND diplomates). Business functions and operations management are the two main themes of this course. Years 1 and 2 subjects include: service industry operations, food and beverage systems management, quantitative analysis for business, human resources, marketing, finance, and tourism. Year 3 is spent in industry. Priority is given to project work in year 4, in addition to which students study corporate policy, and four further subjects – the choice of which determines the title of the degree: licensed retail management, management of hotel operations, international hotel development, heritage studies, the leisure society, tourism management, human resource management, strategic marketing, and financial planning and control. A European language is an option in each year of the course.

10
More about postgraduate qualifications

This chapter describes the programmes available for those who already have management experience in the industry, and, or an HND or degree, and are seeking a professional qualification, postgraduate diploma, or masters degree. Also described are the postgraduate diplomas designed as conversion courses, for those who have a degree in another field and now seek a hotel, catering or tourism qualification.

The universities and some of the other institutions described on the following pages offer MPhil and PhD research degrees.

Directory of postgraduate diplomas, DMS and masters degrees

The information that follows is arranged in alphabetic order, by the city or town in which the institution is located. Addresses are given in Chapter 12. Details of the Open University's programmes are given at the end of the chapter.

The University of Birmingham

MSocSc Leisure Services and Tourism

Full-time, one year; part-time, two years. Intended for those who already have knowledge of the subject area and wish to develop their skills and knowledge. Three courses: leisure services and tourism, plus two options from a range which includes: economic development and policy; economics and society: interpreting change; research methods in social science; housing policy and practice.

Bournemouth University

Postgraduate Diploma/MA European Tourism Management

Full-time, one year. The introductory programme (four weeks) and the first semester (eighteen weeks) are spent at Bournemouth and students study law, financial management, marketing, managing people, tourism planning and languages. Alternatively a broadly parallel course is offered at the Netherlands Institute of Tourism and Transport in Breda.

The second semester is spent in Germany (at the Fachhochschule Heilbronn), or in France (at the Université de Savoie, Chambéry), or in Spain (at the Escuela Oficial de Turismo, Madrid), where lessons are in German/French/Spanish. The course is supported by the European Community's ERASMUS scheme (see Chapter 5).

Case studies focus on the management issues faced by three broad divisions of tourism organizations: *direct providers* – of accommodation, transport, catering and attractions; *intermediaries* – tour operators, travel agents, conference organizers, information services; *strategic bodies* – managers in the public sector.

Students undertake the MA by carrying out a piece of individual research and presenting a thesis. This may be undertaken in any appropriate location.

Brighton: University of Brighton

Diploma International Hospitality Operations

Full-time, one year. This programme offers the option of studying partly in France, in conjunction with INFATH. Business and management skills are developed through the study of marketing, financial management, human-resource management, organizational behaviour and hospitality management – much of it case-study based. Students also develop their abilities to cope with everyday business situations in a second language.

Buckingham: University of Buckingham

MSc International Hotel Management

Full-time, two years for non-hotel graduates, otherwise one year. Non-hotel graduates spend five months at the César Ritz Institute and the rest of the year in a work placement with a major European hotel. The programme is designed to familiarize students with all aspects of hotel operations and their management.

The common year for all participants is based at Buckingham. Advanced hotel management and operations courses are selected from international hotel operations, hotel systems, management, finance, strategic planning, human-resource planning and international tourism. A major project, accounting for 50 per cent of the final marks, completes the course.

Cardiff: University of Wales College of Cardiff

Diploma in Tourism

Part-time, two years: four weekend courses per year plus tutorials and seminars. Designed for those aged twenty-three or over, with at least three years practical tourism experience, and who do not have the opportunity for full-time study. Part I of the programme includes: financial aspects, communication systems, tourism industry legislation; part II: leisure and recreation; part III: passenger transportation, travel agents and tour operators; part IV: planning development and marketing.

MSc Tourism

Full-time, one year. The three modules of this programme include: *structure and organization of tourism* – history, significance and dimensions of tourism, visitor attraction and leisure management; *professional studies* – passenger transportation, accommodation and hospitality management, tourist information technology, planning and development, financial management and tourism project funding, marketing; *related studies* – language study and elective courses.

Edinburgh: Queen Margaret College

Postgraduate Diploma Hospitality Management

Full-time, one year. This programme, designed for non-catering graduates, aims to foster a professional and imaginative attitude to management practices. It is divided into two semesters and includes an industrial placement and project. Six modules must be completed from the following: hospitality practice and operations; finance and business systems; marketing and the hospitality consumer; management for the hospitality and tourism industry; tourism and leisure; management information systems.

The first of the two fifteen-week semesters covers financial and business operations, marketing and the hospitality consumer, hospitality practice and operations. A four-week industrial placement immediately precedes the second semester, which covers financial and business management, applied and creative hospitality management, and includes a hospitality enterprise project.

Glasgow: The Queen's College

Postgraduate Diploma Hotel, Catering and Accommodation Management

Full-time, one year. Catering studies form a major part of the college-based studies: food production, food service including beverage provision, menu planning, hygiene, nutrition and microbiology. Accommodation studies covers the planning and control of buildings, the provision of utilities and services, the organization of cleaning and maintenance, and the welfare of guests. Other subjects are management principles and strategic management, finance and accountancy, legal studies and social science. During the second term, students spend five weeks in a supervised industrial placement.

Glasgow: University of Strathclyde

Postgraduate Diploma/MSc Hotel Administration

Full-time: PgD nine months, MSc one year. The curriculum comprises five classes. Four are compulsory: hotel operations, hotel administration, hotel finance and control, and hotel cuisine. The fifth is chosen from: international tourism, evaluation of tourist facilities, tourism administration, marketing, or an approved class offered by the Strathclyde Business School.

Students for the MSc continue to complete their thesis (dissertation) under the guidance of a supervisor.

Postgraduate Diploma/MSc Tourism

Full-time, PgD nine months, MSc one year; part-time, PgD two years. There are three required classes in this programme: international tourism, tourism administration, and evaluation of tourist facilities. The fourth class can be selected from: tourism in developing countries, tourism in the UK, or other acceptable postgraduate course within Strathclyde Business School.

Guildford: University of Surrey

Postgraduate Diploma/MSc: modular course in tourism and hotel management

Full-time, one year plus. The main course extends over two terms of ten weeks each during the autumn and spring terms. Successful candidates can then proceed to prepare an individual thesis (dissertation) during the final term to qualify for the MSc award. All students are required to study the three core modules: principles of tourism, financial management, and organizational behaviour, and a minimum of fourteen modules overall.

To specialize, students must pass at least six preferred modules. For those opting for the International Hotel Management route, for example, the choice includes hotel management, international hotel finance, hotel and restaurant marketing, accommodation operations, profiles of accommodation, information management, statistical analysis in tourism, and marketing principles. The other qualification routes are: Tourism Management, Tourism Planning and Development, Tourism Marketing, Tourism Studies (for those who do not wish to specialize).

A one-year foundation course is available for those who have professional qualifications and experience somewhat below the standard requirement. It is primarily aimed at overseas students, and covers six areas of study: tourist industry/tourism and development, economics, aspects of management, management science, research method, and accommodation management.

Postgraduate Diploma/MSc Tourism and Hospitality Education

Short courses/distance learning; full-time, one year plus. Designed specifically to meet the needs of educators in further and higher education, this programme provides an understanding of the complex field of tourism including economic, social, cultural, environmental, political, technological and physical aspects.

Apart from the two core modules, there are a variety of specialized modules in tourism and hospitality, such as marketing for tourism, passenger transportation systems and management, hotel management, marketing for hospitality; and in education, such as curriculum and course design, distance learning, education management and administration.

Huddersfield: The University of Huddersfield

Postgraduate Diploma Catering and Applied Nutrition

Full-time, one year. This course is designed for those who have qualifications in the natural or applied sciences, and wish to retrain for the catering industry, or upgrade existing knowledge in the general areas of catering systems, catering technology and applied nutrition.

Postgraduate Diploma International Hospitality Management

Full-time, one year. Emphasis on the international dimension of the industry – for students with a management, financial or social science qualification.

Jordanstown and Londonderry: University of Ulster

Postgraduate Diploma Hotel and Catering Management

Full-time, one year; part-time, two years. The taught element covers such subjects as catering management, the hotel and catering industry, personnel, marketing and financial management, and operational studies – an examination of the technical and managerial aspects of food and beverage production and service and accommodation. The second element of the course is an individual project undertaken in conjunction with a company or organization in the industry. Students who reach an acceptable standard may be eligible to transfer to the MSc programme.

MSc Hotel and Catering Management

Full-time, one year; part-time, two to four years. Students' analytical and interpretive abilities will be enhanced on this programme. Supervision for the dissertation is available for a wide range of areas in hospitality management, tourism and food studies.

Lancaster University

MA Tourism and Recreation

Full-time, one year; part-time, two years. This course is designed for people from a wide variety of disciplines, as well as professionals from the industry. There are three core modules: the geography of tourism and leisure; tourism and history; cultural change and contemporary tourism and leisure. Students are then able to concentrate on particular aspects for further study, choosing three modules from the following: art and nature, aesthetics of the environment, land as a community, tourism, design and leisure, the environment, recreation and tourism, and research methods.

Leeds Metropolitan University

Postgraduate Diploma Hotel, Catering and Institutional Management

Full-time, one year; part-time, variable. Modules concentrate on the management of all resources, and business studies including finance, law, marketing and information technology. The programme structure encourages self-development and problem-solving skills. In addition, students are expected to work on their own using specialized computer software packages and research techniques.

Postgraduate Diploma/MA in Leisure and Human Potential

Full-time, one year; part-time, five semesters. Alternative sets of core modules are offered: recreation, health and lifestyle; and leisure theory, policy and management. The last group is aimed at those interested in strategic decision-making in leisure industries.

London: Middlesex University

Master of Business Administration (with option in tourism management)

Part-time, three years. With its emphasis on an integrated approach to decision making, this course is for managers in the private and public sectors, and for professional people whose work involves management. Year 1 concentrates on the foundation business disciplines which will be applied later in the course, including: the firm and its economic environment, organizational behaviour, accounting and finance, and quantitative methods. Year 2 includes a module on the international business environment with a special focus on Europe, together with a team mini-project and four business functions: marketing, financial, human resource and operations management. Year 3 concentrates on business problem analysis.

The tourism management option, available in year 3, examines how different organizations meet the growing demand for international and domestic tourism. Students evaluate the economic, social and political importance of the tourism business and examine research into visitors' behaviour, approaches to destination planning and development and competitive strategy.

A residential week of full-time study is an integral part of year 2, when it focuses on managerial skills; and year 3, when it is based overseas and focuses on a specific area of business. The dissertation or thesis normally relates to a project carried out in the student's own organization.

Holders of an honours degree in Business Studies or closely related subject, DMS and certain other postgraduate diplomas, may be admitted direct to year 2. A minimum of two years management experience is required for entry to the course, or work in a responsible position.

London: Roehampton Institute

Graduate Diploma/MA Sociology and Anthropology of Travel and Tourism

Full-time, one year; part-time, two years. Applicants should have a second class honours degree or equivalent in sociology, anthropology or related social science. The programme is divided into seven taught modules. Compulsory are: introduction to the sociology and anthropology of travel and tourism; the political economy of travel and tourism; and thesis writing (MA students only). The options include: tourism, heritage and environment; tourism and the third world; tourism and the elderly; tourism and pilgrimage; inner city tourism; tourism, ritual and myth; the economic and social history of tourism. MA students are also required to write a dissertation of about 20,000 words. Awarding body is the University of Surrey.

London: Schiller International University

MBA International Hotel and Tourism Management

MIM Hotel and Tourism Management

Full-time, one year. The emphasis in the MBA is on business subjects such as managerial finance and accounting, marketing management, organizational behaviour, management planning and control, methods of business research and analysis. Hotel management courses include food service systems, international travel and tourism, tourism planning and marketing.

There are rather more hotel management courses on the MIM – Master of International Management – and three business subjects from a choice which includes organizational behaviour, micro and macroeconomics, management and the economic environment, economics of developing countries.

London: Thames Valley University

Postgraduate Diploma in Hospitality Studies

Full-time, one year. Designed as a conversion course for non-hotel and catering graduates, the first semester concentrates on the fundamental skills and disciplines required for effective management in the hospitality industry. The second semester is spent in industry, and for the third, students choose a subject option and complete a project.

London: University of North London

Diploma in Management Studies (Leisure)

Part-time, two years. This programme is designed for those working in the leisure industry, or pursuing a career path with the end goal of a managerial job in leisure. Subjects studied in part one of the course (two terms) include: introduction to management; economics: finance; quantitative analysis; organization behaviour; leisure meanings, motivations and behaviour. Part two, which extends over the remaining four terms and the summer vacation of the second year, includes: finance; marketing; leisure providers, policies and practices; operational management; employee relations; and a specialist leisure option.

MA Leisure and Tourism Studies

Full-time, one year; part-time, two years. This programme introduces a range of disciplinary perspectives on leisure and tourism, and examines the subject in an inter-disciplinary manner. Part 1 units (terms one to three) include: leisure, tourism and lifestyle; public policy; leisure and tourism and the environment; economics; research issues and methods. Part 2 units (terms four to six) include: resource allocation: the political economy of leisure and tourism; tourism development.

Manchester Metropolitan University

Postgraduate Diploma/MSc Hotel and Catering Studies

PgD: full-time, one year; MSc: part-time, one to three years. Three themes: *operational management* – food and beverage management, accommodation studies and management techniques; *business management* – manpower studies, marketing, financial management, law and information technology; *external environment* – marketing statistics, sociology, economics. Four-week period of industrial experience.

Postgraduate Diploma/MSc Tourism

PgD: full-time, one year; MSc: part-time, one to five years. This programme has two strands: tourism and management. The first includes the economics, geography and sociology of tourism; the second, marketing, finance, information technology, personnel and law. There is a four-week period of industrial experience and an overseas field study.

Middlesbrough: University of Teesside

Leisure Management: Certificate in Management/Diploma in Management Studies/Master of Business Administration

Part-time: one year per stage plus one semester for major project for MBA. Any of the modules on this linked programme can be taken individually if desired. The academic year is divided into two semesters of fifteen weeks each, requiring attendance on an afternoon and evening basis one day per week, or two evenings per week.

The integrated programme allows for a systematic progression through courses according to the level of individual career development. Also it enables key themes to be developed at different levels – in particular, the development of a strategic approach, and managing in an international context. Other subjects covered include: *on the CIM* – information technology, managing self in a social context, managing people at work, managing in a competitive environment, making decisions, leisure and people, leisure environment; *on the DMS* – managing the value chain, managing behavioural change, project preparation and management, leisure technology and operations, services marketing, financial management, leisure planning and provision. The DMS also includes a residential conference in The Netherlands; *on the MBA* – management of organizations, developing organizations, strategic management, decision support systems, entrepreneurship and new business development, public policy and management, strategic marketing.

Newcastle: University of Northumbria at Newcastle

Postgraduate Diploma/MA Tourism Management

Full-time, one year. The emphasis is on developing skills and knowledge relevant for people working in organizations concerned with incoming tourism: local authorities, regional tourist boards, museums, resorts, and so forth. Two full terms are taken up with formal teaching in core subjects such as marketing, tourism environment, tourism resources, quantitative methods, tourism research, promotion, planning and policy. One option is also studied: arts management, leisure management or general tourism management. The final six weeks involve a project in which the student takes on the role of tourism management consultant within a tourism firm or organization.

Nottingham: The Nottingham Trent University

Postgraduate Diploma/MA Tourism Studies (Planning and Management)

Full-time, one year; part-time, two years. Primarily designed for people who work in tourism or tourism-related industries, this course aims to develop an advanced understanding of the planning dimensions of tourism, tourism policy and tourism development.

Much of the course is concerned with the impact of the industry on its economics, social, cultural and geographical environment and emphasis is placed on tourism planning from both the viewpoint of government bodies and from that of tourism operators. The nature of the tourism experience is explored, and the need for quality of provision.

Oxford Brookes University

Postgraduate Diploma/MSc Hotel and Catering Management

Block release, PgD one year, MSc two years. Applicants must normally be a minimum of 25-years-old, take a postgraduate entry test and, either possess a graduate or equivalent professional qualification together with at least two years managerial experience, or possess at least five years managerial experience. The applicant's employer agrees to assume financial responsibility and to provide the necessary support for work-based learning and project work.

Polytechnic-based studies are organized in a series of one-week residential course units, eight for the Diploma and fourteen for the MSc. Topics covered include personal diagnosis, marketing management, financial management, human-resource management, and management skills (for the Diploma and MSc); advanced management skills, business development, project development, organizational change, implementation of policies, and personal action plan (for the MSc). A thesis (dissertation) also has to be completed for the MSc.

Portsmouth: University of Portsmouth and Highbury College

Postgraduate Diploma Hotel and Catering Management

Full-time, one year. Designed for graduates from disciplines other than hotel and catering, the key areas of study include food, beverage and accommodation systems and management, facilities management, financial and human-resource management, hospitality marketing, business economics, data processing and strategic management. A minimum of six weeks appropriate industrial experience is a pre-course requirement.

Preston: University of Central Lancashire

Postgraduate Diploma Tourism, Leisure and Service Management

Full-time, one year. The two-week induction phase of this (conversion) programme is designed to encourage the development of self-management skills, and includes a two-day residential course together with orientation visits to industry. The teaching phase, from October to March, incorporates seven units: business modelling and information systems, management processes, group industrial consultancy project, managing consumer services, managing leisure operations, tourism marketing and management, and support workshops. This is followed by the two-week conclusion phase, designed to integrate the individual units and prepare students for the sixteen-week placement phase. The focal part of the programme, this provides an opportunity for students to develop the learning of the tourism and leisure industry from practical experience with organizations in Lancashire and elsewhere.

Sheffield Hallam University

MSc Tourism, Food and Hospitality Management

Full-time, four terms. The fourth term is a period of supervised work experience. The university-based studies include information technology, equipment and structure and design of premises, management principles, finance, law, marketing, human-resource management, the provision and management of food and accommodation, transport, recreation and leisure, entertainments and attractions.

Sheffield University

Diploma/MA Leisure Management

Full-time, one year; part-time, two years. The taught element of the course consists of six modules: history and philosophy of leisure, leisure policy, planning and organization, economics of leisure and tourism, financial management, human-resource and operational management, and marketing leisure. Research information and quantitative methods assist with the preparation of coursework and dissertations. In each module the concern is to raise the critical awareness of students on the issues involved, to provide a framework for the analysis of public policy and planning of leisure. Field work gives the opportunities to apply classwork to practical situations. Those who register for the MA degree spend an additional six months on research and their thesis.

Open University

Master of Business Administration (MBA)

Distance learning, from three to four years up to six years. The MBA is at the top of the Open Business School's three-tier structure of management education. The accelerated route to an MBA is open to managers aged twenty-seven or over, with an honours degree or equivalent. For those without qualifications an access route is provided by the OU Professional Certificate and Professional Diploma in Management, which embody the MCI units of competence.

Stage I comprises a broad foundation addressing key management issues, concepts and areas. The accelerated route, for one credit, involves, on average 440 hours of study, the open access route, for two credits, 880 hours. Subjects covered include: managing people, accounting and the PC for managers, marketing in action, planning and managing change, information systems and IT for managers, managing in the competitive environment.

Stage II comprises a core strategic management course (a half credit, 220 hours), and a range of optional courses of a broadly inter-disciplinary nature from which three are selected (for three and a half credits, 1,540 hours in total). Options include creative management, corporate financial strategy, human-resource strategies, the challenge of the external environment, business research project, managing public services, and manufacturing management for strategic advantage.

11

Directory of organizations

Académie Culinaire de France

Founded Paris 1883, the British branch in 1980: a select group of chefs working in senior positions. Aims to maintain and uphold the highest standards in the culinary art; training is a key concern – scheme for young chefs operated with Bournemouth and Poole College, see Chapter 5. Annual competitions: *Awards of Excellence* aimed at the UK's best young commis chefs, patissiers and waiting staff; *Meilleur Ouvrier de Grande Bretagne* (MOGB), the highest and most prestigious award to be bestowed on a chef.

(In 1990, the Académie gave its support, along with government and many other organizations, to the formation of the **Academy of Culinary Arts**. An ambitious programme of professional courses for chefs and restaurant managers was launched, but the recession affected take-up, and after a short time the Academy was forced into liquidation, declaring its intention to re-open in better times.)

C/o Mrs Sara Jayne, 517 Old York Road, London SW18 1TS
Tel: 081 874 8500   Fax: 081 874 8575.

Academy of Wine Service (AWS)

Founded 1988 to raise the standard of education and skills in the service of wine in hotel and catering establishments. Membership: those seeking development and accreditation, with the intention of following a career in the industry; those already making a professional contribution to the sale, service and appreciation of wine. Runs examinations and training schemes at various levels, including home study and trainer training.

Five Kings House, 1 Queen Street Place, London EC4R 1QS
Tel: 0483 302373   Fax: 04867 5666. Training Director: Barrie Larvin, 66 Clissold Court, Greenway Close, London N4 2EZ
Tel: 081 409 4671.

Advisory Body for Social Services Catering

Advises on provision of efficient, economic, high-quality catering service which promotes healthy diets and meets clients' needs in wide range of welfare catering units, including children's homes, old people's homes, day centres, hostels for the mentally ill and physically handicapped. Gives help on food hygiene, kitchen design and equipment, suppliers' contracts and tenders, also staff training support.

Social Service Department, Head Office, Leeds City Council, Sweet Street, Leeds LS11 9DQ
Tel: 0532 348080.

Association of British Travel Agents (ABTA)

Formed 1950. Self-regulatory body, representing around 90 per cent of Britain's tour operators and travel agents. Ensures high standards of training for the industry; runs training courses for all levels of experience. **ABTA National Training Board** (**ABTANTB**), lead body for sector, offers comprehensive qualification scheme, working jointly with C&G, BTEC, SCOTVEC and other awarding bodies. Approved early 1992 as joint awarding body with C&G for level 1 NVQ Travel Services. Operates Youth and Employment Training schemes under its own managing agency; runs direct training courses; publishes range of self-study materials, and computer-based training packages.

55–57 Newman Street, London W1P 4AH
Tel: 071 637 2444   Fax: 071 637 0713.
ABTA National Training Board, Waterloo House, 11–17 Chertsey Road, Woking, Surrey GU21 5AL
Tel: 0483 727321   Fax: 0483 756698.

Association Culinaire Française de Secours Mutuel

Founded 1903 by Georges Auguste Escoffier and Emile Fetu 'de maintenir et répandre la bonne réputation de l'art culinaire français' – to maintain and propagate the good name of French cuisine. Much of its work is about good fellowship – to strengthen the bonds which exist among chefs by sharing information, helping individual members in time of difficulty, collaborating with fellow associations, acknowledging those who have exceptionally distinguished themselves during their career.

Charles Mercier, President, Association Culinaire Française, 1 Old Compton Street, London W1V 5PH
Tel: 071 437 7485.

Association of Domestic Management (ADM)

Professional body for those in domestic services management within National Health Service, local authorities and further education. Current membership around 400. Formed 1974 to take over and build on the work of the Hospitals Domestic Administrators Association (formed 1960s).

Gill Hallsworth, National Secretary, 14 Radbourn Drive, Sutton Coldfield B74 2NE
Tel: 021 355 4731.

Association of Licensed Free Traders (ALFT)

Formed early 1980s. Largest independent purchasing group in the licensed free trade (1992 membership over 12,000). Members also have access to a wide range of advisory services, including obtaining and managing free houses, finance and training.

Dane House, 55 London Road, St Albans, Herts AL1 1LJ
Tel: 0727 41085.

Association of Marine Catering and Supply

With objective of promoting and improving efficiency within the industry, encourages members to pool knowledge and experience. Liaises with colleges and awarding bodies offering catering schemes, and with **Merchant Navy Training Board**, lead body for sector.

30/32 St Mary Axe, London EC3A 8ET (postal address only).

Automatic Vending Association of Britain (AVAB)

Trade body. Represents interests of automatic vending machine manufacturers and distributors, component and commodity suppliers, and contract operators of catering and retail vending machine systems. Annual handbook and buyers guide.

Bassett House, High Street, Banstead, Surrey SM7 2LZ
Tel: 0737 357211   Fax: 0737 370501.

British Accreditation Council for Independent Further and Higher Education (BAC)

Exists to define, monitor and improve standards in private colleges, schools and other independent further and higher education institutions in Britain.

Inspects accommodation and learning resources, administration and staffing, quality control, welfare arrangements, and teaching (involving assessment of professional competence of academic staff). Regularly updated *Directory of Accredited Independent Colleges in Britain* lists around ninety establishments 'recognized as efficient'. Sponsors include British Council, national validating bodies, public and professional examining boards, universities and colleges.

(Middlesex Polytechnic), All Saints, White Hart Lane, London N17 8HR
Tel: 081 368 1299.

Brewers' Society

Formed 1904. Powerful trade association representing most of UK's brewers. Publishes *Innkeeping*, authoritative manual on the licensed trade, also careers information on management opportunities in licensed retailing.

42 Portman Square, London W1H 0BB
Tel: 071 486 4831   Fax: 071 935 3991.

British Association for Commercial and Industrial Education (BACIE)

Membership drawn from industry, commerce, education, Government, employer's associations, trade unions and professional bodies. Exerts powerful influence on national training policy. Publishes monthly journal, books and manuals on specific aspects of vocational training. Offers wide range of courses for training specialists, managers and others wishing to develop inter-personal and management skills. Members have access to comprehensive information service and library.

16 Park Crescent, London W1N 4AP
Tel: 071 636 5351   Fax: 071 436 2624.

British Association of Hotel Accountants (BAHA)

Professional body for those involved in financial aspects of hotel, catering and leisure. Objectives include achievement of uniformity in the industry's accounting. For Associate membership must pass the BAHA training programme, or have over two years appropriate experience, e.g. as assistant financial controller, leading consultant or audit manager. Fellowship conferred on Associate Members of over two years standing who pass BAHA Course of Professional Education (CPE), or have over two years experience as unit financial controller. (CPE programme: three full weekends of lectures and workshops, case work and a final assignment.) Part sponsors annual Hotech exhibition and seminars on the latest computer technology.

PO Box 128, Edgware, Middx HA8 6TR
Tel: 081 952 0673   Fax: 081 952 0673.

British Hospitality Association (BHA)

Powerful trade association, over 22,000 members (including many local hotel and tourist associations). (Before January 1992, *British Hotels, Restaurants and Caterers Association (BHRCA)*. Origins can be traced back to 1907 when the British Hotels and Restaurants Association was formed.) Represented on HOTREC, IHA and FERCO (Federation of European Contract Caterers). Code of practice binds members to maintain specific standards towards their customers and staff. Provides wide range of membership support services including hygiene helpline, advice on legal matters, recruitment and training of staff, annual wages and salaries survey, monthly magazine *Voice* (previously *British Hotelier and Restaurateur*), business files, buyer's guides, notices and stationery, annual hotel and restaurant guide.

40 Duke Street, London W1M 6HR
Tel: 071 499 6641   Fax: 071 355 4596.

British Incoming Tour Operators Association

Founded 1977. Represents interests of companies deriving substantial part of income from provision of tours and tourism services within UK for visitors from overseas.

18a Coulson Street, London SW3 3NB
Tel: 071 581 4101   Fax: 071 225 3834.

British Institute of Innkeeping (BII)

Founded 1981. Professional body for those involved in day-to-day supervision of public houses: free traders, tenants, managers, brewery company executives; also those starting a career. Established training and development framework for licensed retailing, developed membership examinations and distance learning material. Awarding body for on-licensed premises management NVQs/SVQs at levels 3 and 4. Quarterly journal *The Innkeeper*.

51–53 High Street, Camberley, Surrey GU15 3RG
Tel: 0276 684449   Fax: 0276 23045.

British Institute of Management (BIM)

See *Institute of Management*.

British Universities Accommodation Consortium (BUAC)

Marketing consortium of universities providing accommodation for conferences, exhibitions, training facilities, groups, families and individuals.

Box No 737, University Park, Nottingham NG7 2RD
Tel: 0602 504571   Fax: 0602 422505.

Business in the Community (BITC)

Works to develop involvement of business in the community, and extend and foster education–industry links. Helps establish partnership activities between local employers and schools to increase number of work experience placements, encourages teacher secondments to industry, and promotion of career opportunities within industry through participation in initial teacher training. Newsletter *Partnership Points*.

227a City Road, London EC1V 1LX
Tel: 071 253 3716   Fax: 071 253 2309.
Scottish Business in the Community, Romano House, 43 Station Road, Corstorphine, Edinburgh EH2 7AF
Tel: 031 556 9761/2.

Business and Technology Education Council (BTEC)

Established 1983. (Until 1 December 1991 Business and *Technician* Education Council.) Took over roles of BEC (Business Education Council) and TEC (Technician Education Council), including responsibility for Diplomas/Higher Diplomas in hotel and catering. Remit from Government to establish educational qualifications in England, Wales and Northern Ireland and determine criteria for awarding them. Everything connected with a BTEC course needs BTEC approval: college or centre offering it; people who teach it; course structure, content and assessment. Team of over 1,300 part-time staff (moderators: drawn from industry, commerce, and education; specially trained for the job) monitor and report on every course at least twice a year. At any given time over half a million students studying on a BTEC course, at over 700 colleges, universities, polytechnics and training organizations, including some overseas. On-job experience important ingredient of all BTEC qualifications: BTEC has proud record for increasing quality and availability of work-related education, for people who have jobs, or preparing for employment. In late 1991, accredited by NCVQ as awarding body for NVQs levels 1 to 4 in catering and hospitality.

Central House, Upper Woburn Place, London WC1H 0HH
Tel: 071 413 8400   Fax: 071 383 6068.

Careers Research and Advisory Centre (CRAC)

Non-profit-making body. Founded 1964 to create links between education and employment. CRAC publications, research and advisory services provide help to young people, their teachers and parents as they make choices about further education, training and employment. Also offers training, information and advice on wide range of education-business matters.

Sheraton House, Castle Park, Cambridge CB3 0AX
Tel: 0223 460277   Fax: 0223 311708.

Catering Industry Group (CIG)

Formed 1974 under auspices of Industrial Marketing Research Association (IMRA). 'Pan-industry forum': through regular meetings and discussions, seeks to encourage deeper cooperation between all involved in world of catering – caterers, distributors, suppliers and advisers.

c/o Naomi Arnold Consultancy, 12 Freemans Close, Stoke Poges, Bucks SL2 4ER
Tel: 0753 663305   Fax: 0753 663629.

Catering Managers Association (CMA)

Formed 1947 to foster highest standards of efficiency throughout catering industry. Promotes, supports or opposes measures which affect the industry, and provides facilities for education and social cooperation for members' benefit. Full membership: those holding responsible position in the industry. Affiliated membership: manufacturers, suppliers, colleges, training and education providers.

Peter Godbold MBE, National Secretary, Kirby College of Further Education, Roman Road, Linthorpe, Middlesbrough, Cleveland TS5 5PJ
Tel: 0642 813706.

Catering Teachers' Association (CTA)

Formed 1960 to support and strengthen catering education; to foster and maintain good relations among those engaged in teaching catering students, and to represent their views on issues of concern. Conference and meeting programme at national and regional level; newsletter.

Ian Littlewood, Catering Teachers' Association, Runshaw College, Langdale Road, Leyland, Lancashire PR5 2DQ
Tel: 0772 432511   Fax: 0772 622295.

CENTRA

Established 1990 to provide comprehensive service to education and training throughout the north west: staff development and training, youth and community information and advisory services; examination and assessment services on behalf of the North West Regional Association of Education Authorities (formerly the North Western Regional Advisory Council for Further Education incorporating the Union of Lancashire and Cheshire Institutes). Responsible for monitoring some City and Guilds schemes in region. Offers own catering schemes.

Town Hall, Walkden Road, Worsley, Manchester M28 4QE
Tel: 061 702 8700   Fax: 061 703 8815.

Central Bureau for Educational Visits and Exchanges

Deals with European Commission's Young Worker Exchange programme; responsible for UK Centre for European Education. Helps with lecturer, teacher and student exchanges; study visits. Administers bi-lateral programmes in further education. Publishes *Further and Higher Education LINKup* twice yearly.

Seymour Mews House, Seymour Mews, London W1H 9PE
Tel: 071 486 5101.

CERT

Republic of Ireland's state tourism training agency, responsible for recruitment and training of personnel at all levels of the hotel, catering and tourism industry. (Founded in 1963 as the Council for Education, Recruitment and Training.) Objective: to ensure high operational standards in the industry through a professional trained workforce and business support services. Activities include development of national training systems and facilities, on-going identification of manpower and training needs, industry-based training of tourism personnel, recruitment and training of new entrants through college-based programmes, basic skills training for unemployed adults, business development and advisory services to industry.

CERT House, Amiens Street, Dublin 1
Tel: 010 3531 742555   Fax: 010 3531 742821.

Charles Forte Foundation

Set up 1988 (marking Lord Forte's eightieth birthday) to encourage excellence and help people in the industry acquire new professional skills. Support considered for: those who wish to obtain further qualifications, but lack the funds to do so; those planning a project to study marketing or operations to increase their knowledge and skills, but who need a grant for living expenses; those planning research relevant to the industry at postgraduate level, but unable to fund it adequately; teachers planning a sabbatical leave which will broaden their knowledge; educational institutions planning to establish a facility which will improve the effectiveness of their teaching.

The Secretary, Charles Forte Foundation, 166 Holborn, London WC1V 6TT.

Chartered Institute of Marketing (CIM)

Founded 1911. Granted Royal Charter 1989. Professional body: 26,000 members (1992). Objectives: to develop the knowledge of marketing; to raise awareness of the principles and standards of marketing practice throughout industry and commerce. Controls and administers examinations for the Certificate and Diploma in Marketing, and Certificate in Sales Management. Full programme of two to five days residential courses offered at the College of Marketing in Cookham; seminars and workshops throughout the UK; range of publications and membership services.

Moor Hall, Cookham, Maidenhead, Berks SL6 9QH
Tel: 0628 524922   Fax: 0628 531382.

Chefs and Cooks Circle

Founded 1947 to encourage chefs to aim for the highest possible standards of culinary excellence. Helps members to travel and compete all over the world, including the Culinary Olympics, organizes competitions such as the *Junior Master Chef of Great Britain*, and awards medals and diplomas to recognize outstanding success. Officially recognized by Fédération Mondiale des Sociétés de Cuisiners (World Association of Cooks Societies).

PO Box 239, London N14 7NT.

City and Guilds of London Institute (CGLI or C&G)

Independent, non-profit making body, founded 1878 by the Corporation of the City of London and sixteen Livery Companies 'to develop a national system of technical education'. Royal Charter granted by Queen Victoria, 1900. Works closely with industry, commerce and the public services so that C&G qualifications are linked to various levels of competence needed at all stages in a career, from pre-vocational education and foundation programmes for 14- to 16-year-olds, to the highest levels of professional practice, with the senior awards of Licentiateship, Graduateship, Membership and

Fellowship; over one and a half million entries annually for C&G awards, in over 400 subjects, from chemicals and metallurgy, to family and community care, offered in over 7,000 approved colleges and training centres worldwide. Catering and hospitality important provision since 1944–45; C&G schemes (jointly with HCTB) among first to receive provisional accreditation by NCVQ in 1988; full accreditation from late 1991, for NVQs levels 1 to 3; and from early 1992 at level 4, in conjunction with HCIMA. Joint awarding body with ABTANTB for NVQ level 1 in Travel Services. New C&G NVQ awards replaced such schemes as Cookery for the Catering Industry (706–1, 2, 3), Food and Beverage Service (707–1 and 2), Accommodation Services (708), Beverage Sales and Service (717), Hotel Reception and Front Office Practice (720); the specific skills series, e.g. 7001 Call Order Cooking; and the four master schemes – Master Chef, Master Restaurateur, Master Housekeeper and Master Receptionist.

Licentiateship of the City and Guilds of London Institute (LCG) recognizes achievement in education, training and employment. To qualify for the LCG in Catering, a candidate must hold: *C&G catering qualification*, e.g. 706–2, 707–2, or NVQ level 2; *advanced catering certificate*, e.g. 706–3, 720, or NVQ level 3; *level 4 qualification*, e.g. BTEC or SCOTVEC HND, BTEC Certificate in Management Studies, NEBSM Certificate or Diploma; *an agreed form of recognition for achievement in industry*, e.g. completion of recognized training programme with National Health Service, Merchant Navy Training Board, Scottish Health Service, or HM Forces; *over five years relevant work experience.*

76 Portland Place, London W1N 4AA and 46 Britannia Street, London WC1X 9RG
Tel: 071 278 2468   Fax: 071 278 9460 (Britannia Street).

Civic Catering Association (CCA)

Formed 1962 to provide forum for consultation and cooperation between local authorities operating catering services.

Mr G Swift, Secretary, Civic Catering Association, Leisure Department, Trencherfield Mill, Wallgate, Wigan WN3 4EF
Tel: 0942 828500   Fax: 0942 828540.

Club Secretaries and Managers Association (CSMA)

Established 1975. Membership by invitation to those with professional catering backgrounds, working in major private members clubs; seventeen plus four associate members (1991), mostly London. Some member clubs offer bursary scheme for final year college students. Recipients expected to join donor club after completing course, and after two years or so working through various departments, are offered junior management position.

George Irving, Chairman CSMA, c/o The Overseas Bankers Club, 7 Lothbury, London EC2R 7HH
Tel: 071 606 5883   Fax: 071 600 3083.

College Caterers' Association (CCA)

Formed 1967, to promote advancement of catering and accommodation services within the educational sector, and encourage better understanding of the needs of the sector's management and staff.

Peter Railton, Chairman (1990/92), College Caterers' Association, c/o University of Humberside, 'Ivanhoe', 655 Beverley Road, Hull HU7 7RT.

Confederation of Tourism, Hotel and Catering Management (CTH&CM)

Formerly Institute of Hotel, Tourism and Catering Management. Provides examination and qualification scheme for private colleges. Each award linked to membership grade: *Associate* – Certificate in Catering/Tourism/Tourism and Hotel Management; *Membership* – Diplomas in Professional Cookery/ Tourism, Hotel and Catering Management; *Fellowship* – Advanced Diploma in Professional Cookery/Tourism, Hotel and Catering Management. Bakery Certificate also offered.

204 Barnett Wood Lane, Ashtead, Surrey KT21 2DB
Tel: 03722 78572.

Confederation of National Hotel, Restaurant and Catering Associations in the European Community (HOTREC)

Represents interests of members (which include the BHA) in European Parliament and other EC institutions. Stagiaires scheme, for exchange of trainees for work experience within the EC, is a HOTREC initiative.

80 rue de la Roquette, 75544 Paris Cedex 11, France
Tel: 010 33 1 4700-84-57.

Cookery and Food Association (CFA)

Established 1885 to promote and develop the art and technology of cookery; supervisory and management skills related to cookery and associated professions. Publishes *Food and Cookery Review* six times a year. Organizes salons culinaires, culinary contests, demonstrations and talks. Two divisions promote the professional standing of chefs and waiting staff: *Craft Guild of Chefs*, established 1965; *Restaurant Services Guild* established 1985.

1 Victoria Parade, by 331 Sandycombe Road, Richmond, Surrey TW9 3NB
Tel: 081 948 3870.

Council on Hospitality Management Education (CHME)

For higher education colleges in UK offering hotel and catering courses at HND level and above: to encourage development of hospitality management education, training and research in colleges and universities; to foster links between education and employers, and with professional associations.

Mrs Helen Price, Chairman CHME, Thames Valley University, Wellington Street, Slough SL1 1YG
Tel: 0753 34585.
Dolf Morgendorff, Secretary CHME, University of Central England at Birmingham, Business School, Perry Barr, Birmingham B42 2SU
Tel: 021 331 5000.

Council on Hotel Restaurant and Institutional Education (CHRIE)

Established 1946. Principal educational body for hospitality and tourism in USA: over 500 schools of hospitality management, of which one third offer degrees.

1200 17th Street, New Washington 7th floor, Washington DC 20036
Tel: 202 3315990.

Council for National Academic Awards (CNAA)

Established by Royal Charter 1964 as main awarding body outside university sector. First CNAA degree in hotel and catering started 1971. Many others followed, as well as programmes leading to CNAA's Diploma in Higher Education (DipHE), Postgraduate Diploma, and Masters degrees. Government announced in 1991 that as part of its plans to remove the distinction between academic education (at universities) and vocational education (at polytechnics and colleges), CNAA would be closed, and awarding status granted to individual polytechnics and colleges who had achieved the appropriate standard. This was a development of the dual system CNAA had introduced in 1987 for accredited institutions to validate, monitor, review and approve new taught degree, certificate and diploma courses on the Council's behalf, and to modify existing courses. For associated institutions, on the other hand, the Council retained responsibility for the final approval of all courses.

344–354 Gray's Inn Road, London WC1X 8BP
Tel: 071 278 4411   Fax: 071 833 1012.

Court of Master Sommeliers

Established 1977 to encourage improved standards of knowledge and service of beverages, in particular wine, in restaurants and hotels. (First Master Sommelier examination held in 1969.) Small, elite body: less than 100 candidates hold the Diploma, the highest level qualification. USA chapter based in San Francisco.

Brian Julyan, Secretary, Court of Master Sommeliers, 27 St Matthews Road, Chelston, Torquay, Devon TQ2 6JA
Tel: 0803 605031.

East Midlands Further Education Council (EMFEC)

Provides examinations and assessment services, on its own behalf, and for C&G and other bodies, including catering and baking schemes. In January 1992 became company limited by guarantee with charitable objects. Colleges and local education authorities have the right of membership. Through regional networks and databases across key sectors, offers support and information to schools, colleges and other educational and training establishments in areas of specialist expertise and human resource development; undertakes curriculum development and research.

Robins Wood House, Robins Wood Road, Aspley, Nottingham NG8 3NH
Tel: 0602 293291   Fax: 0602 299392.

EUHOFA – Association Internationale des Directeurs d'Ecoles Hôtelières

International Association of Hotel School Directors, founded 1955 by group of German, Austrian and Swiss hotel school directors, to improve and advance hotel and catering training and education, and develop its members. Annual conference. Journal.

Secrétariat: Ecole Hôtelière de Lausanne, Le Chalet-à-Gobet, CH-1000 Lausanne 25, Switzerland
Tel: 021/785 1111   Fax: 021/784 1407.

European Association of Hotel and Tourism Schools (AEHT)

Formed 1988 to promote links between educational institutions offering post-compulsory education and training for the hotel and tourism industry across the whole of Europe; over 230 members, from eighteen countries (1992). Provides training seminars for staff from member institutions; work experience networks for staff and students; exchange activities between institutions; annual conference; bulletin (three times per year).

Permanent secretary: Sybille Schoch, c/o Lycee d'Hôtellerie, BP 149, 75 Route du Rhin, 67400 Illkirch, France
Fax: 010 33 88 67 44 36.
UK representative and Vice-President: John Evans, Assistant Principal, Eastleigh College, Chestnut Avenue, Eastleigh, Hants SO4 5HT
Tel: 0703 644011   Fax: 0703 620654.

European Association for Orientation, Vocational Guidance and Educational and Professional Information (Euro-Orientation)

Formed December 1990 to promote guidance and information through research and training, in cooperation with public and private institutions (regional, national, European and international).

Euro-Orientation, Therese Van Cutsem, Rue de Bruxelles 27, B1300 Wavre, Belgium.

European Catering Association (Great Britain) (ECA)

Founded 1937. Industrial Catering Association (ICA) until 1989, when it affiliated with European Catering Association International to provide a broader scope and extra dimension to benefit the industry and its members: direct caterers, catering contractors, their employees, suppliers and distributors.

1 Victoria Parade, by 331 Sandycombe Road, Richmond, Surrey TW9 3NB
Tel: 081 940 4464.

European Centre for the Development of Vocational Training (CEDEFOP)

Set up by European Commission in 1975 as forum for exchange of information and experience among governments, national and international institutions involved in vocational training. UK agency: BACIE (see above). Work includes establishing comparability of vocational training qualifications – as first step to enabling workers to make better use of their qualifications, in particular for purposes of obtaining suitable employment in another member state (see Chapter 6). Aim is *not* to harmonize vocational training systems within the EC, or to bring training levels directly into line with each other; nor to implement legally binding regulations with regard to recognizing vocational training qualifications for all employees who might possibly be affected.

Bundesallee 22, D-1000 Berlin 50, Germany
Tel: 010 49 30 884120.

European Foundation for the Accreditation of Hotelschools (EFAH)

Established early 1992 to set standards, determine procedures and then undertake accreditation of craft and management courses offered by universities, colleges and schools. HCIMA (see below) represented on EFAH board of management.

European Hotel Managers Association (EHMA)

Founded 1972. For managers in four- and five-star hotels, with over 15 years experience, including five as a general manager; twelve British members, fifty French, sixty Italian, forty-six Spanish and about thirty German (1991).

1991 President: Dario Dell'Antonia, General Manager, Hotel de Paris, Monte Carlo.

European Leisure and Recreation Association (ELRA)

Founded 1972 to promote and develop policies and programmes of leisure and recreation throughout Europe; encourage cross-national, interdisciplinary exchange of information, and the raising of training standards.

ILAM House, Lower Basildon, Reading RG8 9NE
Tel: 0491 874222   Fax: 0491 874059.

Higher Education Accommodation Consortium (HEAC)

Founded 1982 to market conference and training facilities and residential accommodation at over sixty member polytechnics and colleges throughout mainland Britain.

36 Collegiate Crescent, Sheffield, South Yorkshire S10 2BP
Tel: 0742 683759   Fax: 0742 661203.

Hospital Caterers Association (HCA)

Formed 1948 to promote and improve standards of catering in UK hospitals; assist the education and training of those employed in the service; promote career opportunities; protect and improve the professional interests and status of National Health Service catering managers. Regular conferences, seminars, meetings and social events; journal, *The Hospital Caterer* (ten times per year); annual reference book.

Mr I V Taylor, Honorary National Secretary, Hospital Caterers Association, Castle Hill Hospital, Castle Road, Cottingham, Hull, East Yorkshire HU16 5JQ
Tel: 0482 875875, ext 3120.

Hotel and Catering Benevolent Association (HCBA)

Origins go back to 1937, when the London Coffee House Keepers Association was formed for purpose of 'relieving aged and decayed members of the trade, their widows and orphans'. Assisting needy men and women from the industry remains HCBA's main purpose. It operates five sheltered housing schemes; provides monthly and one-off grants for the sick and elderly; convalescence to those recovering from illness or injury; low-cost accommodation at PM Clubs for young people just starting their careers.

52 Ridgway, Wimbledon, London SW19 4QR
Tel: 081 946 7561   Fax: 081 944 6211.

Hotel Catering and Institutional Management Association (HCIMA)

Formed 1971 – following merger of HCI (Hotel and Catering Institute) and IMA (Institutional Management Association) – to identify, promote and maintain the highest professional and ethical standards in the international hotel and catering industry. Priorities: to win greater recognition for professional managers, to set and maintain standards, to help managers and potential managers develop and maintain their knowledge and abilities. Lobbies on behalf of the industry in the British and European spheres. Around 23,000 members (1991). Chapters in many countries of the world, local branches throughout UK. Extensively involved in education, examination schemes, course monitoring and accreditation; *Corpus of Knowledge* research, undertaken initially in 1975–77, and subsequently updated, helped determine the scope and range of knowledge that a competent practitioner should have. The Professional Certificate and Professional Diploma (replaced Part A and Part B from 1990) form benchmark against which other qualifications are assessed and recognized for exemption or partial exemption from education and training requirements for membership. Monthly journal *Hospitality*, quarterly *Bibliography of Hotel and Catering Management*, annual reference book, annual salary review, regular technical briefs and information sheets, reading lists and directories. Members can borrow books from well-stocked library by post, have access to information service, advice on careers, salaries and conditions of employment. Seven grades of membership (there are alternatives to the basic requirements, and equivalent qualifications in most cases): *Fellow FHCIMA* – responsible position over five years, corporate member (MHCIMA) over ten years; *Member MHCIMA* – management position, over two years experience at junior or first line management, HCIMA Professional Diploma, degree or HND in hotel and catering management; *Associate AHCIMA* – position of responsibility in the industry, over two years, and non-hotel and catering degree or HND; *Licentiate LHCIMA* – two types of Licentiate membership: graduate Licentiate-ship open to those who have satisfied the educational requirements (e.g. Professional Diploma, Part B, HND or degree), but not yet gained sufficient management experience to qualify for MHCIMA; and, a points scheme designed for those aged twenty-eight and over who have management experience, but cannot meet the usual educational requirements – points up to 100 are allocated for experience (minimum thirty), and further and higher education courses (minimum forty), e.g. C&G 706–2 gives five education points, DMS between twenty-five and forty-five depending on content, and a year's industrial experience gives one point; *Intermediate* – hold Professional Certificate, Part A, or National Diploma and working at supervisory level; *Affiliate* – established managers, senior managers in service or supply companies, or people working in a specialist function within the industry; *Student* – studying on HCIMA or other hotel and catering management course.

191 Trinity Road, London SW17 7HN
Tel: 081 672 4251   Fax: 081 682 1707.

Hotel and Catering Personnel and Training Association (HCPTA)

Formed in 1970s to promote further education and training for personnel managers and training specialists in the industry. Organizes annual industry awareness competition for schools in the London area.

c/o Sandra Burrows, 24 Chestnut Road, Twickenham, Middlesex TW2 5QZ
Tel: 081 894 1279.

Hotel and Catering Training Company (HCTC)

Established 1989, initially as the commercial arm of the Hotel and Catering Training Board (HCTB), and from March 1991 as a company limited by guarantee and registered charity. (HCTB, previously HCITB – I for Industry dropped in 1986 – set up as a statutory training board in 1966, and survived various Government reviews of ITBs.) Four Trustees have overall control, nominated by Brewers' Society (one), British Hospitality Association (two) and Restaurateurs Association of Great Britain (one). Various other associations represented within committee structure. HCTC has three roles: as lead body, as awarding body, and as a commercial training organization. The *lead body* acts as a focus for training and vocational education. Core activities –

funded out of interest on reserves inherited from HCTB, and profits made by commercial activities – include manpower research, careers initiatives and development of occupational standards. The *awarding division* was set up end of 1991, following accreditation to offer NVQs levels 1 to 4 (jointly with BII for on-licensed premises). In Scotland similar arrangements agreed with SCOTVEC, HCIMA and BII in March 1992. HCTC already had considerable experience of work-based qualifications schemes with *Caterbase* – piloted in 1986–87 and made available generally from 1987. Modular in format, Caterbase required candidates to consistently demonstrate ability to perform the tasks involved in, for example, *Care and Maintenance of Keg Beers*, to the required standards under normal working conditions. Quality control involved approval of organizations to offer Caterbase, and of the assessors and countersigning officers who could recommend the award of Caterbase modules. Certain Caterbase modules and success in the related City and Guilds theory examination led to the award of a joint HCTB/C&G certificate. Such certificates were the first to gain provisional NCVQ accreditation, and were the forerunner of the NVQ and SVQ qualifications that replaced Caterbase in 1991. HCTC's *training division* offers a wide range of courses from craft skills up to MBA, and including youth and employment training, trainer training, customer care, small business operations, hygiene, customer care, business and operational management. It publishes videos, books and training manuals, many of them developed specifically to support NVQs and SVQs in catering and hospitality and the licensed trade.

International House, High Street, Ealing, London W5 5DB
Tel: 081 579 2400   Fax. 081 840 6217.

Hotel Employers Group (HEG)

Heads of personnel and, or training, of the largest hotel companies operating in the UK. Members meet regularly to share views on industry developments and training issues. (Proposals announced in 1991 to form a *Catering and Leisure Employers Group*. Modelled after HEG, CLEG would have three main areas of activity: promoting the image of public catering as a career, lobbying Government and EC legislators, interpreting and influencing the education changes taking place.)

David Gill, Deputy Chairman HEG, Holiday Inns Executive Offices, Ditton Road, Langley, Bucks SL3 8PT
Tel: 0753 544255   Fax: 0753 585484.

Hotel Leisure Managers Association

Formed 1991 to act as a business forum, bringing together managers in an effort to increase awareness of hotel health leisure, raise standards of professionalism, and improve education and training opportunities.

Spokesperson: Tim Mayled, The Lygon Arms, Broadway, Worcs WR12 7DU
Tel: 0386 852255   Fax: 0386 858611.

Industrial Society

Founded 1918. Granted Royal Charter 1985. Members: industrial and commercial companies, trade unions, nationalized industries, central and local Government departments and employers' associations. Work concentrates on management and leadership skills, employee communication systems, productive management–union relations, harmonizing conditions of employment, equal opportunities, total quality management, customer care, education-industry links, and developing young people at work for work. Extensive programme of conferences, seminars and workshops; publishes many books, videos and checklists; advice and information service.

Robert Hyde House, 48 Bryanston Square, London W1H 7LN
Tel: 071 262 2401   Fax: 071 706 1096.

Institute of Baths and Recreation Management (IBRM)

Founded 1921. Professional and examining body for those managing indoor leisure facilities, including sports centres and swimming pools. Membership qualifications at four levels: Leisure Technician, Recreation Management Certificate, Diploma Examination, and Continuing Professional Development.

Giffard House, 36–38 Sherrard Street, Melton Mowbray, Leicestershire LE13 1XJ
Tel: 0664 65531   Fax: 0664 501155.

Institute of Brewing

Founded 1886. Covers the whole spectrum of disciplines concerned with brewing, distilling, wine, cider and vinegar making, and a wide selection of allied activities. Education and training key part of its work, with programme of courses leading to Associate and Diploma Master Brewer examinations.

33 Clarges Street, London W1Y 8EE
Tel: 071 499 8144   Fax: 071 499 1156.

Institute of Careers Guidance (ICG)

Founded 1961. (Institute of Careers Officers until 1991.) Professional body for individuals and organizations who have an interest in careers education and guidance, training and employment. Represents the views of the careers service to Government, statutory and voluntary bodies; helps sustain and strengthen the partnership between industry and education.

27a Lower High Street, Stourbridge, West Midlands DY8 1TA
Tel: 0384 376464   Fax: 0384 440830.

Institute of Commercial Management (ICM)

Founded 1979. Professional and examining body specializing in business and management; offers a wide range of vocational qualifications including hotel and catering, travel and tourism.

PO Box 125, Bournemouth BH2 6JH
Tel: 0202 290999   Fax: 0202 293497.

Institute of Hotel Security Management

Formed 1983 to promote mutual support and cooperation between security managers employed in UK hotels, and to encourage a greater awareness of security issues.

c/o Ivan Clark, Director of Security, London Marriott Hotel, Grosvenor Square, London W1A 4AW
Tel: 071 493 1232.

Institute of Leisure and Amenity Management (ILAM)

Formed 1983 (amalgamation of four smaller bodies). Professional and examining body (ILAM Certificate and Diploma) covering every aspect of leisure and recreation. Wide range of short courses and seminars; monthly journal *The Leisure Manager*.

ILAM House, Lower Basildon, Nr Reading, Berks RG8 9NE
Tel: 0491 874222   Fax: 0491 874059.

Institute of Management (IM)

Formed November 1992 by the merger of *British Institute of Management (BIM)* and *Institution of Industrial Managers* (IIM), to promote the development and exercise of professional management. Membership over 75,000 (1992). Wide range of courses and services include in-house training, research into management techniques, salaries and related matters, management information centre, library, specialist reading lists, management publications, monthly journal *The Professional Manager* (was *Management Today* before November 1992). BIM played an active role in the Management Charter Initiative project to assess the competence of the more experienced manager for NVQs and SVQs. In 1990/91, BIM introduced a new competency-based modular certificate and diploma programme following guidelines of the National Forum for Management Education and Development (NFMED), and validated by BTEC. BIM's Competent Manager programme will be integrated with IIM's Leader Series (accredited by NCVQ).

Management House, Cottingham Road, Corby, Northants NN17 1TT
Tel: 0536 204222   Fax: 0536 201651.

Institute of Travel and Tourism (ITT)

Founded 1956 (as Institute of Travel Agents, present name adopted 1976). Professional body for travel and tourism industry. Approves colleges offering travel and tourism courses. Membership examination takes the form of a three-hour written test based on a seen case study. Offers wide range of seminars. Journal (three or four times yearly).

113 Victoria Street, St Albans, Herts AL1 3TJ
Tel: 0727 54395   Fax: 0727 47415.

Institution of Environmental Health Officers (IEHO)

Founded 1883. Professional and examining body. Encourages the highest possible standards in the training and work of environmental health officers. Provides advice and latest technical information to members.

Chadwick House, Rushworth Street, London SE1 0QT
Tel: 071 928 6006   Fax: 071 928 6953.

International Association of Hotel Management Schools (IAHMS)

Members (fifty in 1991) meet regularly to improve communications between their institutions.

E Th Cassee, Chairman, c/o Hotel School The Hague, Brusselselaan 2, 2587 AH The Hague, Netherlands
Tel: 31/70 512481.

International Flight Catering Association (IFCA)

Established 1980. Worldwide trade association representing the catering departments and subsidiaries of airlines, independent inflight caterers, and suppliers (including duty free).

4 Grendon Close, Horley, Surrey RH6 8JW
Tel: 0293 771872   Fax: 0293 784361.

International Ho-Re-Ca

Founded 1949. Forum for worldwide cooperation among national professional organizations of the hotel and catering industry; over thirty members from eighteen countries (1991). Annual congress. Magazine.

Dr X Frei, General Secretary, International Ho-Re-Ca, Blumenfeldstrasse 20, Postfach, 8046 Zurich, Switzerland
Tel: 01 377 51 11   Fax: 01 371 89 09.

International Hotel Association (IHA)

Founded London 1946 to promote and defend the interests of the industry internationally. 4,700 members (1992). Develops working contracts with other international organizations, governmental and non-governmental.

80 rue de la Roquette, 75544 Paris Cedex 11, France
Tel: 010 33 1 4700/84/57.

Local Authorities Caterers Association (LACA)

Formed 1990, taking over from NASMO as the national professional association for supervisors and managers of school catering. (Until 1989, the National Association of School Meals Organizers existed as a sector-specific group under the umbrella of HCIMA.)

33 Grangefields Road, Jacobs Well, Guildford, Surrey GU4 7NR
Tel: 0483 35523.

Local enterprise companies (lecs)

E.g. Glasgow Development Agency, Grampian Enterprise Ltd. Scotland's equivalent to Training and Enterprise Councils (TECs). Some thirteen have been established under Scottish Enterprise and ten under Highlands and Islands Enterprise.

Central contact point for lecs: Scottish Enterprise, 120 Bothwell Street, Glasgow G2 7PG
Tel: 041 248 2700   Fax: 041 221 3217.

Highlands and Islands Enterprise, Bridge House, 20 Bridge Street, Inverness IV1 1QR
Tel: 0463 234171   Fax: 0463 244469

A list of lecs, TECs, Education Business Partnerships and Compacts is also available from Business in Community (see above).

Local Government Management Board (LGMB)

Formed 1991 to take over work of various local authority organizations including Local Government Training Board. Lead body for its sector and for sports and recreation. Wide range of publications and training packages; provides employment, pay and grading advice; assists in negotiating pay and conditions for local government employees.

Arndale House, The Arndale Centre, Luton, Beds LU1 2TS
Tel: 0582 451166   Fax: 0582 412525.

London Tourism Manpower Project (LTMP) and Springboard

Set up by the Joint London Tourism Forum, following its formation in 1986, to develop a strategy for tourism in London. LTMP's mission is to encourage job seekers to think positively about the hospitality industry, and to ensure adequate training provision for new and existing employees. Backed by over £75,000 from employers, a major LTMP initiative came into being in 1990: *Springboard*, the employment showcase for the industry. In attractive groundfloor premises off Tottenham Court Road, London, Springboard provides careers advice to callers in person, by telephone, or by letter. Staff from the centre visit schools and other establishments in the London area to make career presentations.

1 Denmark Street, London WC2H 8LP
Tel: 071 497 8654.

The Master Innholders

Membership (fifty-two in 1992) is awarded to qualified, practising hoteliers who demonstrate exceptionally high standards of innkeeping. The award (initiated in 1978) is jointly sponsored by HCIMA and The Worshipful Company of Innholders. The main aim – to further professionalism within the hotel industry – is achieved by the standards upheld by its individual members within their own establishments (see code of practice in Chapter 6), and by a programme of conferences, seminars and forums on topical subjects.

David Locket, Clerk to the MI, The Old Bakery, South Road, Reigate, Surrey RH2 7LU
Tel: 0737 245195   Fax: 0737 222989.

Mobile and Outside Caterers Association of Great Britain (MOCA)

Established 1987 as forum for exchange of information between members, to promote closer liaison with local authorities, the IEHO and other industry organizations. Publishes national guidelines for outdoor catering; year book and reference guide.

John Barton, Secretary, Mobile and Outside Caterers Association, 7 Hamilton Way, Wallington, Surrey SM6 9NJ
Tel: 081 669 8121   Fax: 081 647 1128.

National Association of Licensed House Managers (NALHM)

Founded 1969 to secure for members the maximum possible benefit in their terms and conditions of employment. Runs courses; publishes quarterly newspaper *The Licensed House Manager*; provides financial and legal advice, insurance and other services.

9 Coombe Lane, London SW20 8NE
Tel: 081 946 3080/5491.

National Committee of Heads of Catering (NATHOC)

Formed 1988 to provide a national voice for further education hotel and catering departments in the UK and Channel Islands, and promote the development of catering education and training. (For higher education this function is performed by CHME.) Facilitates staff interchanges, curriculum development, special projects and research.

Dr Iain Maclean, Chairman NATHOC, c/o Chichester College of Technology, Westgate Fields, Chichester PO19 1SB
Tel: 0243 786321   Fax: 0243 775783.

National Council for Vocational Qualifications (NCVQ)

Set up by Government in 1986 to improve vocational qualifications by basing them on the standards of competent performance needed in employment, and to establish them in a national framework which everyone can use and understand. NVQ levels 1 to 4 will be widely available by end-1992, level 5 thereafter. (In Scotland the same remit has been given to SCOTVEC. In Northern Ireland, the Department of Education and the Department of Economic Development have jointly established a Vocational Qualifications Unit to liaise with NCVQ. This is based in the Training and Employment Agency, Belfast.) NCVQ works closely with employers, trade unions and awarding bodies to make sure that the qualifications offered measure up to the standards of competence required by business and industry. NCVQ accreditation procedure involves approval of: an NVQ statement of competence agreed by the appropriate lead body, at the level at which it falls in the NVQ framework; and awarding body/bodies/consortia to offer, administer and maintain the quality of NVQs. These details and many others are held on the National Database.

222 Euston Road, London NW1 2BZ
Tel: 071 387 9898   Fax: 071 387 0978.

National Examining Board for Supervisory Management (NEBSM)

Set up 1964 by the Department of Education and Science. (Name changed from National Examinations Board for Supervisory Studies (NEBSS) in 1990.) Concerned with the education and training of supervisory managers, providing examinations and qualifications in cooperation with over 600 centres, including colleges and employers; also NEBSM *Super Series* open learning packages. Administration provided by City and Guilds.

76 Portland Place, London W1N 4AA
Tel: 071 278 2468   Fax: 071 436 7630.

National Federation of Fish Friers (NFFF)

Trade association for proprietors or partners of fried fish businesses. Educational and information service; runs short training courses for newcomers to the trade.

Federation House, 289 Dewsbury Road, Leeds LS11 5HW
Tel: 0532 713291   Fax: 0532 717571.

National Licensed Victuallers' Association (NLVA)

Represents self-employed tenants, free traders and leaseholders of public houses in England and Wales, to safeguard their rights to earn a dignified living. Lobbies Government on issues of concern to the licensed trade. Publishes monthly newspaper: advisory services, including financial and legal; special trade insurance schemes.

Boardman House, 2 Downing Street, Farnham, Surrey GU9 7NX
Tel: 0252 714448   Fax: 0252 723742.

Northern Ireland Hotels and Caterers Association (NIHCA)

Primarily a consultative body, representing members' interests in all issues which affect their livelihood and professional activities.

108/110 Midland Bank Building, Whitla Street, Belfast BT15 1JP
Tel: 0232 351110/351434   Fax: 0232 351509.

Open Learning Foundation (Open Polytechnic)

Established mid-1990 to increase the accessibility of polytechnics and higher education to individuals, companies, and public sector organizations. Does not enrol its own students, but through its activities enables its members (over twenty polytechnics/universities) to create a framework for more flexible learning through the production of high quality teaching and learning materials: e.g. business studies, languages, foundation maths and communication skills, and hospitality management (anticipated).

24 Angel Gate, City Road, London EC1V 2RS
Tel: 071 833 3757   Fax: 071 833 3819.

PETRA

European Commission Action Programme for the Vocational Training of Young People and Their Preparation for Adult and Working Life. Encourages twinning or linking of training initiatives, and cooperative action in the area of research and surveys on the effectiveness of training provision.

PETRA Support Unit, IFAPLAN, Square Ambiorix 32, B-1040 Bruxelles, Belgium
Tel: 32 2/230 71 06.

Restaurateurs Association of Great Britain (RAGB)

Founded 1967 to promote mutual understanding and cooperation, to advance and protect the interests of British-based restaurateurs. A leading campaigner behind 1988 reform of the licensing laws, which made possible all-day service of alcohol in England and Wales.

190 Queen's Gate, London SW7 5EU
Tel: 071 581 2444   Fax: 071 581 8261.

Réunion des Gastronomes

Founded 1898. Membership restricted to owners, managers and managing directors of hotels and restaurants who pledge to 'develop and support the culinary art in every possible way; to promote mutual understanding and the exchange of ideas on professional matters; and to endeavour to raise the status of hotelkeeping and catering'. Admission to its exclusive ranks is jealously guarded – less than 200 members.

c/o Mr M C Thatcher, General Secretary 35 Great Peter Street, London SW1P 3LR.

Royal Environmental Health Institute of Scotland (REHIS)

Formed 1983 by amalgamation of Royal Sanitary Association (founded 1875) and Scottish Institute of Environmental Health (founded 1891). Professional and examining body to: promote the advancement of health and hygiene in all their aspects; stimulate interest in public health; disseminate knowledge on health matters to the benefit of the community; protect the interests of those engaged in environmental health work; secure the proper organization of the recruitment, training and qualifications of EHOs and other officers in the field.

Virginia House, 62 Virginia Street, Glasgow G1 1TX
Tel: 041 552 1533   Fax: 041 553 2525.

Royal Institute of Public Health and Hygiene (RIPHH)

Formed 1937 by amalgamation of Royal Institute of Public Health (founded 1886) and Institute of Hygiene (founded 1903). Educational, standard-setting and examining body concerned to advance the cause of health and hygiene across the complete spectrum of age in the varied settings of home, school, work and leisure. Regular conferences, lectures and training courses; quarterly journal *Health and Hygiene*.

28 Portland Place, London W1N 4DE
Tel: 071 580 2731   Fax: 071 580 6157.

Royal Society of Health (RSH)

Founded 1876 to protect and preserve health, advance health-related sciences, and diffuse knowledge. Caters for all aspects of public health including food and nutrition, environmental health, architecture and planning, town planning, building, housing and engineering. Examining body. Holds conferences, meetings and lectures; publishes bi-monthly journal.

RSH House, 38A St George's Drive, London SW1V 4BH
Tel: 071 630 0121   Fax: 071 976 6847.

Scottish Licensed Trade Association (SLTA)

Founded 1880 to protect and promote the rights and interests of all sections of the licensed trade in Scotland. Provides legal and financial advice; wide range of courses, including one for new entrants to the trade.

10 Walker Street, Edinburgh EH3 7LA
Tel: 031 225 5169   Fax: 031 220 4057.

Scottish Vocational Education Council (SCOTVEC)

Established 1985 by Secretary of State for Scotland. Took over from SCOTEC (Scottish Technical Education Council) and SCOTBEC (Scottish

Business Education Council), including SCOTEC Diploma and Higher Diploma in Hotel, Catering and Institutional Operations/Management and SCOTBEC hotel reception schemes. A private company, limited by guarantee, SCOTVEC is responsible for developing, awarding and accrediting vocational qualifications in Scotland. Works in partnership with all sectors of industry and commerce, Government, training providers and other organizations to ensure that SCOTVEC qualifications are relevant to the needs of employment, flexible to respond to change, and recognized nationally and internationally. Many of its awards are jointly certificated, for example with the HCTC, HCIMA and BII.

Hanover House, 24 Douglas Street, Glasgow G2 7NQ
Tel: 041 248 7900   Fax: 041 242 2244.

Society of Catering and Hotel Management Consultants

Founded 1968. An international association of professionally qualified consultants specializing in hotel, catering and leisure. Enforces high standards of ethical conduct among members, and encourages exchange of knowledge and information to keep members abreast of new technologies and developments. Provides recognition to student achievements through award schemes and lectures.

The Midden, Node Court, Drivers End, Codicote, Herts SG4 8TR
Tel: 0483 821444.

Society of Golden Keys

British branch set up 1952, 170 members, plus associates (1991). Brings head porters throughout the world together: twenty-six countries in the Paris-based Union Internationale des Portiers des Grand Hotels Clefs d'Or.

Tim Broadbent, President, c/o Dukes Hotel, 35 St James's Place, London SW1A 1NY
Tel: 071 491 4840.

The University Catering Officers (TUCO)

Founded 1964 to promote effective catering management in universities (all UK universities belong). Regular meetings; newsletter.

George Donaldson, National Secretary TUCO, c/o Residences Office, University of Dundee, Perth Road, Dundee DD1 4HN
Tel: 0382 23181 ext 4040   Fax: 0382 202605.

Tourism Society

Established 1977. Professional body for managers and potential managers in tourism. National and regional seminar and conference programme; quarterly bulletin and biennial handbook.

26 Chapter Street, London SW1P 4ND
Tel: 071 834 0461   Fax: 071 233 6551.

Training and Employment Agency

From 1990 responsible for the administration and delivery of all Government training programmes in Northern Ireland. (Took over work of Northern Ireland Training Authority and a number of Industrial Training Boards including Catering ITB.) An executive agency within the Department of Economic Development, bringing together all employment and training services. Priorities include: improving access to employment and training opportunities; liaising with NCVQ with regard to NVQs; raising quality and relevance of training; providing the unemployed and those entering the labour market with skills to find jobs; and promoting more effective management development.

Clarendon House, 9/21 Adelaide Street, Belfast BT2 8DJ
Tel: 0232 244300.

Training and Enterprise Councils (TECs)

Eighty-two established throughout England and Wales (in Scotland similar functions are carried out by local enterprise companies). Employer-led groups, with wide-ranging responsibilities for vocational education and training in their area: administering the Training Credit scheme; managing Youth and Employment Training schemes; providing training for small businesses; closely involved in careers work, the Technical and Vocational Education Initiative, and in decisions about the provision of work-related further education in local colleges.

Central contact for TECs: The TEC Development Branch, TEED, Moorfoot, Sheffield S1 4PQ
Tel: 0742 753275.
A list of TECs, lecs, Education Business Partnerships and Compacts is also available from Business in Community (see above).

Training Enterprise and Education Directorate (TEED)

Took over from Training Agency (previously Manpower Services Commission) in 1990, as a division within the Employment Department. Works with employers, the education service, voluntary organizations, training providers and trade unions to improve the training system. Responsible for appointment of lead bodies.

Moorfoot, Sheffield S1 4PQ
Tel: 0742 753275   Fax: 0742 758316.

Travel and Tourism Programme (TTP)

Partnership between a group of major service industries and the education establishment, responsible for devising and introducing the Travel and Tourism GCSE, UK's first industry-sponsored secondary qualification. Also involved more generally in curricular development in UK and internationally. American Express, BTA, ETB, International Leisure Group, and Forte Hotels are business partners.

3 Redman Court, Bell Street, Princes Risborough, Aylesbury, Bucks HP17 0AA.
Tel: 08444 4208   Fax: 0844 274340.

United Kingdom Bartenders Guild (UKBG)

Founded 1933. 'Run by bartenders for bartenders ... for the advancement of the bartending profession.' Provides bar skills and cocktail-making courses; registration scheme for new cocktails; competitions, tastings and new product presentation; publishes newsletter.

91–93 Gordon Road, Harborne, Birmingham B17 9HA
Tel: 021 427 8099.

United Kingdom Housekeepers Association

Formed 1985, with support of *Caterer & Hotelkeeper*, to improve professional status of housekeepers, provide a forum for exchange of ideas and information, and promote housekeeping as a career.

Lynn Yambao, National Secretary, UK Housekeepers Association, Flat 7, 14–15 Molyneux Street, London W1H 5HU
Tel: 071 723 6668.

Vegetarian Society (UK) Ltd

Formed 1969 to improve knowledge of the benefits of a vegetarian diet in terms of ethics, health, economics, ecology and a reduction of famine in Third World countries. Runs cookery courses, sponsors scientific research in the field of nutrition, publishes cookbooks, leaflets, a bi-monthly magazine, vegetarian handbook and *International Travel Guide*, with listing of vegetarian restaurants, hotels, guesthouses and health food shops.

Parkdale, Dunham Road, Altrincham, Cheshire WA14 4QG
Tel: 061 928 0793   Fax: 061 926 9182.

Wine Guild of the United Kingdom

Formed by Lord Montagu of Beaulieu in 1984 to promote the communication of the love, knowledge and understanding of wine to the public at large.

190 Queen's Gate, London SW7 5EU
Tel: 071 584 9925   Fax 071 581 8261.

Wine and Spirit Education Trust (WSET)

Founded 1969 to provide education and product knowledge for those employed, or seeking employment, in wine and spirit trade and ancillary occupations. Students may prepare for WSET examinations on courses run by the Trust itself, by approved colleges, or by distance learning.

Five Kings House, 1 Queen Street Place, London EC4R 1QS
Tel: 071 236 3551.

Yorkshire and Humberside Association for Further and Higher Education (YHAFHE)

Provides regional administration for various C&G schemes.

Bowling Green Terrace, Leeds LS11 9SX
Tel: 0532 440751.

12
Directory of colleges

This chapter is organized in seven sections:

1–4   For England, the Channel Islands and Isle of Man (1), Wales (2), Scotland (3) and Northern Ireland (4): the colleges of further and higher education, polytechnics, central institutions and universities in the public sector which offer courses in any of the subjects covered in this book; entries are in alphabetic order by county/region, and then by city/town.

5   Institutions specializing in distance learning: note many of the awarding bodies (see Chapter 4) and an increasing number of colleges also publish distance learning material.

6   Private schools, colleges and universities.

7   Private cookery schools.

To find colleges that are offering a particular course, first consider what locations would be suitable. Then use the subject and level guide (printed in italics after the name of the college) as the first step only in deciding which colleges to telephone or write to for more details and a prospectus – by keeping an open mind at this stage you might find a course you hadn't first thought of to be very suitable for your needs. If you are looking for colleges that offer:

- cookery, food and beverage service, housekeeping, reception, or similar craft or specific skills, select levels 1 or 2,
- BTEC First, select level 2,
- National Diploma/Certificate, or advanced craft, select level 3,
- Higher National Diploma/Certificate, select level 4,
- degrees, select level 4,
- postgraduate, select level 5.

If you are writing for details, it makes your request easier to process if you use a postcard. State briefly what you are interested in, and give your name and address clearly, so that the college staff can address the envelope accurately when they send you the details.

Some courses are available on a full-time basis only, others only part-time, and some colleges offer a choice of both. If only one or the other is suitable, tell this to the college when you ask for course details – this will save time and help the college to give you the best advice.

1   England

Avon

BATH   Bath College of Higher Education
Food management, level 4
Newton Park, Newton St Loe, BA2 9BN
Tel: 0225 873701.

BATH   City of Bath College of Further Education
Hotel and catering, levels 1–3
Avon Street, BA1 1UP
Tel: 0225 312191.

BRISTOL   Brunel College of Technology
Hotel and catering, levels 1–4
Ashley Down Road, BS7 9BU
Tel: 0272 241241.

BRISTOL   Soundwell College
Tourism, leisure, levels 2, 3
St Stephen's Road, BS16 4RL
Tel: 0272 675101.

BRISTOL   South Bristol College
Leisure, level 2
Marksbury Road, Bedminster, BS3 5JL
Tel: 0272 639033.

BRISTOL   University of West England at Bristol
Tourism, level 4
Coldharbour Lane, Frenchay, BS16 1QY
Tel: 0272 656261.

WESTON-SUPER-MARE   Weston-Super-Mare College of Further Education
Hotel and catering, leisure, levels 1–3
Knightstone Road, BS23 2AL
Tel: 0934 621301.

Bedfordshire

BEDFORD   Bedford College of Higher Education
Hotel and catering, levels 1–3
Cauldwell Street, MK42 9AH
Tel: 0234 45151.
Leisure and recreation, level 4
Lansdowne Site, Lansdowne Road, MK40 2BZ
Tel: 0234 351966.

DUNSTABLE   Dunstable College
Tourism, leisure, level 2
Kingsway, LU5 4HG
Tel: 0582 696451.

LUTON   Barnfield College
Hotel, catering, tourism, leisure, levels 1–4
New Bedford Road, LU3 2AX
Tel: 0582 507531.

LUTON   Luton College of Higher Education
Hotel and catering, leisure, tourism, level 4
Faculty of Business, Park Square, LU1 3JU
Tel: 0582 34111.

Berkshire

BRACKNELL   Bracknell College
Hotel, catering, leisure, tourism, levels 1–3
Church Road, RG12 1DJ
Tel: 0344 420411.

LANGLEY   Langley College
Tourism, leisure, level 3
Station Road, SL3 8BY
Tel: 0753 49222.

NEWBURY   Newbury College of
   Further Education
*Hotel, catering, tourism, leisure, levels
   1–3*
Oxford Road, RG13 1PQ
Tel: 0635 42824

READING   Reading College
Hotel and catering, leisure, levels 1–3
Crescent Road, RG1 5RQ
Tel: 0734 583501.

SLOUGH   Thames Valley University
Hotel and catering, levels 2–5
Wellington Street, SL1 1YG
Tel: 0753 534585.

WINDSOR/MAIDENHEAD   Windsor
   and Maidenhead College
Tourism, leisure, levels 2, 3
Claremont Road, SL4 3AZ
Tel: 075 35 62111.

Buckinghamshire

AMERSHAM   Amersham College of
   Further Education, Art and Design
Tourism, leisure, levels, 2, 3
Stanley Hill, HP7 9HN
Tel: 024 03 21121.

AYLESBURY   Aylesbury College
*Hotel, catering, tourism, leisure, levels
   1–4*
Oxford Road, HP21 8PD
Tel: 0296 434111.

HIGH WYCOMBE   The
   Buckinghamshire College
Leisure and tourism, level 4
Queen Alexandra Road, HP11 2JZ
Tel: 0494 22141.

MILTON KEYNES   Milton Keynes
   College
Hotel and catering, levels 1–4
Bletchley Centre, Sherwood Drive,
   Bletchley, MK3 6DR
Tel: 0908 668998.

Cambridgeshire

CAMBRIDGE   Cambridge Regional
   College
*Hotel, catering, tourism, leisure, levels
   1–3*
Newmarket Road, CB8 5EG
Tel: 0223 324455.

PETERBOROUGH   Peterborough
   Regional College
*Hotel, catering, tourism, leisure, levels
   1–3*
Park Crescent, PE1 4DZ
Tel: 0733 67366.

Channel Islands

JERSEY   Highlands College
Hotel and catering, levels 1–4
PO Box 1000, St Saviour, JE4 9QA
Tel: 0534 71800.

GUERNSEY   Guernsey College of
   Further Education
Hotel and catering, levels 1–4
Route des Coutanchez, St Peter Port
Tel: 0481 727121.

Cheshire

CHESTER   West Cheshire College
*Hotel, catering, tourism, leisure, levels
   1–3*
Eaton Road, Handbridge, CH4 7ER
Tel: 0244 677677.

CREWE   South Cheshire College
*Hotel, catering, leisure, tourism, levels
   1–4*
Dane Bank Avenue, CW2 8AB
Tel: 0270 69133.

MACCLESFIELD   Macclesfield
   College of Further Education
*Hotel, catering, tourism, leisure, levels
   1–3*
Park Lane, SK11 8LF
Tel: 0625 427744.

NORTHWICH   Mid-Cheshire College
of Further Education
*Hotel, catering, tourism, leisure, levels
1–3*
Hartford Campus, CW8 1LJ
Tel: 0606 75281.

WARRINGTON   North Cheshire
College
Leisure, level 4
Padgate Campus, Fearnhead, WA2 0DB
Tel: 0925 814343.

WIDNES   Halton College of Further
Education
Hotel and catering, levels 1–3
Kingsway, WA8 7QQ
Tel: 051 423 1391.

Cleveland

HARTLEPOOL   Hartlepool College
of Further Education
Tourism, leisure, levels 2, 3
Stockton Street, TS25 7NT
Tel: 0429 275453.

MIDDLESBROUGH   Kirby College
*Hotel, catering, tourism, leisure, levels
1–3*
Roman Road, TS5 5PJ
Tel: 0642 813706.

MIDDLESBROUGH   Longlands
College of Further Education
Leisure, levels 2–4
Douglas Street, TS4 2JW
Tel: 0642 248351

MIDDLESBROUGH   Teesside
University
Leisure, levels 4, 5
Teesside Business School, Flatts Lane,
Normanby, TS6 0QS
Tel: 0642 342900.

REDCAR   Cleveland Technical
College
Tourism, leisure, levels 1–3
Corporation Road, TS10 1EZ
Tel: 0642 473132.

Cornwall

REDRUTH   Cornwall College
*Hotel, catering, tourism, leisure, levels
1–4*
TR15 3RD
Tel: 0209 712911.

ST AUSTELL   Mid-Cornwall College
*Hotel, catering, tourism, leisure, levels
1–3*
Palace Road, PL25 4BW
Tel: 0726 67911.

Cumbria

BARROW-IN-FURNESS   Furness
College
Hotel and catering, leisure, levels 1–3
Howard Street, LA14 1NB
Tel: 0229 826782.

CARLISLE   Carlisle College
*Hotel, catering, leisure, tourism, levels
1–3*
Victoria Place, CA1 1HS
Tel: 0228 24464.

CARLISLE   Cumbria College of Art
and Design
Heritage management, level 4
Brampton Road, CA3 9AY
Tel: 0228 25333.

KENDAL   Kendal College of Further
Education
Hotel and catering, tourism, levels 1–5
Milnthorpe Road, LA9 5AY
Tel: 0539 724313.

WORKINGTON   West Cumbria
College
Hotel and catering, leisure, levels 1–3
Park Lane, CA14 2RW
Tel: 0900 64331.

Derbyshire

BUXTON   High Peak College
*Hotel, catering, leisure, tourism, levels
1–4*
Harpur Hill, SK17 9JZ
Tel: 0298 71100.

DERBY   University of Derby
Hotel and catering, tourism, level 4
Derbyshire Business School, Kedleston
  Road, DE3 1GB
Tel: 0332 47181.

CHESTERFIELD   Chesterfield College
  of Technology and Arts
*Hotel, catering, tourism, leisure, levels
1–3*
Infirmary Road, S41 7NG
Tel: 0246 231212.

CHESTERFIELD   North Derbyshire
  Tertiary College
Hotel and catering, levels 1–3
Rectory Road, Clowne, S43 4BQ
Tel: 0246 810332.

DERBY   Derbyshire College of Higher
  Education
Tourism, level 4
Kedleston Road, DE3 1GB
Tel: 0332 47181.

DERBY   Derby Tertiary College
*Hotel, catering, tourism, leisure, levels
1–3*
London Road, Wilmorton DE2 8UG
Tel: 0332 757570.

ILKESTON   South East Derbyshire
  College
Leisure, level 3
Field Road, DE7 5RS
Tel: 0602 324212.

Devon

BARNSTAPLE   North Devon College
*Hotel, catering, tourism, leisure, levels
1–3*
Sticklepath Hill, EX31 2BQ
Tel: 0271 45291.

BUDLEIGH SALTERTON   Bicton
  College of Agriculture
Leisure, level 3
East Budleigh, EX9 7BY
Tel: 0395 68353.

EXETER   Exeter College
*Hotel, catering, tourism, leisure, levels
1–4*
Hele Road, EX4 4JS
Tel: 0392 384904/5.

NEWTON ABBOT   University of
  Plymouth
Hotel, catering, leisure, tourism, level 4
Faculty of Agriculture, Food and Land
  Use, TQ12 6NQ
Tel: 0626 52323.

PLYMOUTH   Plymouth College of
  Further Education
*Hotel, catering, leisure, travel, levels
1–4*
Kings Road, Devonport, PL1 5QG
Tel: 0752 385186.

TIVERTON   East Devon College of
  Further Education
Hotel and catering, leisure, levels 1–3
Bolham Road, EX16 6SH
Tel: 0884 254247.

TORQUAY   South Devon College of
  Arts and Technology
*Hotel, catering, tourism, leisure, levels
1–4*
Newton Road, TQ2 5BY
Tel: 0803 217511.

Dorset

BOURNEMOUTH   The Bournemouth
  and Poole College of Further
  Education
Hotel and catering, tourism, levels 1–4
The Lansdowne, BH1 3JJ
Tel: 0202 747600.

BOURNEMOUTH/POOLE
Bournemouth University
Hotel, catering, leisure, tourism, levels 4, 5
Department of Food and Hospitality Management, Talbot Campus, Fern Barrow, BH12 5BB
Tel: 0202 524111.

WEYMOUTH   Weymouth College
Hotel, catering, leisure, tourism, levels 1–3
Newstead Road, DT4 0DX
Tel: 0305 208978.

Durham

BISHOP AUCKLAND   Bishop Auckland Technical College
Leisure, levels 2, 3
Woodhouse Lane, BL14 6JZ
Tel: 0388 603052.

CONSETT   Derwentside College
Hotel and catering, levels 1–3
Park Road, DH8 5EE
Tel: 0207 502906.

DARLINGTON   Darlington College of Technology
Hotel and catering, leisure, levels 1–3
Cleveland Avenue, DL3 7BB
Tel: 0325 467651.

DURHAM   Durham College of Agriculture and Horticulture
Tourism, level 4
Houghall, DH1 3SG
Tel: 091 386 1351.

DURHAM   New College Durham
Hotel, catering, tourism, leisure, levels 1–4
Department of Community Services, Framwellgate Moor Centre, DH1 5ES
Tel: 091 386 2421.

PETERLEE   Peterlee College
Hotel and catering, levels 1–3
Department of Service Industries, SR8 1NU
Tel: 091 586 2225.

East Sussex *see* Sussex, East

Essex

BARKING   Barking College of Technology
Cookery, tourism, levels 1–3
Dagenham Road, RM7 0XU
Tel: 0708 766841.

BASILDON   Basildon College of Further Education
Leisure, levels 1–3
Nethermayne, SS16 5NN
Tel: 0268 289281.

BRAINTREE   Braintree College of Further Education
Hotel and catering, levels 1–3
Church Lane, CM7 5SN
Tel: 0376 21711.

CHELMSFORD   Anglia Polytechnic University
Leisure, level 4
Victoria Road South, CM1 1LL
Tel: 0245 493131.

CHELMSFORD   Chelmsford College of Further Education
Hotel and catering, leisure, levels 1–4
Princes Road, CM2 9DX
Tel: 0245 265611.

CHELMSFORD   Writtle College
Leisure, level 4
CM1 3RR
Tel: 0245 420705.

CLACTON ON SEA   Colchester Institute
Hotel, catering, leisure, tourism, levels 2–4
Marine Parade East, CO15 6JQ
Tel: 0255 220444.

GRAYS   Thurrock Technical College
Hotel and catering, levels 1–3
Woodview, RM16 4YR
Tel: 0375 391199.

HARLOW   Harlow College
Hotel and catering, leisure, levels 1–3
College Square, The High, CM20 1LT
Tel: 0279 441288.

LOUGHTON   Epping Forest College
Leisure, level 3
Borders Lane, IG10 3SA
Tel: 081 508 8311.

REDBRIDGE   Redbridge Technical
   College
Hotel and catering, levels 1–3
Little Heath, RM6 4XT
Tel: 081 559 5231.

ROMFORD   Havering College of
   Further and Higher Education
Hotel and catering, leisure, levels 1–3
Tring Gardens, Harold Hill, RM3 9ES
Tel: 04023 81460.

SOUTHEND ON SEA   The South
   East Essex College of Arts and
   Technology
Hotel and catering, tourism, levels 1–4
Carnarvon Road, SS2 6LS
Tel: 0702 432205.

Gloucestershire

CHELTENHAM   Cheltenham and
   Gloucester College of Higher
   Education
Hotel, catering, tourism, leisure, level 4
PO Box 220, The Park, GL50 2QF
Tel: 0242 532904/532700.

CHELTENHAM   Gloucestershire
   College of Arts and Technology
Hotel and catering, tourism, levels 1–3
Park Campus, 73 The Park, GL50 2RR
Tel: 0242 532073.

COLEFORD   The Royal Forest of
   Dean College
Hotel, catering, leisure, levels 1, 2
Five Acres Campus, Berry Hill,
   GL16 7JT
Tel: 0594 33416.

STROUD   Stroud College of Further
   Education
Cookery, leisure, levels 1–3
Stratford Road, GL5 4AH
Tel: 0453 763424.

Hampshire

ANDOVER   Cricklade College
Hotel and catering, levels 1–3
Charlton Road, SP10 1EJ
Tel: 0264 63311.

BASINGSTOKE   Basingstoke College
   of Technology
*Hotel, catering, tourism, leisure, levels
   1–3*
Worting Road, RG21 1TN
Tel: 0256 54141.

BROCKENHURST   Brockenhurst
   College
Hotel and catering, levels 1–3
Lyndhurst Road, SO42 7ZE
Tel: 0590 23565.

EASTLEIGH   Eastleigh College
*Hotel, catering, tourism, leisure, levels
   1–3*
Chestnut Avenue, SO5 5HT
Tel: 0703 644011.

FAREHAM   Fareham Tertiary College
Hotel and catering, leisure, levels 1–3
Bishopsfield Road, PO14 1NH
Tel: 0329 822483.

FARNBOROUGH   Farnborough
   College of Technology
*Hotel, catering, tourism, leisure, levels
   1–4*
Boundary Road, GU14 6SB
Tel: 0252 515511.

HAVANT   South Downs College of
   Further Education
Hotel and catering, tourism, leisure
College Road, PO7 8AA
Tel: 0705 257011.

PORTSMOUTH   Highbury College of
Technology
*Hotel, catering, tourism, leisure, levels
1–4*
Dovercourt Road, Cosham, PO6 2SA
Tel: 0705 383131.

PORTSMOUTH   Portsmouth
University
Hotel and catering, levels 4, 5
Business School, Locksway Road,
Milton, PO4 8JF
Tel: 0705 827681.

SOUTHAMPTON   Southampton
Institute of Higher Education
Leisure, level 4
For degree: Maritime Division,
Newtown Road, Warsash, SO3 6ZL
Tel: 0489 576161.
For CMS: Management Centre, East
Park Terrace, SO9 4WW
Tel: 0703 229381.

SOUTHAMPTON   Southampton
Technical College
Hotel and catering, levels 1–3
St Mary Street, SO9 4WX
Tel: 0703 636728.

Hereford and Worcester

EVESHAM   Evesham College of
Further Education
Tourism, level 3
Cheltenham Road, WR11 6LP
Tel: 0386 41091.

HEREFORD   Herefordshire College of
Technology
*Hotel, catering, tourism, leisure, levels
1–4*
Folly Lane, HR1 1LS
Tel: 0432 352235.

REDDITCH   North East
Worcestershire College
*Hotel, catering, tourism, leisure, levels
1–4*
Redditch Campus, Peakman Street, B98
8DW
Tel: 0527 63607.

WORCESTER   Worcester College of
Technology
*Hotel, catering, tourism, leisure, levels
1–4*
Department of Hospitality, Deansway,
WR1 2JF
Tel: 0905 723383.

Hertfordshire

BROXBOURNE   Hertford Regional
College
Hotel and catering, leisure, levels 1–3
Broxbourne Centre, Turnford,
EN10 6AF
Tel: 0992 466451.

HERTFORD   University of
Hertfordshire
Travel and tourism, level 4
Business School, Mangrove Road,
SG13 8QF
Tel: 0992 558451.

LETCHWORTH   North Hertfordshire
College
Hotel and catering, leisure, levels 1–4
Broadway, SG6 3PB
Tel: 0462 683911.

WARE   Hertford Regional College
Hotel and catering, leisure, levels 1–3
Ware Site, Scotts Road, SG12 9JF
Tel: 0920 465441.

WATFORD   Watford College
Hotel, catering, leisure, level 4
Hempstead Road, WD1 3EZ
Tel: 0923 57500.

WATFORD   West Herts College
Hotel and catering, tourism, levels 1–3
Cassio Campus, Langley Road,
WD1 3RH
Tel: 0923 240311.

Humberside

BEVERLEY   Beverley College of
   Further Education
Hotel and catering, levels 1–4
Gallons Lane, HU17 7DT
Tel: 0482 868362.

BEVERLEY   Bishop Burton College of
   Agriculture
Tourism, level 3
HU17 8QG
Tel: 0964 550481.

BRIDLINGTON   East Yorkshire
   College
Hotel and catering, levels 1–4
St Mary's Walk, YO16 5JW
Tel: 0262 672676.

GRIMSBY   Grimsby College of
   Technology and Arts
Hotel and catering, tourism, levels 1–4
Nuns Corner, DN34 5BQ
Tel: 0472 79292.

HULL   Hull College of Further
   Education
Hotel and catering, levels 1–3
Queens Gardens, HU1 3DG
Tel: 0482 29943.

HULL   University of Humberside
Hotel, catering, tourism, leisure, level 4
School of Social and Professional
   Studies, Inglemire Avenue, HU6 7LU
Tel: 0482 440550.

SCUNTHORPE   North Lindsey
   College
*Hotel, catering, tourism, leisure, levels
   1–4*
Kingsway, Scunthorpe DN17 1AJ
Tel: 0724 281111.

Isle of Man

DOUGLAS   Isle of Man College
Hotel and catering, levels 1–3
Homefield Road
Tel: 0624 623113.

Isle of Wight

NEWPORT   Isle of Wight College of
   Arts and Technology
Hotel and catering, travel, levels 1–3
Medina Way, PO30 5TA
Tel: 0983 526631.

Kent

BROADSTAIRS   Thanet Technical
   College
Hotel and catering, levels 1–3
Ramsgate Road, CT10 1PN
Tel: 0843 65111.

CANTERBURY   Canterbury Christ
   Church College of Higher Education
Tourism and leisure, level 4
Department of Tourism Studies,
   CT1 1QU
Tel: 0227 767700.

CANTERBURY   Canterbury College
   of Technology
Hotel and catering, leisure, levels 1–3
New Dover Road, CT1 3AJ
Tel: 0227 766081.

CHATHAM   Mid-Kent College of
   Further Education
Hotel and catering, leisure, levels 1–3
Horsted, Maidstone Road, ME5 9UQ
Tel: 0622 691555.

DARTFORD   North West Kent
   College of Technology
*Hotel, catering, tourism, leisure, levels
   1–3*
Miskin Road, DA1 2LU
Tel: 0322 25471.

GRAVESEND   North West Kent
   College of Technology
Hotel and catering, levels 1–3
Pelham Road, Gravesend DA11 0HM
Tel: 0474 365233.

FOLKESTONE   South Kent College
Hotel and catering, tourism, levels 1–3
Shorncliffe Road, CT20 2NA
Tel: 0303 850061.

ORPINGTON   Orpington College of
Further Education
Hotel and catering, leisure, levels 1, 2
The Walnuts, High Street, BR6 0TE
Tel: 0589 39336.

TONBRIDGE   West Kent College
*Hotel, catering, leisure, tourism, levels
1–4*
Brook Street, TN9 2PW
Tel: 0732 358101.

Lancashire

ACCRINGTON   Accrington and
Rossendale College
Hotel and catering, leisure, levels 1–3
Sandy Lane, BB5 2AW
Tel: 0254 393521.

BLACKBURN   Blackburn College
Hotel and catering, leisure, levels 1–3
Feilden Street, BB2 1LH
Tel: 0254 55144.

BLACKPOOL   Blackpool and The
Fylde College
*Hotel, catering, tourism, leisure, levels
1–3*
Department of Hotel and Food Studies,
Park Road, FY1 4JN
Tel: 0253 293071.
Hotel and catering, tourism, levels 3–4
Department of Management Studies,
Ashfield Road, Bispham, FY2 0HB
Tel: 0253 52352.

BURNLEY   Burnley College
Tourism, leisure, levels 1–3
Shorey Bank, Ormerod Road,
BB11 2RX
Tel: 0282 36111.

LANCASTER   Lancaster and
Morecambe College
*Hotel, catering, leisure, tourism, levels
1–3*
Morecambe Road, LA1 2TY
Tel: 0524 66215.

LANCASTER   The University
Tourism and recreation, level 5
LA1 4YW
Tel: 0524 65201.

LEIGH   Leigh College
*Hotel, catering, tourism, leisure, levels
1–3*
Railway Road, WN7 4AH.
Tel: 0942 608811.

LEYLAND   Runshaw College
Hotel and catering, levels 1–3
Langdale Road, PR5 2DQ
Tel: 0772 432511.

NELSON   Nelson and Colne College
Hotel and catering, leisure, levels 1–3
Scotland Road, BB9 7YT
Tel: 0282 603151.

PRESTON   Lancashire College of
Agriculture and Horticulture
Leisure, level 4
Byerscough Hall, Bilsborrow, PR3 0RY
Tel: 0995 40611.

PRESTON   Preston College
*Hotel, catering, travel, leisure, levels
1–3*
St Vincent Road, Fulwood, PR2 4UR
Tel: 0772 58855.

PRESTON   University of Central
Lancashire
*Hotel, catering, tourism, leisure, levels
4, 5*
School of Organizational Studies,
PR1 2TQ
Tel: 0772 201201.

WIGAN   Wigan College of
Technology
*Hotel, catering, leisure, tourism, levels
1–3*
Parson's Walk, WN1 1RS
Tel: 0942 494911.

Leicestershire

COALVILLE   Coalville Technical College
Hotel and catering, leisure, levels 1–2
Bridge Road, LE6 2QR
Tel: 0530 36136.

HINCKLEY   Hinckley College of Further Education
Hotel and catering, levels 1–2
London Road, LE10 1HQ
Tel: 0455 251222.

LEICESTER   Charles Keene College of Further Education
Leisure, levels 2, 3
Painter Street, LE1 3WA
Tel: 0533 516037.

LEICESTER   South Fields College of Further Education
Hotel and catering, levels 1–3
Aylestone Road, LE2 7LW
Tel: 0533 541818

LOUGHBOROUGH   Loughborough College
Hotel, catering, tourism, leisure, levels 1–3
Division of Hotel and Catering, Radmoor, LE11 3BT
Tel: 0509 215831.

MELTON MOWBRAY   Melton Mowbray College of Further Education
Hotel and catering, levels 1–3
Asfordby Road, LE13 0HJ
Tel: 0664 67431.

Lincolnshire

BOSTON   Boston College
Hotel and catering, levels 1–3
Rowley Road, PE21 6JF
Tel: 0205 365701.

GRANTHAM   Grantham College
Hotel, catering, tourism, leisure, levels 1–3
Stonebridge Road, NG31 9AP
Tel: 0476 63141.

LINCOLN   North Lincolnshire College
Hotel and catering, tourism, levels 1–4
Cathedral Street, LN2 5HQ
Tel: 0522 510530.

STAMFORD   Stamford College
Hotel and catering, leisure, levels 1, 3
Drift Road, PE9 1XA
Tel: 0780 64141.

London

ACTON   Acton College
Hotel and catering, levels 1, 2
Mill Hill Road, London W3 8UX
Tel: 081 993 2344.

BARNET   Barnet College
Hotel and catering, levels 1–3
Russell Lane, Whetstone, London N20 0AX
Tel: 081 361 5101.

BATTERSEA   Westminster College
Hotel and catering, leisure, levels 1–4
Battersea Park Road, London SW11 4JR
Tel: 071 720 2121.

BELVEDERE   Erith College of Technology
Tourism, leisure, levels 2–3
Tower Road, DA17 6JA
Tel: 03224 42331.

BOUNDS GREEN   College of North East London
Cookery, levels 1, 2
Park Road, London N11 2QF
Tel: 081 888 7123.

BROMLEY   Bromley College of Technology
Tourism, leisure, level 3
Rookery Lane, BR2 8HE
Tel: 081 462 6331.

COLINDALE   Hendon College
Hotel, catering, tourism, leisure, levels 1–3
Corner Mead, Grahame Park Way, London NW9 5RA
Tel: 081 200 8300.

EALING   Thames Valley University
Hotel, catering, leisure, tourism, levels 3–5
Faculty of Hospitality Studies, St Mary's Road, London W5 5RF
Tel: 081 579 5000.

ENFIELD   Enfield College
Tourism, leisure, levels 1–3
Montagu Road, N18 2LY
Tel: 081 803 7311.

ELTHAM AND ROEHAMPTON   University of Greenwich
CertEd
Avery Hill Campus, Bexley Road, London SE9 2PQ
Tel: 081 854 2030.

HARROW   Harrow College of Higher Education
Leisure, level 4
Watford Road, Northwick Park, HA1 3TP
Tel: 081 864 5422.

HARROW   Weald College
Hotel, catering, tourism, leisure, levels 1–3
Brookshill, Harrow Weald, Middlesex HA3 6RR
Tel: 081 954 9571.

HENDON   Middlesex University
Hotel and catering, tourism, levels 4, 5
The Burroughs, London NW4 4BT
Tel: 081 368 1299.

HOLBORN   Kingsway College
Leisure, level 3
Grays Inn Centre, Sidmouth Street, LondonWC1H 8JB
Tel: 071 278 0541.

HOLLOWAY   University of North London
Hotel, catering, leisure, tourism, levels 4, 5
The Business School, 277–281 Holloway Road, N7 8HN
Tel: 071 607 2789.

ISLEWORTH   Hounslow Borough College
Hotel and catering, leisure, levels 1–3
London Road, Isleworth, Middlesex TW7 4HS
Tel: 081 568 0244.

KILBURN   Kilburn College
Hotel and catering, levels 1–2
Priory Park Road, Colindale, London NW6 7UJ
Tel: 071 328 8241/5.

LEWISHAM   Lewisham College
Hotel and catering, leisure, levels 1–3
Breakspears Road, Lewisham Way, London SE4 1UT
Tel: 081 692 0353.

MORDEN   Merton College
Hotel and catering, tourism, levels 1–3
London Road, Morden, Surrey SM4 5QX
Tel: 081 640 3001.

NORWOOD   South London College
Leisure, level 3
Knight's Hill, West Norwood, London SE27 0TX
Tel: 081 670 4488.

ROEHAMPTON   Roehampton Institute
Travel and tourism, level 5
Southlands College, Wimbledon Parkside, London SW19 5NN
Tel: 081 946 2234.

SOUTHALL   Southall College of Technology
Leisure, tourism, levels 1–3
Beaconsfield Road, Southall, Middlesex UB1 1DP
Tel: 081 574 3448.

SOUTHGATE   Southgate College
Hotel and catering, leisure, levels 1–3
High Street, London N14 6BS
Tel: 081 886 6521.

SOUTHWARK   South Bank
University
Hotel and catering, levels 1–4
103 Borough Road, London SE1 0AA
Tel: 071 928 8989.

SOUTHWARK   Southwark College
Tourism, leisure, levels 2, 3
The Cut, London SE1 8LE
Tel: 071 928 9561.

STRATFORD   Newham Community
College
Cookery, levels 1–2
Welfare Road, Stratford, London
E15 4HT
Tel: 081 555 1422.

TOTTENHAM   Tottenham College of
Technology
Tourism, leisure, levels 1–3
High Road, London N15 4RU
Tel: 081 802 3111.

TWICKENHAM   Richmond upon
Thames Tertiary College
Hotel and catering, leisure, levels 1–4
Egerton Road, Twickenham, Middlesex
TW2 7SJ
Tel: 081 892 6656.

TWICKENHAM   West London
Institute of Higher Education
Leisure, level 4
Department of Business and
Management Studies, Gordon House,
300 St Margarets Road,
Twickenham, Middlesex TW1 1PT
Tel: 081 891 0121.

UXBRIDGE   Uxbridge College
Hotel and catering, leisure, levels 1–3
Park Road, UB8 1NQ
Tel: 0895 30411.

WALTHAMSTOW   Waltham Forest
College for Further and Higher
Education
Hotel and catering, tourism, levels 1–3
Forest Road, London E17 4JB
Tel: 081 527 2311.

WATERLOO   Central Catering
College
Hotel and catering, levels 1–4
(part of South Bank University)
Cornwall Road, SE1 8TE
Tel: 071 928 9686.

WEST END   The London Institute
Tourism, level 4
388–396 Oxford Street, W1R 1FE
Tel: 071 491 8533.

WESTMINSTER   Westminster College
Hotel and catering, leisure, levels 1–4
Vincent Square, London SW1P 2PD
Tel: 071 828 1222.

Manchester, Greater

ALTRINCHAM   South Trafford
College
*Hotel, catering, tourism, leisure, levels
1–3*
Manchester Road, West Timperley,
WA14 5PQ
Tel: 061 973 7064.

ASHTON-UNDER-LYNE   Tameside
College of Technology
Hotel, catering, leisure, levels 1–4
Beaufort Road, OL6 6NX
Tel: 061 330 6911.

BOLTON   Bolton Institute of Higher
Education
Tourism, leisure, level 4, CertEd
Deane Road, BL3 5AB
Tel: 0204 28851.

BOLTON   Bolton Metropolitan
College
*Hotel, catering, tourism, leisure, levels
1–3*
Manchester Road, BL2 1ER
Tel: 0204 31411.

BURY   Bury Metropolitan College
*Hotel, catering, tourism, leisure, levels
1–3*
Whitfield Centre, Albert Road,
Whitfield, M25 6NH
Tel: 061 766 7296.

MANCHESTER   Manchester College of Arts and Technology
Hotel, catering, tourism, leisure, levels 1–3
Lower Hardman Street, M3 3ER
Tel: 061 953 5995.

MANCHESTER   The South Manchester College
Hotel, catering, tourism, leisure, levels 1–3
Fielden Park Centre, 141 Barlow Moor Road, West Didsbury, M20 8PQ
Tel: 061 434 4821.

MANCHESTER   Manchester College of Arts and Technology
Hotel and catering, leisure, levels 1–3
Moston Campus, Ashley Lane, Moston, M9 1WU
Tel: 061 205 7525.

MANCHESTER   Manchester College of Arts and Technology
Hotel and catering, levels 1, 2
Openshaw Centre, Whitworth Street, Openshaw, M11 2WH
Tel: 061 223 8282.

MANCHESTER   Manchester Metropolitan University
Hotel and catering, tourism, levels 4, 5
Hollings Faculty, Old Hall Lane, M14 6HR
Tel: 061 247 2603/2000/2722

OLDHAM   Oldham College
Hotel and catering, leisure, levels 1–3
Rochdale Road, OL9 6AA
Tel: 061 624 5214.

ROCHDALE   Hopwood Hall Tertiary College
Hotel and catering, leisure, levels 1–3
St Mary's Gate, OL12 6RY
Tel: 0706 345346.

SALFORD   Salford College of Technology
Hotel, catering, tourism, leisure, levels 1–4
Department of Food and Consumer Studies, Frederick Road, M6 6PU
Tel: 061 736 6541.

STOCKPORT   Stockport College of Technology
Tourism, leisure, levels 2–4
Wellington Road South, Cheshire SK1 3UQ
Tel: 061 480 7331.

Merseyside

BIRKENHEAD   Wirral Metropolitan College
Hotel and catering, levels 1–2
Borough Road, L42 9QD
Tel: 051 653 5555.

EASTHAM   Wirral Metropolitan College
Hotel and catering, levels 1–3
Carlett Park Site, Eastham, L62 0AY
Tel: 051 327 4331.

LITHERLAND   Hugh Baird College
Hotel and catering, leisure, levels 1–3
Church Road, L21 5HA
Tel: 051 928 3013.

LIVERPOOL   City of Liverpool Community College
Hotel and catering, levels 1–3
Colquitt Centre, L1 4DB
Tel: 051 709 0541.

LIVERPOOL   City of Liverpool Community College
Hotel and catering, levels 1, 2
Mabel Fletcher Centre, Sandown Road, L15 4JB
Tel: 051 733 7211.

LIVERPOOL   South Mersey College
Travel, leisure, levels 1–3
Riversdale Road, L19 3QR
Tel: 051 427 1227.

ROBY   Knowsley Community College
Hotel and catering, leisure, levels 1–3
Rupert Road, Huyton, L36 9TD
Tel: 051 443 2600.

ST HELENS   St Helens Community
    College
Hotel and catering, tourism, levels 1–4
Brooks Street, WA10 1PZ
Tel: 0744 33766.

SOUTHPORT   Southport College
*Hotel, catering, tourism, leisure, levels
    1–3*
Mornington Road, PR9 0TT
Tel: 0704 500606.

Midlands see West Midlands

Norfolk

GREAT YARMOUTH   Great
    Yarmouth College of Further
    Education
Hotel and catering, leisure, levels 1–3
Southtown, NR31 0ED.
Tel: 0493 655261

KINGS LYNN   Norfolk College of
    Arts and Technology
*Hotel, catering, tourism, leisure, levels
    1–3*
Tennyson Avenue, PE30 2QW
Tel: 0553 761144.

NORWICH   Norwich City College of
    Further and Higher Education
*Hotel, catering, tourism, leisure, levels
    1–4*
Ipswich Road, NR2 2LJ
Tel: 0603 660011.

Northamptonshire

CORBY   Tresham College
*Hotel, catering, tourism, leisure, levels
    1–3*
George Street, NN17 1QA
Tel: 0536 402252.

NORTHAMPTON   Northampton
    College
*Hotel, catering, tourism, leisure, levels
    1–3*
Booth Lane, NN3 3RF
Tel: 0604 403322.

Northumberland

ASHINGTON   Northumberland
    College of Arts and Technology
*Hotel, catering, tourism, leisure, levels
    1–3*
College Road, NE63 9RG
Tel: 0670 813248.

Nottinghamshire

MANSFIELD   West Nottinghamshire
    College
Hotel and catering, levels 1–3
Derby Road, NG18 5BH
Tel: 0623 27191.

NEWARK   Newark Technical College
Leisure, levels 1, 2
Chauntry Park, NG24 1BP
Tel: 0636 705921.

NOTTINGHAM   Broxtowe College
    of Further Education
Tourism, leisure, levels 1–3
High Road, Chilwell, NG9 4AH
Tel: 0602 228161.

NOTTINGHAM   Clarendon College
Hotel and catering, leisure, levels 1–4
Pelham Avenue, Mansfield Road,
    NG5 1AL
Tel: 0602 607201.

NOTTINGHAM   The Nottingham
    Trent University
Hotel and catering, tourism, levels 4, 5
Nottingham Business School, Burton
    Street, NG1 4BU
Tel: 0602 418418.

NOTTINGHAM   South
Nottinghamshire College of Further
Education
Leisure, levels 3, 4
Greythorn Drive, West Bridgford,
NG2 7GA
Tel: 0602 812125.

WORKSOP   North Nottinghamshire
College of Further Education
*Hotel, catering, tourism, leisure, levels
1–3*
Carlton Road, S81 7HP
Tel: 0909 473561.

Oxfordshire

ABINGDON   Abingdon College
Hotel and catering, levels 1, 2
Northcourt Road, OX14 1NN
Tel: 0235 555585.

BANBURY   North Oxfordshire
College and School of Art
Hotel and catering, levels 1, 2
Broughton Road, OX16 9QA
Tel: 0295 252221.

HENLEY-ON-THAMES   Henley
College
Hotel and catering, levels 1, 2
Deanfield Avenue, RG9 1UH
Tel: 0491 579988.

OXFORD   Oxford Brookes University
Hotel, catering, tourism, levels 4, 5
Gipsy Lane, Headington, OX3 0BP
Tel: 0865 741111.

OXFORD   Oxford College of Further
Education
*Hotel, catering, leisure, tourism, levels
1–3*
Oxpens Road, OX1 1SA
Tel: 0865 245871.

Shropshire

BRIDGNORTH   Bridgnorth and
South Shropshire College of Further
Education
Hotel and catering, levels 1, 2
Sourbridge Road, WV15 6AL
Tel: 0746 764431.

OSWESTRY   Oswestry College
Leisure, level 3
College Road, SY11 2SA
Tel: 0691 653067.

SHREWSBURY   Shrewsbury College
of Arts and Technology
Hotel and catering, leisure, levels 1–3
Radbrook Centre, Radbrook Road,
SY3 9BL
Tel: 0743 232686.

TELFORD   Telford College of Arts
and Technology
Cookery, leisure, levels 1–3
Haybridge Road, Wellington, TF1 2NP
Tel: 0952 641122.

Somerset

BRIDGWATER   Bridgwater College
Food service, leisure, levels 1–3
Bath Road, TA6 4PZ
Tel: 0278 455464.

FROME   Frome College
Leisure, level 2
Bath Road, BA11 2HQ
Tel: 0373 62456.

TAUNTON   Somerset College of Arts
and Technology
*Hotel, catering, tourism, leisure, levels
1–3*
Wellington Road, TA1 5AX
Tel: 0823 283403.

YEOVIL   Yeovil College
Hotel and catering, leisure, levels 1–3
Ilchester Road, BA21 3BA
Tel: 0935 23921.

Staffordshire

BURTON UPON TRENT   Burton upon Trent Technical College
Hotel, catering, tourism, leisure, levels 1–3
Lichfield Street, DE14 3RL
Tel: 0283 45401.

CANNOCK   Cannock College
Hotel, catering, tourism, leisure, levels 1, 2
The Green, WS11 1UE
Tel: 0543 462200.

LEEK   Leek College of Further Education and School of Art
Leisure, levels 1–3
Stockwell Street, ST13 6DP
Tel: 0538 382506.

NEWCASTLE   Newcastle-under-Lyme College
Cookery, leisure, levels 1–3
Liverpool Road, ST5 2DF
Tel: 0782 715111.

STAFFORD   Stafford College
Hotel and catering, leisure, levels 1–4
Earl Street, ST16 2QR
Tel: 0785 223800.

STOKE-ON-TRENT   Staffordshire University
Tourism, level 4
Leek Road, ST4 2DF
Tel: 0782 412515.

STOKE-ON-TRENT   Stoke-on-Trent College
Hotel, catering, leisure, tourism, levels 1–3
Cauldon Campus, Stoke Road, Shelton, ST4 2DG
Tel: 0782 202561.

TAMWORTH   Tamworth College
Hotel, catering, leisure, tourism, levels 1–3
Croft Street, Upper Gungate, B79 8AE
Tel: 0827 310202.

Suffolk

BURY ST EDMUNDS   West Suffolk College
Hotel, catering, leisure, tourism, levels 1–3
Out Risbygate, IP33 3RL
Tel: 0284 701301.

IPSWICH   Suffolk College
Hotel and catering, leisure, levels 1–4
Rope Walk, IP4 1LT
Tel: 0473 255885.

LOWESTOFT   Lowestoft College
Hotel, catering, leisure, tourism, levels 1–3
St Peter's Street, NR32 2NB
Tel: 0502 583521.

Surrey

CARSHALTON   Carshalton College
Hotel, catering, tourism, leisure, levels 1–3
Nightingale Road, CM5 2EU
Tel: 081 770 6800.

CROYDON   Croydon College
Hotel, catering, tourism, leisure, levels 1–4
Fairfield, CR9 1DX
Tel: 081 686 5700.

EWELL   North East Surrey College of Technology
Cookery, leisure, levels 1–3
Reigate Road, KT17 3DS
Tel: 081 394 1731.

GUILDFORD   Guildford College of Technology
Hotel, catering, leisure, tourism, levels 1–4
Stoke Park, GU1 1EZ
Tel: 0483 31251.

GUILDFORD   University of Surrey
Hotel and catering, tourism, levels 4, 5
Stag Hill, GU2 5XH
Tel: 0483 300800.

REDHILL   East Surrey College
Hotel and catering, tourism, levels 1–3
Gatton Point South, College Crescent,
   RH1 2FA
Tel: 0737 772611.

WEYBRIDGE   Brooklands College
Hotel and catering, leisure, levels 1–3
Heath Road, KT13 8TT
Tel: 0932 853300.

Sussex, East

BRIGHTON   Brighton College of
   Technology
Hotel and catering, tourism, levels 1–5
Faculty of Art, Catering and Service
   Industries, Pelham Street, BN1 4FA
Tel: 0273 667788.

EASTBOURNE/BRIGHTON
   University of Brighton
Hotel and catering, tourism, levels 4, 5
49 Darley Road, Eastbourne
BN20 7UR
Tel: 0273 600900.

EASTBOURNE   Eastbourne College
   of Arts and Technology
Hotel and catering, levels 1–3
Kings Drive, BN21 2UN
Tel: 0323 644711.

HASTINGS/ST LEONARDS-ON-
   SEA   Hastings College of Arts and
   Technology
Hotel and catering, levels 1–3
Archery Road, St Leonards-on-Sea,
   TN38 0HX
Tel: 0424 423847.

LEWES   Lewes Technical College
Tourism, leisure, levels 2–3
Mountfield Road, BN7 2XH
Tel: 0273 476121.

Sussex, West

CHICHESTER   Chichester College of
   Technology
*Hotel, catering, leisure, tourism, levels
   1–3*
Westgate Fields, PO19 1SB
Tel: 0243 786321.

CRAWLEY   Crawley College
Hotel and catering, levels 1–4
College Road, RH10 1NR
Tel: 0293 612686.

WORTHING   Northbrook College of
   Design and Technology
Hotel and catering, tourism, levels 2–4
Littlehampton Road, Goring-by-Sea,
   BN12 6NV
Tel: 0903 830057.

Tyne and Wear

NEWCASTLE UPON
   TYNE   Newcastle College
*Hotel, catering, tourism, leisure, levels
   1–5*
Sandyford Road, NE1 8QE
Tel: 091 235 8239.

NEWCASTLE UPON
   TYNE   University of Northumbria
   at Newcastle
Travel and tourism, levels 4, 5
The Newcastle Business School, Ellison
   Building, Ellison Place, NE1 8ST
Tel: 091 235 8433/8434.

SOUTH SHIELDS   South Tyneside
   College
Hotel and catering, leisure, levels 1–3
St Georges Avenue, NE34 6ET
Tel: 091 456 0403.

SUNDERLAND   Monkwearmouth
   College
Hotel and catering, leisure, levels 1–3
Swan Street, SR5 1EB
Tel: 091 548 7119.

SUNDERLAND   Wearside College of
   Further Education
Leisure, levels 1, 2
Sea View Road West, Grangetown,
   SR2 9LH
Tel: 091 567 0794.

TYNE AND WEAR   Gateshead
Technical College
Leisure, levels 1–3
Durham Road, NE9 5BN
Tel: 0632 770524.

WALLSEND   North Tyneside College
Hotel, catering, tourism, leisure, levels 1–3
Embleton Avenue, NE28 9NJ
Tel: 091 262 4081.

Warwickshire

NUNEATON   North Warwickshire
College of Technology and Art
Hotel and catering, leisure, levels 1–3
Hinckley Road, CV11 6BH
Tel: 0203 349321.

RUGBY   East Warwickshire College of
Further Education
Hotel and catering, levels 1, 2
Lower Hillmorton Road, CV21 3QS
Tel: 0788 541666.

STRATFORD UPON AVON   South
Warwickshire College
Hotel, catering, leisure, tourism, levels 1–4
The Willows North, Alcester Road,
CV37 9QR
Tel: 0789 266245.

West Midlands

BIRMINGHAM   Birmingham College
of Food, Tourism and Creative
Studies
Hotel, catering, tourism, leisure, levels 1–4
Summer Row, B3 1JB
Tel: 021 235 2951/2774.

BIRMINGHAM   Bournville College of
Further Education
Hotel, catering, leisure, levels 1, 2
Bristol Road South, B31 2AJ
Tel: 021 411 1414.

BIRMINGHAM   Brooklyn College
Leisure, level 3
Aldridge Road, Great Barr, B44 8NE
Tel: 021 360 3543.

BIRMINGHAM   East Birmingham
College
Hotel and catering, leisure, levels 1–3
Garretts Green Lane, B33 0TS
Tel: 021 743 4471.

BIRMINGHAM   Hall Green College
Leisure, level 3
Colebank Road, Hall Green, B28 8ES
Tel: 021 778 2311.

BIRMINGHAM   Handsworth College
Cookery, travel, leisure, levels 1–3
The Council House, Soho Road,
B21 9DP
Tel: 021 551 6031.

BIRMINGHAM   Matthew Boulton
College
Leisure, levels 2–4
Sherlock Street, B5 7DB
Tel: 021 446 4545.

BIRMINGHAM   The University of
Birmingham
Tourism, leisure, levels 4–5
Edgbaston, B15 2TT
Tel: 021 414 6619.

BIRMINGHAM   University of Central
England at Birmingham
Hotel and catering, level 4
Perry Barr, B42 2SU
Tel: 021 331 5000.

COVENTRY   Coventry University
Leisure, level 4
Priory Street, CV1 5FB
Tel: 0203 631313.

COVENTRY   Henley College
Coventry
Hotel, catering, leisure, tourism, levels 1–4
Henley Road, CV2 1ED
Tel: 0203 611021.

DUDLEY   Dudley College of Technology
Cookery, tourism, leisure, levels 1–3
The Broadway, DY1 4AS
Tel: 0384 455433/453585.

HALESOWEN   Halesowen College
Hotel, catering, tourism, leisure, levels 1–3
Whittingham Road, B63 3NA
Tel: 021 550 1451.

SOLIHULL   Solihull College of Technology
Hotel, catering, tourism, leisure, levels 1–3
Blossomfield Road, B91 1SB
Tel: 021 711 2111.

SUTTON COLDFIELD   Sutton Coldfield College of Further Education
Hotel and catering, leisure, levels 1, 2
Lichfield Road, B74 2NW
Tel: 021 355 5671.

WALSALL   Walsall College of Technology
Hotel, catering, tourism, leisure, levels 1–3
St Paul's Street, WS1 1XN
Tel: 0922 720824.

WEST BROMWICH   Sandwell College of Further and Higher Education
Hotel, catering, travel, leisure, levels 1–3
High Street, B70 8DW
Tel: 021 556 6000.

WOLVERHAMPTON   Bilston Community College
Hotel and catering, leisure, levels 1–3
Westfield Road, Bilston, WV14 6ER
Tel: 0902 353877.

WOLVERHAMPTON
Wolverhampton University
Hotel, catering, tourism, leisure, level 4
Wolverhampton Business School, Compton Road West, WV3 9DY
Tel: 0902 321059/321000.
CertEd
Faculty of Education, Gorway Road, Walsall WS1 3BD
Tel: 0902 321050/321000.

West Sussex *see Sussex, West*

Wiltshire

CHIPPENHAM   Chippenham Technical College
Hotel and catering, leisure, levels 1–3
Cockelbury Road, SN15 3QD
Tel: 0249 444501.

CHIPPENHAM   Lackham College
Tourism, level 3
Lacock, SN15 2NY
Tel: 0249 443111.

SALISBURY   Salisbury College of Technology
Hotel and catering, tourism, levels 1–3
Southampton Road, SP1 2LW
Tel: 0722 323711.

SWINDON   Swindon College
Hotel, catering, tourism, leisure, levels 1–3
North Star Avenue, SN2 1DY
Tel: 0793 491591.

TROWBRIDGE   Trowbridge College
Hotel and catering, tourism, levels 1–3
College Road, BA14 0ES
Tel: 0225 766241.

Worcester *see Hereford and Worcester*

Yorkshire, North

HARROGATE   Harrogate College of Arts and Technology
Hotel, catering, travel, leisure, levels 1–3
Hornbeam Park, Hookstone Road, HG2 8QT
Tel: 0423 879466.

SCARBOROUGH   Scarborough
Technical College
Hotel and catering, leisure, levels 1–3
Lady Edith's Drive, YO12 5RN
Tel: 0723 372105.

SELBY   Selby College
Hotel and catering, levels 1, 2
Abbot's Road, YO8 8AT
Tel: 0757 702606.

SKIPTON   Craven College of Further
Education
Hotel, catering, tourism, leisure, levels 1–3
High Street, BD23 1JY
Tel: 0756 791411.

YORK   York College of Arts and
Technology
Hotel, catering, tourism, leisure, levels 1–3
Dringhouses, YO2 1VA
Tel: 0904 704141.

Yorkshire, South

BARNSLEY   Barnsley College
Hotel and catering, leisure, levels 1–3
Church Street, S70 2AX
Tel: 0226 730191.

DONCASTER   Doncaster College
Hotel and catering, levels 1–3
Waterdale, DN1 3EX
Tel: 0302 322122.

ROTHERHAM   Rockingham College
of Further Education
Hotel, catering, tourism, leisure, levels 1, 2
West Street, Wath upon Dearne,
S63 6PX
Tel: 0709 760310.

ROTHERHAM   Rotherham College
of Arts and Technology
Hotel and catering, levels 1–3
Eastwood Lane, S65 1EG
Tel: 0709 822760.

SHEFFIELD   Castle College
Hotel and catering, levels 1–4
Granville Road, S2 2RL
Tel: 0742 760271.

SHEFFIELD   Loxley College
Tourism, level 3
Myers Grove Lane, S6 5JL
Tel: 0742 323163.

SHEFFIELD   Rother Valley College of
Further Education
Hotel, catering, tourism, leisure, levels 1–3
Doe Quarry Lane, Dinnington, S31 7NH
Tel: 0909 550550.

SHEFFIELD   Sheffield Hallam
University
Hotel, catering, tourism, levels 4, 5
Pond Street, S1 1WB
Tel: 0742 720911.

SHEFFIELD   Stradbroke College
Travel, levels 2, 3
Richmond Centre, Spinkhill Drive,
S13 8FD
Tel: 0742 392621.

SHEFFIELD   The University of
Sheffield
Leisure, level 5
Leisure Management Unit, Room F22,
Hicks Building, S3 7RH
Tel: 0742 768555.

Yorkshire, West

BRADFORD   Bradford and Ilkley
Community College
Hotel and catering, leisure, levels 1–4
Great Horton Road, BD7 1AY
Tel: 0274 753288.

DEWSBURY   Dewsbury College
Hotel and catering, leisure, levels 1–3
Halifax Road, WF13 2AS
Tel: 0924 465916.

HALIFAX   Calderdale College
Hotel, catering, tourism, leisure, levels 1–3
Francis Street, HX1 3UZ
Tel: 0422 358221.

HUDDERSFIELD   Huddersfield
Technical College
Hotel, catering, travel, leisure, levels 1–3
New North Road, HD1 5NN
Tel: 0484 536521.

HUDDERSFIELD   The University of
Huddersfield
Hotel, catering, applied nutrition, levels 4, 5, CertEd
Queensgate, HD1 3DH
Tel: 0484 422288.

LEEDS   Airedale and Wharfedale
College
Leisure, levels 1–3
Calverley Lane, Horsforth, LS18 4RQ
Tel: 0532 581723.

LEEDS   Leeds Metropolitan University
Hotel, catering, tourism, leisure, levels 4, 5
Calverley Street, LS1 3HE
Tel: 0532 832600.

LEEDS   Park Lane College
Tourism, levels 2, 3
Park Lane, LS3 1AA
Tel: 0532 443011.

LEEDS   Thomas Danby College
Hotel and catering, leisure, levels 1–4
Roundhay Road, Sheepscar, LS7 3BG
Tel: 0532 494912.

WAKEFIELD   Wakefield District
College
Hotel and catering, levels 1–4
Margaret Street, WF1 2DH
Tel: 0924 370501.

2 Wales

Clwyd

COLWYN BAY   Llandrillo College
Hotel and catering, levels 1–4
Llandudno Road, LL28 4HZ
Tel: 0492 46666.

CONNAH'S QUAY   North East
Wales Institute of Higher Education
Hotel and catering, levels 1–3
Deeside, CH5 4BB
Tel: 0244 831531.

WREXHAM   North East Wales
Institute of Higher Education
Hotel and catering, leisure, levels 1–3
Plas Coch, Mold Road, LL11 2AW
Tel: 0978 290666.

Dyfed

ABERYSTWYTH   Ceredigion College
of Further Education
Hotel, catering, tourism, leisure, levels 1–3
Llanbadarn Fawr, SY23 3PB
Tel: 0970 624511.

CARDIGAN   Ceredigion College of
Further Education
Hotel and catering, levels 1, 2
Park Place, SA43 1AB
Tel: 0239 621059/60.

CARMARTHEN   Carmarthenshire
College of Technology and Art
Hotel and catering, leisure, levels 1–4
Pibwrlwyd Campus, SA31 2NH
Tel: 0554 759165.

HAVERFORDWEST   Pembrokeshire
College
Hotel and catering, levels 1–3
College Campus, Dew Street, SA16 1SZ
Tel: 0437 765247.

Glamorgan mid, south and west

ABERDARE   Aberdare College
Hotel and catering, levels 1–3
Cwmdare Road, CF44 8ST
Tel: 0685 873405.

BARRY   Barry College
Hotel and catering, levels 1–3
Colcot Road, CF6 8YJ
Tel: 0446 733251.

BRIDGEND   Bridgend College of
Technology
Hotel and catering, tourism, levels 1–3
Cowbridge Road, CF31 3DF
Tel: 0656 766588.

CARDIFF   Cardiff Institute of Higher
Education
Hotel and catering, tourism, levels 2–4
Colchester Avenue Centre, CF3 7XR
Tel: 0222 551111.

CARDIFF   University of Wales College
of Cardiff
Hotel, catering, tourism, levels 4, 5
65–67 Park Place, CF1 3AS
Tel: 0222 874846.

MERTHYR TYDFIL   Merthyr Tydfil
College
Hotel and catering, leisure, levels 1–3
Ynysfach, CF48 1AR
Tel: 0685 723663.

NEATH   Neath College
Hotel and catering, leisure, levels 1–3
Dwt-y-Felin Road, SA10 7RF
Tel: 0639 634271.

PORT TALBOT   Afan College
Tourism, leisure, levels 2, 3
Margam, SA13 2AL
Tel: 0639 882107.

RHYDFELEN   Pontypridd Technical
College
Hotel and catering, leisure, levels 1–3
Ynys Terrace, CF37 5RN
Tel: 0443 486121.

SWANSEA   Gorseinon College
Leisure, level 3
Belgrave Road, SA4 2RF
Tel: 0792 898283.

SWANSEA   Swansea College
Hotel and catering, leisure, levels 1–3
Tycoch Road, Sketty, SA2 9EB
Tel: 0792 206871.

SWANSEA   West Glamorgan Institute
of Higher Education
Tourism, leisure, level 4
Townhill Campus, Townhill Road,
SA2 0UT
Tel: 0792 203482.

TONYPANDY   Rhondda College
Hotel and catering, levels 1, 2
Llwynpia, CF40 2TQ
Tel: 0443 432187.

YSTRAD MYNACH   Ystrad Mynach
College
Hotel and catering, levels 1–3
Twyn Road, Hengoed, CF8 7XR
Tel: 0443 816888.

Gwent

CROSSKEYS   Crosskeys Tertiary
College
*Hotel, catering, tourism, leisure, levels
1–3*
Risca Road, Crosskeys, NP1 7ZA
Tel: 0495 270295.

EBBW VALE   Ebbw Vale College of
Further Education
Hotel and catering, levels 1, 2
College Road, NP3 6LE
Tel: 0495 302083.

NEWPORT   Newport College of
Further Education
Hotel and catering, levels 1–3
Nash Road, NP9 0TS
Tel: 0633 274861.

PONTYPOOL   Pontypool College
Hotel and catering, leisure, levels 1–3
Blaendare Road, NP4 5YE
Tel: 0495 755141.

Gwynedd

BANGOR   Gwynedd Technical
College
Hotel and catering, levels 1–3
Ffriddoedd Road, LL57 2TP
Tel: 0248 370125.

DOLGELLAU   Coleg Meirionnydd
Hotel and catering, leisure, levels 1–3
Barmouth Road, LL40 2SW
Tel: 0341 422827.

LLANGEFNI   Coleg Pencraig
Hotel and catering, leisure, levels 1–3
Ynys Mon, LL77 7HY
Tel: 0248 750101.

Powys

BRECON   Coleg Powys Brecon
Hotel and catering, levels 1, 2
Penlan, Brecon, LD3 9SR
Tel: 0874 5252.

NEWTOWN   Coleg Powys
  Montgomery Coleg Site
Hotel and catering, levels 1–3
Llanidloes Road, SY16 1BE
Tel: 0686 622722.

3   Scotland

Borders Region

HAWICK   Borders College of Further
  Education
Hotel and catering, tourism, levels 1–3
Henderson Building, Commercial Road,
  TD9 7AW
Tel: 0450 74191.

Central Region

ALLOA   Clackmannan College of
  Further Education
Hotel and catering, levels 1–3
Branshill Road, FK10 3BT
Tel: 0259 215121.

FALKIRK   Falkirk College of
  Technology
*Hotel, catering, tourism, leisure, levels
  1–4*
Grangemouth Road, FK2 9AD
Tel: 0324 24981.

Dumfries and Galloway Region

DUMFRIES   Dumfries and Galloway
  College of Technology
Hotel and catering, tourism, levels 1–3
Heathhall, DG1 3QZ
Tel: 0387 61261.

Fife Region

CUPAR   Elmwood College
Hotel and catering, levels 1–3
Carslogie Road, KY15 4SB
Tel: 0334 52781.

DUNFERMLINE   Lauder College
Hotel and catering, levels 1–4
Halbeath, KY11 5DY
Tel: 0383 726201.

GLENROTHES   Glenrothes College
Hotel and catering, levels 1–3
Stenton Road, KY6 2RA
Tel: 0592 772233.

KIRKCALDY   Fife College of
  Technology
Hotel and catering, levels 1–3
St Brycedale Avenue, KY1 1EX
Tel: 0592 268591.

Grampian Region

ABERDEEN   Aberdeen College of
  Further Education
Hotel reception, level 2
Holburn Street, AB9 2YT
Tel: 0224 572811.

ABERDEEN   Aberdeen College of
  Further Education
Hotel and catering, levels 1–3
Gallowgate, AB9 1DN
Tel: 0224 640366.

ABERDEEN   The Robert Gordon
University
Hotel and catering, food science, level 4
Queen's Road, AB9 2PG
Tel: 0224 633611.

ELGIN   Moray College of Further
Education
Hotel and catering, levels 1–3
Hay Street, IV30 1NQ
Tel: 0343 543425.

FRASERBURGH   Banff and Buchan
College of Further Education
Hotel and catering, levels 1–3
Henderson Road, AB43 5RF
Tel: 0346 25777.

Highland Region

INVERNESS   Inverness College of
Further and Higher Education
Hotel and catering, tourism, levels 1–3
3 Longman Road, Longman South,
IV1 1SA
Tel: 0463 236681.

THURSO   Thurso College
Hotel and catering, levels 1–3
Ormlie Road, KW14 7EE
Tel: 0847 83555.

Lothian Region

BATHGATE   West Lothian College of
Further Education
Hotel and catering, levels 1–3
Majoribanks Street, EH48 1QJ
Tel: 0506 634300.

DALKEITH   Jewel and Esk Valley
College
Hotel and catering, levels 1–3
Eskbank Centre, Newbattle Road,
EH22 3AE
Tel: 031 663 1951.

EDINBURGH   Napier University
*Hotel and catering, tourism, levels 4
and 5*
Merchiston Campus, 10 Colinton
Road, EH10 5DT
Tel: 031 455 2570/444 2266.

EDINBURGH   Queen Margaret
College
Hotel and catering, levels 4, 5
Clerwood Terrace, EH12 8TS
Tel: 031 317 3000.

EDINBURGH   Stevenson College
Tourism, levels 1–4
Bankhead Avenue, Sighthill, EH11 4DE
Tel: 031 453 6161.

EDINBURGH   Telford College of
Further Education
Hotel and catering, tourism, levels 1–4
Crew Toll, EH4 2NZ
Tel: 031 332 2491.

Strathclyde Region

AYR   Ayr College
Hotel and catering, levels 1–4
Dam Park, KA8 0EU
Tel: 0292 265184.

CLYDEBANK   Clydebank College
Hotel and catering, tourism, levels 1–3
Kilbowie Road, G81 2AA
Tel: 041 952 7771.

CUMBERNAULD   Cumbernauld
College
Hotel and catering, levels 1–3
Town Centre, G67 1HU
Tel: 0236 731811.

EAST KILBRIDE   Cambuslang
College
Hotel and catering, levels 1–3
East Kilbride Annexe, Main Street,
G74 4JZ
Tel: 03552 43018.

GLASGOW   Anniesland College
Tourism, levels 1–3
Hatfield Drive, G12 0YE
Tel: 041 357 3969.

GLASGOW   Central College of
   Commerce
Tourism, levels 1–4
300 Cathedral Street, G1 2TA
Tel: 041 552 3941.

GLASGOW   Glasgow College of Food
   Technology
Hotel and catering, tourism, levels 1–4
230 Cathedral Street, G1 2TG
Tel: 041 552 3751.

GLASGOW   John Wheatley College
Cookery, levels 1, 2
1346 Shettleston Road G32 9AT
Tel: 041 778 2426.

GLASGOW   Jordanhill College of
   Education
Teaching qualification in FE
School of Further Education, Southbrae
   Drive, G13 1PP
Tel: 041 959 1232.

GLASGOW   The Queen's College
Hotel and catering, levels 4, 5
1 Park Drive, G3 6LP
Tel: 041 337 4000.

GLASGOW   Springburn College
Tourism, levels 1–3
110 Flemington Street, G21 4BX
Tel: 041 558 9001.

GLASGOW   Stow College
Leisure, level 4
43 Shamrock Street, G4 9LD
Tel: 041 332 1786.

GLASGOW   University of Strathclyde
Hotel and catering, tourism, levels 4, 5
Scottish Hotel School, Curran Building,
   94 Cathedral Street G4 0LG
Tel: 041 552 4400.

GREENOCK   James Watt College
*Hotel, catering, tourism, leisure, levels
   1–4*
Finnart Street, PA16 8HF
Tel: 0475 24433.

HAMILTON   Bell College of
   Technology
Tourism, level 4
Almada Street, ML3 0JB
Tel: 0698 283100.

IRVINE   Kilmarnock College
Hotel and catering, tourism, levels 1–3
Irvine Campus, Bank Street, KA12 0LP
Tel: 0294 73839.

MOTHERWELL   Motherwell College
Hotel and catering, tourism, level 1–4
Dalzell Drive, ML1 2DD
Tel: 0698 59641.

PAISLEY   Reid Kerr College
Hotel and catering, levels 1–4
Renfrew Road, PA3 4DR
Tel: 041 889 4225.

Tayside Region

ARBROATH   Angus College of
   Further Education
Hotel and catering, levels 1–3
Keptie Road, DD11 3EN
Tel: 0241 72056.

DUNDEE   Duncan of Jordanstone
   College of Art
Hotel and catering, level 4
13 Perth Road, DD1 4HT
Tel: 0382 23261.

DUNDEE   Dundee College of Further
   Education
Hotel and catering, tourism, levels 1–4
Old Glamis Road, DD3 8LE
Tel: 0382 819021.

PERTH   Perth College of Further
   Education
Hotel and catering, levels 1–4
Brahan Estate, Crieff Road, PH1 2NX
Tel: 0738 21171.

Orkney

KIRKWALL   Kirkwall Grammar
  School
Hotel and catering, levels 1–3
Further Education Centre, KW15 1QM
Tel: 0856 2839.

Shetland

LERWICK   Shetland College of
  Further Education
Hotel and catering, levels 1–3
Gressy Loan, ZE1 0B
Tel: 0595 5514.

Western Isles

STORNOWAY   Lews Castle College
Hotel and catering, levels 1–3
Stornoway, Isle of Lewis, PA86 0XR
Tel: 0851 703311.

4   Northern Ireland

Belfast

BELFAST   Belfast Institute of Further
  and Higher Education
Hotel and catering, levels 1–4
Brunswick Street, BT2 7GX
Tel: 0232 245891.

BELFAST   Belfast College of
  Technology
Leisure, level 3
College Square East, BT1 6DJ
Tel: 0232 327244.

BELFAST   Castlereagh College
Hotel and catering, levels 1–3
Montgomery Road, BT6 9JD
Tel: 0232 797144.

BELFAST   Rupert Stanley College of
  Further Education
Hotel and catering, tourism, levels 1–3
Tower Street, BT5 4FH
Tel: 0232 452111.

JORDANSTOWN &
  LONDONDERRY   University of
Ulster
Hotel and catering, tourism, levels 4, 5
Department of Hotel and Catering
  Management, Shore Road,
  Newtonabbey, BT38 0QB
Tel: 0232 365131.

North Eastern

ANTRIM   Antrim Technical College
Hotel and catering, levels 1, 2
Fountain Street, BT41 4AL
Tel: 08494 63916.

BALLYMENA   Ballymena Technical
  College
Hotel and catering, levels 1, 2
Trostan Avenue, BT43 7DN
Tel: 0266 652871.

BALLYMONEY   The New Technical
  College
Hotel and catering, level 1
Coleraine Road, BT53 6BT
Tel: 02656 62258.

COLERAINE   Coleraine Technical
  College
Hotel and catering, tourism, levels 1–3
Union Street, BT52 1QA
Tel: 0265 54717.

LARNE   Larne College of Further
  Education
Hotel and catering, levels 1, 2
32–34 Pond Street, BT40 1SQ
Tel: 0574 72268.

MAGHERAFELT   Magherafelt
  College of Further Education
Cookery, levels 1, 2
22 Moneymore Road, BT45 6AE
Tel: 0648 32462.

NEWTONABBEY   Newtonabbey
  Technical College
Hotel and catering, levels 1, 2
400 Shore Road, BT37 9RS
Tel: 0232 864331.

PORTRUSH   Northern Ireland Hotel and Catering College
Hotel and catering, tourism, levels 1–4
Ballywillam Road, BT56 8JL
Tel: 0265 823768.

South Eastern

BANGOR   North Down and Ards College of Further Education
Hotel and catering, levels 1–3
Castle Park Road, BT20 4TF
Tel: 0247 271254.

DOWNPATRICK   Down College of Further Education
Hotel and catering, levels 1, 2
Market Street, BT30 6ND
Tel: 0396 615815.

LISBURN   Lisburn College
Hotel and catering, leisure, levels 1–3
39 Castle Street, BT27 4SU
Tel: 0846 677225.

NEWCASTLE   Newcastle College of Further Education
Cookery, leisure, levels 1–3
2 Donard Street, BT33 0AP
Tel: 03967 22451.

NEWTOWNARDS   North Down College of Further Education
Hotel and catering, levels 1, 2
Victoria Avenue, BT23 3ED
Tel: 0247 812116.

Southern

ARMAGH   Armagh College of Further Education
Cookery, levels 1, 2
Lonsdale Road, BT61 4TF
Tel: 0861 522205.

BANBRIDGE   Banbridge College of Further Education
Cookery, leisure, levels 1, 2
Castlewellan Road, BT32 4AY
Tel: 08206 62289.

COOKSTOWN   Cookstown Further Education College
Cookery, levels 1, 2
Loy Street, BT80 8PE
Tel: 06487 62620.

DUNGANNON   Dungannon Further Education College
Hotel and catering, levels 1, 2
Circular Road, BT71 6BQ
Tel: 0868 722323.

LURGAN   Lurgan College of Further Education
Hotel and catering, levels 1, 2
Kitchen Hill, BT66 6AZ
Tel: 0762 326135.

NEWRY   Newry College of Further Education
Hotel and catering, leisure, levels 1–3
East Campus, Patrick Street, BT35 8DN
Tel: 0693 61071.

PORTADOWN   Portadown College of Further Education
Hotel and catering, levels 1, 2
24–44 Lurgan Road, Craigavon BT63 5BL
Tel: 0762 337111.

Western

ENNISKILLEN   Fermanagh College of Further Education
Hotel and catering, travel, leisure, levels 1–3
Fairview Avenue, BT74 6AE
Tel: 0365 322431.

LIMAVADY   Limavady College of Further Education
Hotel and catering, levels 1, 2
Main Street, BT49 0EX
Tel: 05047 62334.

LONDONDERRY   North West
  College of Technology
Hotel and catering, leisure, levels 1, 2
Strand Road, BT48 7BY
Tel: 0504 266711.

OMAGH   Omagh College of Further
  Education
Hotel and catering, levels 1–3
Mountjoy Road, BT79 7AH
Tel: 0662 245433.

5 Specialist providers of distance learning

INTERNATIONAL
CORRESPONDENCE SCHOOLS
Intertext House, 8 Elliot Place,
  Clydeway Centre, Glasgow G3 8EF
Tel: 041 221 2926.

OPEN COLLEGE
3rd Floor, St James' Buildings, Oxford
  Street, Manchester M1 6FQ
Tel: 061 228 6415.

OPEN UNIVERSITY
PO Box 188, Milton Keynes MK7 6AA
Tel: 0908 274066.

6 Private schools, colleges and universities

BOURNEMOUTH   Hotel Career
  Centre
*Hotel, catering, travel, tourism, levels
1–3*
43 Norwich Avenue West, BH2 6AJ
Tel: 0202 291877.

BUCKINGHAM   University of
  Buckingham
Hotel and catering, levels 4, 5
MK18 1EG
Tel: 0280 814080.

BUSHEY   United States International
  University-Europe
Hotel, catering, tourism, levels 4, 5
The Avenue, Bushey, Herts, WD2 2LN
Tel: 0923 249067.

LONDON   Belair Education Centre
Hotel reception, tourism, level 2
10 Denmark Street, WC2H 8LS
Tel: 071 836 1316.

LONDON   City College of Higher
  Education
Hotel and tourism, levels 2, 3
67/83 Seven Sisters Road, Holloway,
  N7 6BU
Tel: 071 263 5937/8.

LONDON   Greenwich College
*Hotel, catering, travel, tourism, levels 2,
3*
Meridian House, Royal Hill,
  Greenwich, SE10 8RT
Tel: 081 853 4484.

LONDON   Lakefield Catering and
  Educational Centre
Hotel and catering, levels 2, 3
41a Maresfield Gardens, NW3 5RY
Tel: 071 794 5669.

LONDON   London City College
*Hotel, catering, travel, tourism, levels 2,
3*
Royal Waterloo House, 51–55
  Waterloo Road, SE1 8TX
Tel: 071 928 0029/0938.

LONDON   Schiller International
  University
Hotel, catering, tourism, levels 3–5
Royal Waterloo House, 51–55
  Waterloo Road, SE1 8TX
Tel: 071 928 8484.

LONDON   Speedwing Training
International House, Ealing Broadway
  Centre, W5 5DB
Tel: 081 840 7077.

7 Private cookery schools

EASTBOURNE Eastbourne College
of Food and Fashion
1 Silverdale Road, Eastbourne, East
Sussex BH20 7AA
Tel: 0323 30851.

LITLINGTON L'Ecole de Cuisine
Française – Sabine de Mirbeck
Clapham House, Litlington, East Sussex
BN26 5RQ
Tel: 0323 870047.

LONDON Le Cordon Bleu
114 Marylebone Lane, W1M 6HH
Tel: 071 935 3503.

LONDON Leith's School of Food and
Wine
21 St Alban's Grove, W8 5BP
Tel: 071 229 0177.

WOKING Tante Marie School of
Cookery
Woodham House, Carlton Road,
Woking, Surrey GU21 4HF
Tel: 0483 726957.

Index